Suggs is a singer, TV presenter and radio broadcaster. As the frontman of the hugely successful band Madness he helped create a distinctive London sound. He lives in North London.

SUGGS

AND THE CITY

My journeys through disappearing London

SUGGS

headline

First published in 2009
by HEADLINE PUBLISHING GROUP

First published in paperback in 2010
by HEADLINE PUBLISHING GROUP

1

Cataloguing in Publication Data is available from the British Library

ISBN 978 0 7553 1926 8

Typeset in Aldine 401 by Avon DataSet Ltd,
Bidford-on-Avon, Warwickshire

Printed and bound in Great Britain by
Clays Ltd, St Ives plc

Headline's policy is to use papers that are natural, renewable and recyclable
products and made from wood grown in sustainable forests. The logging and
manufacturing processes are expected to conform to the environmental
regulations of the country of origin.

HEADLINE PUBLISHING GROUP
An Hachette UK Company
338 Euston Road
London NW1 3BH

www.headline.co.uk
www.hachette.co.uk

Acknowledgements

I would like to thank Wavelength Films, who conceived the original idea for the television documentary series *Disappearing London*, out of which this book has grown. Thanks to Emma Barker at ITV London and Barbara Gibbon at Sky for commissioning the series; it gave me a chance to explore my city and its past, and opened doors to some extraordinary places and some wonderful people.

A number of the stories recounted here first featured in the series, and because of that I'd like to acknowledge the contributions of everyone who appeared in *Disappearing London*. I also want to thank the production crew, including Mike Mortimer, Kate Smith, Micaela Blitz and Justin Coleman. The programmes were a starting point but the book has expanded way beyond them. Consequently, I am indebted to the huge amount of additional research and work that the team at Wavelength Films undertook to help me produce this book; specifically Philip Crocker, Patrick McGrady and Lucy Ward. I could not have written it without them.

I would also like to thank Andrea Henry at Headline for her belief in this book from the start, and David Wilson and Jo Whitford for helping to pull it all together at the end.

Above all, thanks to Anne for putting up with me for all these years.

Contents

To Alf Masterson, the last rag-and-bone man

Introduction

I've lived and worked most of my life in London. I grew up here, met my wife, got married, saw my children born, and in the last 40-odd years I must have traversed most of the city's highways and byways at one time or another. As a musician I've written numerous songs about the place and over the years I've played with Madness in most of its venues, from its smallest to its grandest. I've made television and radio programmes about London, and from rather humble beginnings I've had the great privilege to live and work among its many walks of life, from the top to the bottom, experiencing all the colour and diversity on offer. London has been an unending inspiration, and – for good or ill – it has made me the man I am today.

It's a city that's changed a lot since I took my first heady breath of perfumed carbon dioxide: old buildings have come down, new buildings have gone up, fads and fashions have come and gone like the wind up the Thames. This is a city that never stays still, and its knack for relentless reinvention is what makes it such an exciting place to live in. It's been constantly evolving for thousands of years, as new waves of Londoners settle here from all corners of Britain and beyond, just as my ancestors came in days gone by to seek their fortune in the big smoke. Each fresh arrival adding a new note to the ongoing song of London life.

But sometimes in the rush to the future, important things get lost along the way: old buildings that no longer serve their original purpose, old trades, old ways of doing things. Often they're the things you barely notice sliding away. They seem to have been there forever, until one day you wake up and they've gone, victims of the wrecking ball, hikes in rent or the endless domination of the high-street brands. By the time you realise what's happened it is, of course, too late to do anything about it.

This book is my attempt to celebrate some of those people and places that have floated into my firmament while they're still around, and to remember others that have already disappeared from the map. Sadly time's constant march was all too evident during the writing, as a number of the places I was featuring slipped away even in the course of completing the book. At times I started to dread documenting another endangered spot, for fear I was the curse that would finish them off!

But I'm very glad I didn't stop. This book is a love letter not a lecture; I'm no historian, and London's past has been covered by much finer minds than mine. We shall be crossing paths with very few of the capital's great landmarks and public buildings – if it's the tourist trail you're after, you've picked up the wrong book. But if, like me, you have a fascination for the ordinary and extraordinary locations that give London its heart and soul, a love of paths not quite so beaten, and an appetite for eccentric, quirky, implausible and often unintentionally hilarious stories of the city, hopefully there's something here for you.

One of the reasons I'm so fascinated by the wonderful interplay between London's past and present can be blamed, I guess, on my day job as a musician. It all starts with song-writing. London, in one form or another, has always been a character in the lyrics I've written. In the early Madness stuff it was usually only there in the background – the natural setting for the characters whose lives and loves I wanted to sing about. The backdrop then was the London of now, a city seen through the eyes of a young cove from Camden with all the usual preoccupations of young coves from Camden, or anywhere else for that matter. More recently though, it appears as though I may have mellowed a bit, and London's past has stepped out from the shadows to claim a share of the limelight. For evidence of this unexpected turn of events, I refer you to Madness's latest musical offering – an album called *The Liberty of Norton Folgate*.

The first time I encountered those words they instinctively

sounded to me like a great title, something Syd Barrett might have come up with in his psychedelic pomp. It happened a couple of years back, while me and the rest of the band – all miraculously still on speaking terms after 30 plus years together – were kicking around the idea of a concept album about London, despite the observation of my esteemed colleague, a certain C. J. Foreman, who enquired as to what the f**k we thought the majority of the songs that make up our enormous canon of work are about if they aren't about London anyway. What excited me about this project though was the thought of writing a song about a street or an area in its historical context: not just a song about now, but from then until now. An X-ray snapshot, going down through the surface of today's city streets, peeling back the layers of grime and history, shrapnel and shoes, broken pots and broken dreams.

Strange that inspiration should strike when I found myself browsing in a second-hand bookshop in Whitstable, on a weekend getaway from it all down on the south coast. I spotted those words – The Liberty of Norton Folgate – in a book called *This Bright Field*, written by a chap called William Taylor and published in 2000. I flicked through its pages after being grabbed by the picture on its cover, which showed a Max Wall-type character, with arms outstretched, singing at the moon in a way only those who've had one too many do. It also had a pleasingly intriguing byline which read 'a travel book in one place'.

It's the tale of a trainee vicar who was sent to Shoreditch by the Bishop of Oxford, who suggested it might be a good place to do a little 'exploring', in order to test his vocation. He ended up living and working there for seven years and went on to become the chaplain to the Guildhall University, so the test was obviously passed.

While Taylor was discovering his ultimate vocation, he also set about discovering the lives and history of the people and the area around Spitalfields. He got a job in the fruit and veg market and was there when it closed down. He also worked behind the bar of the Jack the Ripper pub, which is now the Ten Bells (and well worth a visit, by the way). All in all, it's a charming book and full of great anecdotes, local culture and dialogue, written by a middle-class man struggling to understand the alien culture of the working classes in their rawest form, almost like an eighteenth-century explorer going up the Amazon and discovering the locals. It's also a great first-hand historical record of an incredibly ancient part of London going through enormous change.

But Spitalfields has always been a place of great change. Standing just outside the walls of the old City of London, it was originally a rubbish tip. As the centuries passed, it became a point of entry for newcomers fresh off the boats at the docks in Shadwell or Limehouse Basin and hoping to get a foothold in the city proper. Eventually the area became an unofficial town, independent of the conventions of the city: a place where anything and everything was allowed and where notables and worthies from elsewhere in the capital would slip to quietly of an evening to conduct their own nefarious activities.

Even after the walls came down and generations of immigrants made new lives for themselves in the ever-expanding city, a small area of Spitalfields remained a liberty, outside the normal restrictions and laws of the rest of London. Built up as a collection of courts and alleyways off Bishopsgate, a few strides east of the modern-day Liverpool Street Station, the Liberty of Norton Folgate in the 1700s had its own school, church, hospital and almshouses for destitute silk weavers, which are depicted on the back wall of the Ten Bells pub. It even had a daily rubbish collection, which is more than can be said of Camden today! Utterly self-contained and well run by a group of trustees, it also became a refuge for actors, writers, thinkers, louts, lowlifes and libertines – outsiders and troublemakers all. Sounds like our kind of place, does it not?

Being close to the docks and libertarian in its attitude to new arrivals, every race and creed has been through here at one time or another. And some of them settled in Brick Lane: the Huguenot silk weavers exiled from France came with their needles and thread; then came the Jewish settlers, yet more stitches in time; they were then replaced by the Bangladeshis, who kept those sewing machines turning with their leatherwear. A perfect example of London's strange social continuum as an area passes hands again and again down through the ages.

Here are a few words from the song 'The Liberty of Norton Folgate'.

Whether one calls it Spitalfields, Whitechapel, Tower
   Hamlets or Banglatown,
We're all dancing in the moonlight, we're all on
   borrowed ground.
Oh, I'm just walking down to, I'm just floating down
   through,
Won't you come with me to the Liberty of Norton
   Folgate?
'Cause you're a part of everything you see, yes you're a
   part of everything you see.

Strangely, no sooner had we put our song-writing pens down
than the phone started ringing. Over the course of a couple of
days in the spring of 2008 we had just about every news outlet
in London on the line asking why we'd written a song about
the campaign to save Folgate Street. I didn't know what they
were talking about at first – what campaign? Then I discovered
that there was a controversial plan cooked up by architect
Norman Foster to build a huge skyscraper on the site and
everyone assumed that we had joined the fight against it by
penning a protest song to rouse the rabble.

   It had never been our intention to get involved in the fight,
but in the end we couldn't really help it. Having just
discovered more about the fabulous history of this little slice of
the city, it seemed churlish to let it disappear for good so soon
after I'd made its acquaintance. For us it wasn't a battle against
development necessarily, more a case of trying to protect one
of the last best bits of familiar old London – shabby most

definitely, but soulful too, and far too precious to be buried under 50 storeys of concrete, regardless of whether or not it was to have a waterfall on the top.

As it turns out, the battle to save Folgate Street was successful, although I don't think our song can claim credit for the victory. Rather marvellously, in the process of preparing their case for opposing the building, someone dug up a set of ancient documents which suggested that Norton Folgate may still have rights to act as an independent state. It was like *Passport to Pimlico*, twenty-first-century style. If you're ever walking east down Bishopsgate towards Shoreditch High Street and take a turn to the right just before you reach Commercial Road, you'll still find Folgate Street in all its Edwardian glory. I urge you to do it sometime soon, because next time the builders come to call it may not be so lucky.

In many ways this book is an extension of that Folgate Street song – my attempt to piece together the story of some other special London places, and discover what the modern-day city can reveal about the past. But it's not only the fabric of the city that I'll be exploring, it's also the tales of the people who've helped build and preserve it. As I've come to realise over the years, it's often the same story with flesh and blood as it is with bricks and mortar: it's all too easy to take them for granted until you wake up one day and find out they're gone.

The Last Rag-and-Bone Man

I have lived in north London on and off for most of my life. It's an area rich in street characters of all sorts, but one gentleman in particular provided one of the finest sights for about as long as I can remember: the huge silhouette of Alf Masterson, the rag-and-bone man, coming up over one of Highgate's hills, pushing his handcart, loaded up with everything from trombones to globes and bits of furniture of every shape and size. His Jack Russell, Lucky, up front, snout forward, sniffing the air, like a miniature figurehead on the prow of Alf's creaking and clanking ship of the road, riding the high seas of north London in search of booty. And even without sails he could shift; take your eye off him for a second and he was gone, over the hill and far away, leaving just the echoes of his handbell and his strange, timeless cry. Whooah ooha! The words that were once hidden in this indecipherable call have long since been lost in the generations, but the cry remained as much part of Alf as his cart and his faithful dog.

Alf's various rounds brought him down my street every Tuesday morning at 9 a.m. on the dot, whooahing and ring-a-dinging. And if you wanted to know anything that was going on in the area, he was your man. He spent every day trudging these streets, come rain or shine, and could tell you everything from forthcoming council parking plans to the dodgy dealings of just about everyone in the borough. For all the disparate people hanging about at home all day – the old, young mums, out of work actors, the unemployed, the mad, me – he was like a beam of sunshine coming down the road and he treated everybody exactly the same. He was always up for a chat, with one eye over your shoulder to see what might be lurking in your hallway. He permanently had a cigar on the go and if he was in the mood he'd offer you one too, though they were normally reserved for people who had given him something substantial. I once gave him a decent piece, an oak chest of drawers, and I would always get an extra ring of his bell when he passed by my front door. But it would never be long before his feet would be itching and he'd be off up the road.

Once my nephew, Jerome, and a few of his pals from school were discussing possible projects for their film club and I suggested that Alf doing his round might make an interesting subject. We met at Alf's place in Kentish Town one crisp February morning, as arranged. The teacher in charge of the club wasn't able to make it, so I stood in to supervise. Alf was very obliging, which was lucky since the camera equipment was quite new to the boys and I didn't have a clue. It took a little time to set up and Alf had finished unchaining his barrow from the lamppost and was starting to get a bit fidgety. Lucky was starting to whine. Apart from race days at Ascot – Alf was a great horse-racing fan – this daily routine had been the same for years. Now he was starting to wonder what treasures he was being held back from discovering and Lucky couldn't understand why the sights and smells of the back streets of north London were not flying past his nostrils yet.

Finally the film crew were ready. We'd set up at the end of his road and on the shout of 'Action!' he was off. The boys got a lovely shot of him coming down the hill chugging on a cigar butt, brown fedora on the back of his head, the metal-rimmed wheels of the barrow rattling and rolling round the corner into Kentish Town Road. Beautiful, they were off to a flyer. Jerome picked up the camera on its tripod and we jogged round to the main road to see where Alf had headed. Well, he hadn't gone left to Camden Town, so he must have turned right heading for Highgate. We set off in hot pursuit but soon realised he hadn't gone that way either. We looked left and right again, he was nowhere to be seen. He'd simply vanished. We hadn't anticipated how fast he could go, but Alf later told me that he reckoned to cover 15 miles or more on a good day. And up some pretty steep hills too. No mean feat pushing that lumbering cart.

Sadly, Alf passed away in 2007. I heard the news from a reporter at the *Camden New Journal* who'd done a piece on him. It was a big shock, because Alf always seemed indestructible to me, an ox of a man and a constant in an ever-changing world.

When I got home that evening from rehearsing with Madness for a gig at Ascot racecourse at the weekend I found a box of cigars and this note on my doorstep.

Hi Graham (aka Suggs),
I am sorry that we have all lost Alf. I know you have a lot on. My dad had some dreams in his last weeks. He loved Ascot; this will be the first Ascot race meeting that he will not attend in 43 years. This year Ascot is on his birthday,

11 August, and there is a race meeting that day. One of his wishes was that his best friend and I go to the race meeting that day. My dad had a dream that he and myself called to see you. In the dream he said to you, 'Hi, play me a song, I am not well.' I had to tell him it was just a dream. He said I was to give you a box of cigars that he had kept for you, if he did not get a chance to call and see you. Could you please play him a song that night at Ascot? My dad would have loved that. One for the rag-and-bone man. Thanks so much.

Lots of love,

Damian, Alf's son

I did sing him a song that night and even added a bit of 'wooah ooah!' for good measure. Before he died I had the chance to ask Alf what it was he had been shouting for 40-odd years as he came down the road ringing his bell. He thought for a moment and said, 'D'you know what? I haven't got a clue.' Now that Alf has gone, there's no one else left who could answer the question. He was greatly loved and is sorely missed. He did as much, if not more, for the community as anyone paid by the council. Alf, the last of that noble London breed, the rag-and-bone man.

So this book is also a celebration of the people like Alf who are just as much a part of the fabric of London as its streets and buildings.

You can't stop the clock of progress, or travel back in time – and nor would I want to. I love this city as it is today, and I can't wait to find out what it'll be like tomorrow. But sometimes it's good to stop for a breather and take the time to celebrate the best bits of the past before they head off over the hill like Alf and his cart, a last ring of the bell swallowed up by the sound of the traffic.

1 New Piccadilly Cafe *
2 Torino's Cafe *
3 The Gargoyle Club *
4 Quo Vadis
5 The Colony Room Club *
6 The Caves de France
7 The Groucho Club
8 The French House
9 Gerry's Club
10 Lorelei
11 Bar Italia
12 Jimmy's Greek
13 Ronnie Scott's
14 The Theatre Girls Club *
15 The Gay Hussar
16 The Coach and Horses

Central London

250 metres

* No longer operating as described in text

CHAPTER ONE

Soho-itis

I have a pad in Soho; well, it's a helipad actually, located on the roof of the 24-storey tower block where I have an apartment. There are dozens of heli garages on the rooftop of my building, so the skies above the glass-canopied streets of Soho can get a little congested if all my neighbours decide to take their helicopters for a whirl at the same time, especially if the people in the five identical tower blocks nearby decide to take flight too. Still, if I'm venturing no further than the French House for a cold drink, I usually navigate my way by high-tech gondola along the network of rooftop canals and, if I've remembered to bring my Speedos along, I'll take a dip in the vast, glass-bottomed swimming pool that looks like a tropical fish tank in the sky.

No, I haven't been at one of Sherlock Holmes's pipes, nor have I had one too many absinthe shandies: this fantastical plan for a 'Brave New Soho' was actually put forward by the Pilkington Glass Company in 1954. Back in post-war, bombsite-ridden Soho, Pilkington's proposal to turn the district into something approaching a modern-day shopping mall with a touch of *Thunderbirds* thrown in was just one of many redevelopment schemes that were considered for the district. It might seem incredible to us that such a radical idea was ever conceived, but if you were to tell those Pilkington chaps that one day it would be illegal to smoke in pubs, they'd probably choke on their cigars.

If you fancy a glimpse of how Soho might've turned out, take a look at the only piece of the jigsaw to have slipped out of the box: Kemp House on Berwick Street. This incongruous, 17-storey block of flats was as close as plans for a futuristic Soho came to being realised. All I can say to that is phew. The building, which features on the cover of the Oasis album *(What's the Story) Morning Glory?*, was once home to the infamous Soho-ite and bibulous journalist Jeffrey Bernard, who made a career out of writing about his alcoholic escapades in Soho and was a drinking buddy of many of the 1950s bohemian brigade, including the painter Francis Bacon. I don't know what he thought of the place but I thank God Mr Pilkington and his glass company's attention was diverted to the Westfield shopping centre, because a high-rise Soho would've been a no-go for me – an abomination of epic proportions. After all, what makes this tiny district of London so special is its village-in-the-city appeal. It's one of the few areas of London that is not traversed by any bus route, never mind rooftop gondolas, so the pavements are full of pedestrians.

To outsiders, life in Soho might appear to be the world turned upside down, but to me it's the world turned the right way up and that's because my experience of this bastion of bohemia began at a very young age. In fact, Soho's been a part of my life since I was knee-high to a barstool. It's here that I got a lot of my education, and because the place is so full of surprises lurking around every corner, I don't suppose I shall ever stop learning. And I owe it all to my mum, who beamed down to planet Soho in the mid-1960s.

Mum was a jazz singer when she arrived here from Liverpool, and she's been singing and working in Soho's clubs ever since. We didn't actually live in the district, but moved first to Clerkenwell and later to a flat on Tottenham Court Road, which was no more than a long throw-in from Soho if launched by Chelsea legend Ian 'The Windmill' Hutchinson. One of my earliest memories of the place is being taken by Mum to the Colony Room Club on Dean Street in 1968, and to this day I clearly remember the legs of those old barstools, at eye-level to a youngster like me. This also meant that I was well below the thick fug of cigarette smoke that hung across the tiny bar, so that I couldn't really see or hear what was going on at adult level. On reflection, that was probably all for the best. Occasionally a giant hand would reach down through the nicotine clouds and ruffle my hair, or better still proffer a two shilling coin. If the atmosphere was particularly convivial, that might even rise to a ten bob note. Now there's a thing to conjure with, and conjure you could as ten shillings would buy a lad a lot of magic tricks.

The décor of the place didn't bear too close scrutiny. Arguments still rage today on Dean Street, among those without more important things to do, as to who was the first person to find their feet physically stuck to the Colony carpet. I can say without fear of contradiction that my credentials, sir, are impeccable. Now whose round is it?

I shall be returning to the Colony later, but I mention it now because of its association with the so-called 'golden age' of Soho back in the 1950s. During this period, some of the most charismatic, dissolute and infamous characters in Soho's already lively history were doing the rounds including, as I've said, Bacon and Bernard, along with Muriel Belcher, the redoubtable founder of the Colony Room Club, and George Melly, who were both still knocking about in my time. Another regular from that era was writer and broadcaster Daniel Farson, who wrote the definitive book on Soho in that decade entitled, funnily enough, *Soho in the Fifties*. Farson was a talented journalist, writer and photographer and wrote the authorised biography of his pal Francis (*The Gilded Gutter Life of Francis Bacon*). He could also be a nightmare when under the influence. I didn't know Farson personally, but I often used to see him in Soho's pubs and clubs before his death in 1997. His reputation as a hellraiser was of sufficient standing for his obituary in the *Daily Telegraph* to contain the following description: 'Television interviewer, writer and photographer who turned into a monstrous drunk in his beloved Soho.'

Part of Farson's book chronicles a Soho 'Life in a Day' kind of journey set in 1951, the year he first set foot in the district. Farson appears to have nicked this idea from James Joyce's *Ulysses*, so in the same spirit of recycling I thought I'd attempt to follow in his footsteps to see which places remain from those far-off days and to mull over just how much the area has changed in my lifetime. It's the sort of journey that would come with a government health warning these days, but attitudes to alcohol were different back then and, as Farson said himself: 'A Soho type of person would never contemplate going out "just for the one" unless it was the one day.' So, having done a fair bit of training in my time, I'm ready to give it my best shot, but please don't try this at home.

It came as a bit of a shock to read that Farson's perfect 1951 Soho day began with a coffee at a cafe; I'd have bet good money that he would've been off in search of the hair of the dog. But, of course, back in the 50s, and for decades to come, you couldn't get a drink in Soho until the pubs opened at 11 a.m., which is why serial hooch-hounds used to head to Covent Garden for an early morning livener, because prior to the fruit and veg market getting the heave-ho in 1974, the Garden's pubs were permitted to open at 5 a.m. This quirk in the licensing laws applied to pubs adjacent to many London markets, like Smithfields meat market (and probably still does in some instances). There was, however, one major proviso during Farson's day: landlords were only permitted to serve market workers.

This stumbling block didn't prevent a number of Soho characters I knew in the early 70s from regularly chancing their drinking arms in the hope of hoisting a few before the milkman delivered and, for others, the pubs of Covent Garden were the last port of call after a night out. It didn't work for everyone though: apparently the barman of the Coach and Horses on Wellington Street in Covent Garden was gunned down by a Canadian soldier during the Second World War after refusing to serve him an early-morning drink. Which seems a trifle harsh, even by Soho standards.

Daniel Farson took his coffee at Torino's cafe on the corner of Dean Street and Old Compton Street. This was a popular rendezvous for poets and artists in the 50s and was run, as most Soho cafes were back then, by an Italian family. The attraction of this place was that the owners not only allowed credit, they also permitted customers to sit and talk for hours over a small cup of 'real' coffee. Unfortunately, Soho said *arrivederci* to Torino's long ago, but not to worry, there's an establishment of a similar vintage and cultural ancestry just around the corner that we can visit instead.

Bar Italia is a Soho institution which has been run by three generations of the Polledri family since it first opened for business on Frith Street in 1949. Over the centuries, Soho's been home to a huge number of different cultures following the lead of the French Huguenots, who first arrived here in the seventeenth century having fled religious

6

persecution in their homeland. Greek Cypriots, Chinese, Russians, Poles, Spaniards, Maltese and Bengalis have all prospered and made their mark in this oasis of toleration. However, if you were to pressure me into revealing who I think has made the biggest impact on Soho, I'd have to go with the Italians. This judgement is not governed by the fact that I have a penchant for all things Italian – no, it's all down to the coffee bars the Italians introduced to Soho, which brought a welcome splash of colour and style to a dour post-war London and set the capital on its way to becoming the world's hippest city. Soho's coffee bars were a breeding ground for British rock'n'roll and hosted early gigs by the country's pop pioneers. Without them there would've been no Tommy Steele or Billy Fury, no Cliff and the Shadows, no Johnny Kidd and, further on up pop's long and winding road, no me. What a cultural vacuum there could've been.

I've been going to Bar Italia for aeons and, being the hardy individual I am, I like to take my coffee *al fresco*. Partly because of a pathological aversion to offices, I try to have all my meetings there, much to the consternation of my agent. It can be quite cramped as we huddle round tables and it can get a bit fresh in the winter, but I am sure it's extremely efficient. But more important than efficiency, there are few finer places to sit and watch the kaleidoscopic street theatre of Soho unfold.

Because the concept of sitting at a pavement table was as remote as closing down a post office in 1951, Daniel Farson watched the Soho world go by from inside Torino's Cafe, and what a different world it was. In the days before freezers and fridges were commonplace, ice used to be delivered in huge blocks by robust geezers who, in Soho, were usually of Italian descent. Farson mentions blocks of ice that were left outside shuttered restaurants and had 'started to dribble across the pavements'. Rather as the modern out-of-town revellers do now on a Friday night.

He also talks about the large number of musicians who'd venture into Soho on Monday mornings armed with instruments in their cases, making their way to the Musicians' Union offices on Archer Street in the hope of securing employment in a dance band, theatre orchestra, club band and so on.

Around this period, Bar Italia was set to take delivery of a new-fangled machine made by Gaggia, thus making it one of the first espresso bars in London and, to paraphrase the famous song that featured in the show written by the ex-jailbird and Soho drinking accomplice of Daniel Farson, Frank Norman, with lyrics and music provided by Lionel Bart, the arrival of frothy coffee meant that fings weren't what they used to be.

Unfortunately, things nowadays aren't what they used to be either when it comes to classic, family-run cafes. In the 1950s Soho had the greatest concentration of Formica-festooned Italian coffee bars in London, but over the past decade or so many of my old favourites have served their last fried slice. Perhaps the most shocking closure in recent times was the much-loved New Piccadilly Cafe on Denman Street, which first opened its doors coincidentally in 1951. Described by classic-cafe connoisseur Adrian Maddox as a 'cathedral amongst caffs', the New Piccadilly's populuxe interior remained intact right up until 2007 when a rent hike of Land's End to John O'Groats proportions forced its owner, Lorenzo Marioni – who'd put in over 50 years' service at the cafe – to throw in the tea towel. This great cafe, with its iconic 50s décor, was like a set straight out of *Expresso Bongo*, a film that starred Cliff Richard in that famous, not-to-be-reprised role of Bongo Herbert. Cliff is still clinging to his youthful looks but the New Piccadilly has bitten the dust. Its closure sounds a bit of a warning. I feel I ought to remove my bowler as a sign of respect when I mention it. And, to be honest, every time its name does pass my lips or comes to my mind I feel sickened that I/we/they didn't do more to save such an important cultural icon.

Fortunately for us another caff that belongs to old Soho and is still open for business is the Lorelei on Bateman Street. The wood-panelled exterior of this A-list anachronism is painted in the colours of the Italian flag, and its village-hall-like interior features a large, tobacco-stained mural of a mermaid that covers one wall. Also on the menu, décor or otherwise, are faux-leather banquettes, dodgy light fittings, a linoleum floor, creaky chairs, perfect pasta and pizzas, excellent espresso, great chips, an elderly owner and, just when you thought things couldn't get more authentic, you have to take a walk in the open air to get to the lavs, which are located in an outside yard. There used to be tons of caffs like the Lorelei in

Soho, but nearly all of them have done a vanishing act in recent times due to the inexorable march of the global coffee conglomerates.

It's one of life's great mysteries to me as to who wants to pay £6.90 for the privilege of having 'coffee' in a gallon of warm milk served in a bucket with a straw. It always amazes Italian friends of mine, when they're over here on a visit, to see office workers in contortions on benches in Soho Square, balancing one of those super-sized mocha frappuccinos between their knees while trying to eat a sandwich and talk on a mobile phone at the same time. Mind you, talking of contortions, you should have seen their faces when they came out of one of the brighter Soho clubs later that evening.

The sterile, uniform surroundings of the coffee-chain cafes don't pass muster either. Do you know what I want? I want to hear the dull chink of Pyrex crockery and the rattle of cutlery trays; I want wall-to-wall laminate surfaces and chrome and vitriolite espresso machines; I want steamed-up windows and the whiff of a fat fryer; I want tea urns and tomato-shaped sauce dispensers; I want a bit of banter with a familiar face behind the counter instead of being told to 'have a nice day' by remote. Above all, I want the charismatic caffs of yesteryear over the bland, branded coffee combines that have stripped our high streets, back streets, avenues and alleyways of their individuality. Give me a coffee outside Bar Italia underneath its big neon clock that directs lost latte lovers to its two-tone Formica charms and I'll greet all passers-by with a contented smile.

Sitting on Frith Street with the froth blowing off cappuccinos all around me, it's evident that catering is king in Soho these days, because just about every retail outlet opposite me is either a coffee concession, club, bar, takeaway or restaurant. Thirty years ago sex shops ruled the retail roost in Soho, with over 200 outlets dotted around the district selling a different variety of takeaway wrapped in a brown paper bag. A balance had to be found. Soho needed to be cleaned up a smidge, because its sleazy reputation was not only killing other businesses, it was also destroying the sense of community that had long existed among residents and tradespeople. The district was reborn in the 1980s, thanks to the concerted efforts of the Soho Society. However, Soho's resurgence was accompanied by the rise of commercial rents, which had been artificially low during the period the district was in the grip of vice and, inevitably, there were some casualties.

Most of the small businesses that used to supply goods and provisions to the local community – butchers, fishmongers and ironmongers – are long gone. There used to be a fair number of back-street tailors and specialist instrument-makers too, of which only a few still survive. Recently I've noticed that the record shops of Berwick Street have all but vanished, which has special resonance for me. Berwick Street used to be a Mecca for vinyl and CD junkies, and in the 70s I used to buy obscure singles on the Bluebeat label here. Initially I bought a couple out of curiosity, because it certainly wasn't the sort of thing that would've been played on the self-proclaimed 'Nation's Favourite' pop music station, BBC Radio One. Of course, had I been around a few years earlier, I would've been able to walk into Soho's mod clubs, like the Scene or the Flamingo, not more than a few yards away, and hear this kind of music every night. Anyway, by the time I was about 17, my collection of Bluebeat singles had grown to a couple of hundred and a fair proportion of these 45s were by Prince Buster, including one called 'Madness'. I can even recall the number of the single: BB 170. Of course, this later became the name of a very successful and tremendously talented British pop group. I'm wondering now whatever did happen to BB 170!

Obviously the demise of small business isn't just a Soho phenomenon – it's a familiar tale on the high streets of cities everywhere – but because Soho is essentially a village, their passing is more noticeable and keenly felt. However, Bar Italia is still doing business after all this time and will probably do so for many years to come, because not only is it popular with the hip brigade, it also has very strong ties with London's Italian community – you only have to be around when Italy are playing a footie match to see that. Thousands of Italians gathered outside the cafe for the 2006 World Cup final between France and Italy, despite the fact that there was little or no chance of seeing any of the game on the two TV screens which are located at the back of the bar. Those of you who haven't yet seen the game and don't want to know the result, please turn away now. Italy won! Funnily enough, I watched the game on TV in a bar in southern Italy and it was followed by the news, which included a report from London showing the Italian crowd celebrating outside Bar Italia. Quite a surreal moment for me and, by all accounts, a pretty messy affair for them. Having failed to stock up on ticker tape, the Polledri family decided to throw the next best thing from the windows above: pasta. Good job England didn't win: King Edwards could have done some serious damage.

After my caffeine fix and a spot of people-watching, it's time once again to follow in the footsteps of Farson. His next port of call was the York Minster. A trek to the cathedral of Yorkshire's county town does seem an awfully long way to go just for a tiny measure of claret and a wafer-thin canapé, but fortunately I don't have to go that far: the York Minster is the former name of the famous French House pub on Dean Street, which is a relief because I believe you have to confirm your membership of the former club in order to partake of the wine, and I didn't even make it to the font.

Back in 1951, Daniel Farson moseyed over to 'the French', as it has always been known, as soon as the doors opened at 11.30 a.m. for a few glasses of shampoo and a chinwag with the pub's legendary landlord, Gaston Berlemont. The pub was a rendezvous for the French Resistance during the Second World War and, allegedly, the location where Charles de Gaulle drew up his Free French call-to-arms speech. Gaston, who was born in an upstairs room shortly after his father took over the pub in 1914, sported a huge handlebar moustache and was a master of diplomacy when it came to ejecting troublesome customers. 'I'm afraid one of us is going to have to leave, and it's not going to be me' was his signature line when such action needed to be taken. Indeed, Daniel Farson was diplomatically banished from the French by Gaston on many occasions, which is no surprise when you understand that he was cut from the same cloth as his contemporaries, whom he describes as being such reckless drinkers 'that when they met the next morning they had to ask if they needed to apologise for the day before'.

I remember Gaston well because he was still running the pub right up until his retirement on Bastille Day 1989. Unlike Farson, I don't think I was ever benignly booted out of the pub, but we do share something in common at the French: among the many black-and-white photographs of movie stars, politicians, aviators, boxers and legendary drinkers that adorn the walls of this bijou boozer, there happens to be one of him and another featuring my ugly mug.

All the legendary Soho drinkers of the 50s were regulars at the French, including Dylan Thomas, who, before he went plastered into that dark night, left his one and only manuscript of *Under Milk Wood* under a table in the bar following a night on the lash. Amazing he managed to misplace it, as that's where he ended up most evenings. Apparently, Gaston retrieved the script and kept it safe until the grateful head of BBC radio drama came to collect it.

When Gaston retired it seemed as if the lights were about to go out all over Soho, but the new owners, Lesley Lewis and Noel Botham, fitted into his seemingly irreplaceable shoes rather well. Lesley formerly made clothes for strippers at a club on Old Compton Street, having acquired the skill of dropping stitches in all the right places, and Noel is an author and journalist. The French has been a second home for thirsty journalists across the years and the source of many a missed deadline no doubt; it's a tradition that Noel has worked hard to perpetuate and resulted in him establishing Anti-Alcoholics Anonymous. This august organisation consists only of its founder member, who allows acquaintances to phone him if they feel in danger of climbing on the wagon, in which case Noel, being the altruistic soul that he is, promises to deter them from going through with it at any time of the day or night.

The reason the French has lost none of its *je ne sais quoi* is down to the fact that Lesley and Noel have kept the place pretty much how it was in Gaston's time, and even maintained the arcane practice of serving beer in half-pint glasses only. I've always believed this to be a Gallic custom that had some special significance but I recently discovered how off-kilter my theory has been all these years: beer is served in halves at the French because Gaston didn't have room for pint glasses behind the bar. One good thing about having a rule is that you can break it. So every year, on 1 April, the shelving is extended and they break with tradition and have a Pints Day. For the last three years I have pulled the first pint of the day, hence my photo on the wall. It's all for charity, and always a very jolly affair, but I don't tend to hang around too long, as it's not just beer you can order by the pint, it's anything you want. I'm usually gone by the first order for gin.

★

Well, that's enough digression, we have an onerous schedule to follow. Come on, keep up at the back! Man cannot live by drink alone. Although many round here have tried. Including Ian Board, the second manager of the Colony following the redoubtable Jewish lesbian Muriel Belcher, who reckoned the only nourishment he was getting for many years of his life was from the lemon in his gin and tonic.

Back in 1951 Daniel Farson moved on to Wheeler's fish restaurant on Old Compton Street at 2 p.m. In its time Wheeler's was one of London's premier eateries, with a menu which boasted 32 different ways of serving lobster and sole. Once there, he met up with some of his arty chums – like Lucien Fried, I mean Freud – and he paints quite a picture of the place (geddit?) in its heyday. However, Wheeler's rolled out of Soho a few years ago and there are only a handful of restaurants that remain from that time. Jimmy's Greek restaurant on Frith Street is still going (without Jimmy though) and I often used to go to this basement eatery with my mum for a slap-up plate of moussaka and chips and a vintage bottle of retsina. Legend has it that Jimmy's subterranean vaulted ceiling was originally built as a section of an unsuccessful tube line. Maybe they could sell it to Crossrail: just imagine, you could then drop your kebab before you've even left the tube station!

It's fair to say that I wasn't really a gastronome in my teens or early 20s. But I wasn't alone in that: the food revolution was some years off. The only gastronomy you could find in pubs back then came in the form of ham or cheese rolls in a Perspex bread bin on the bar, not forgetting a pickled egg starter, of course. However, exotic food and I made up a few years later and are now the best of friends. Though I still keep my distance from the jellied eel, much as I have tried to embrace that particular delicacy.

Out of the vast array of restaurants that the district has to offer, one of my current favourites is Quo Vadis on Dean Street, which has also added its own rather terrific members' club to Soho's firmament. Quo Vadis was not only around in the early 1950s, it was a Soho fixture before the talkies arrived. The building itself has its own global claim to fame, as it was upstairs here that Karl Marx put the finishing touches to his romantic comedy *Das Kapital*. But this classy establishment has changed greatly since its first owner, Peppino Leoni, passed away a few years ago, so I think a visit to another Farson favourite is in order, the Gay Hussar on Greek Street.

I'm not a regular at the Gay Hussar, although every time I set foot in the place I feel I should become one because this small, dimly lit, wood-panelled, banquette-lined restaurant has real atmosphere. The layout of the dining area has barely changed in 60 odd years and nor, by the looks of things, has the menu, which makes this place a real retro experience. There can't be many finer sights, on a cold winter's day, than a plate piled high with roast duck, mashed potato and red cabbage, and a quaffable glass of Hungarian red or three.

The Gay Hussar began life as the Budapest in the late 40s,

before its founder, Victor Sassie, opted for the new name in the early 50s. The Happy Hussar would probably have saved a lot of confusion over the years. Being a late convert to the Gay Hussar, I didn't get to meet Victor, who sold the place in 1988, but I recently shared a glass there with actress Amanda Barrie – she of *Carry On* and *Coronation Street* fame – who remembers him from the early days, thanks to the kindness he showed her when she was an impoverished aspiring dancer and actress.

I decided to take Amanda back to the Gay Hussar for the first time in over 50 years. Sharing a bottle of Bull's Blood in this restaurant beloved by journalists, media figures and left-wing politicians, many of whom feature in the huge collection of framed caricatures that hang from the walls, Amanda revealed how, as a waif-like teenager, Victor Sassie took pity on her and used to give her cheese and crackers in the restaurant because the food provided at the Theatre Girls Club where she lodged was not what you might call *haute cuisine*. Just think, had it not been for Victor's generosity, Amanda might well have jacked the acting lark in and we'd never have got to see her Cleopatra, the role she was born to play.

Some film buffs might argue that Liz Taylor and Richard Burton are the classic classical lovers in the Hollywood blockbuster *Cleopatra*, but for me it has to be Amanda and her dashing Mark Antony, played by Sid James. No film can be entirely without merit if it includes the classic line 'Infamy, infamy, they've all got it in for me!' And speaking of old cheese, the cheese that Victor fed her wasn't just any old cheese: no, this was a special, soft, reddish Hungarian cheese that was served on an oval silver platter and resembled a mousse. Over the course of our lunch Amanda recalled the cheese so vividly, in spite of the fact that she hadn't eaten it since, that I decided there and then to investigate whether or not a little reunion might be possible.

As I mentioned, the menu has barely altered at the Gay Hussar, so I thought there was a fair chance that the mystery cheese was still being served. I secretly described it to the manager, who informed me that it was called Liptauer and, yes, it was still on the menu. When he plonked the cheese mousse surprise down in front of Amanda five minutes later, the look on her face was not unlike that of a startled rabbit, which you'll be glad to hear is not on the menu here. Do not underestimate the power of cheese. A Proustian experience was triggered the moment Amanda dug her cracker into the orange globe and the memories came flooding back.

Astonishingly, Amanda first arrived in Soho in 1948, aged just 13, having been expelled from her school in Lancashire. She moved into the Theatre Girls Club, which was situated directly opposite Victor's restaurant. This building, which today provides accommodation for the homeless, was initially built as the Soho Club and Home for Working Girls in 1883 and provided short- and long-term accommodation for 'young women engaged in business, and students'. In the 1920s it became the Theatre Girls Club and provided the same service as above, but exclusively for women working in the theatre. In the 20s, acting was a precarious occupation for women and the link between this profession and the oldest profession in the book hadn't yet gone away.

The key function of the Theatre Girls Club was to prevent unemployed actresses from considering a rather different 'role' between jobs out of financial necessity. The seamier side of the district wouldn't have escaped their notice, owing to the fact that, prior to the introduction of the Street Offences Act (1959), scores of prostitutes openly touted for trade on the pavements of Soho. Girls didn't have too far to travel in order to fall from grace, so to speak. Amanda remembers the ladies of the night as being rather friendly and said that because she was so young they used to look out for her and made sure she got home safely.

The Theatre Girls Club was also the temporary home of former Tiller Girl and future Speaker of the House of Commons Betty Boothroyd. My all-roller-skating, all-dancing, cartwheeling late mother-in-law, Christina Martin (the cartwheels normally took place at parties – when a chap was being a bit tedious she would hand him her glass, do a cartwheel, retrieve the glass and say, 'As you were saying...'), also lived at this charitable institution when she was between jobs in variety theatre.

Amanda lived at the Theatre Girls Club for several years and left when her career began to take off. I got the chance to go inside this white-stone and red-brick building with Amanda, but sadly no trace remains of the fabulous Victorian interior she remembers from her time at the club. However, one thing that's changed very little is the view from the fourth floor, where her dormitory used to be, although the slap-and-tickle goings-on she used to witness occurring in the upstairs rooms across the street appear to be a thing of the past. Looking out to the north end of Greek Street you can see Soho Square and just before it sits the Gay Hussar.

Having feasted on wild cherry soup, goulash and a nibble of cheese, it's 3 p.m. and time for a couple of sherbets at one of the most remarkable survivors from Daniel Farson's 1951 Soho sojourn. I'm off to the Colony Room Club on Dean Street which has barely changed in 60 years . . . well, until very recently, that is. It is with the gravest of expressions that I have to report that since this visit the Colony has served up its last beverage and has gone the way of the dodo, and with it Soho has lost its bohemian heartbeat and one of its best friends. Back in the days of Prohibition – well, that's what I call the era when pubs shut at 2.30 p.m. and didn't open again till 5.30 p.m. – a Soho drinker could potentially die of thirst in the afternoon, but none did thanks to a loophole in the licensing laws that permitted private members' clubs to sell alcohol from 3 p.m. till 11 p.m. And the most celebrated Soho private members' drinking den of the period was the Colony. Opened in 1948 by the formidable Muriel Belcher, this watering hole soon became the favoured afternoon hangout of committed hedonists and will be forever woven into the fabric of Soho's history.

One of the club's strictest rules remained to the very end: members must not be boring. Belligerent, bevvied-up, bellicose, bombastic, boisterous and bonkers were all by the by, but boring . . . um, no! Unfortunately, the selection process wasn't foolproof because I managed to slip through the net, but, as I mentioned earlier, I first started coming here before Neil Armstrong set foot on the moon and I think I was finally rewarded on account of my persistence. Yes, I'm nothing if not persistent and often ended up in that state after a session at the Colony.

I well remember the first time I went through the Colony's emerald-green door on Dean Street and up the dingy staircase to the tiny club room on the first floor, its walls covered with artefacts donated by the constant stream of artists who'd been seduced by the club's raffish charm over the years. I was seven years old when I entered the claustrophobic, bilious-green club room that day in 1968, and when I left a couple of hours later I'd probably aged another ten in terms of life experience. The Colony was the sort of place that you either instantly fell in love with and felt right at home in, or took fright at and couldn't wait to get out of. I fell straight away into the former category and have fallen in, and indeed out of, it ever since.

The first obstacle to overcome when venturing into the Colony was the stream of expletives that Muriel Belcher hurled at you on arrival from her 'throne', which was a barstool by the door. If you could handle that, which many couldn't, you were in. My mum had no problems with the language or behaviour at the Colony as she worked in a similar club just down the road called the Kismet, which had a navy-blue hardboard ceiling with stars and moons cut out. The

Kismet was located in an airless, damp, smoky cellar off the Charing Cross Road and was nicknamed 'the iron lung' and 'death in the afternoon' by those who'd had the pleasure. It was a place where the low life met the elite. In the *Daily Telegraph* obituary of the fiery, red-haired journalist, writer and Soho addict Sandy Fawkes (December 2005), who had a liking for such drinking establishments and was a friend of my mum's, a story is recounted of a passing visitor asking what the strange smell was at the Kismet. 'Failure,' was the reply.

The atmosphere and clientele of the Colony that I remember from my first visit probably hadn't altered much since Daniel Farson first stepped over Muriel's threshold in 1951. The place very quickly became a popular hangout for budding artists after a skint Francis Bacon walked into the newly opened club in 1948 and Muriel offered him a tenner a week to attract new members to the club. Bacon encouraged fellow painters and their wealthy patrons to join the Colony where they socialised with a diverse array of characters whom Muriel felt would complement their artistic bent, all of them packed tightly inside that dark, smoky room. There were jazz musicians, painters, toffs, strippers (still wearing their feather boas), poets and gangsters. If homosexuality was still 'the love that dared not speak its name' on the streets of London, here in the Colony it could sing, shout, dance and paint its name and address.

This was the only place an outsider could go to mix with other like-minded souls with no fear of discrimination, unless you were boring, of course, in which case you would last precisely ten seconds until Muriel or indeed Bacon got you in their sights. This place needed no bouncers. The whole scene was, for me, perfectly summed up in the Kinks song 'Lola' which recounts the story of a naive heterosexual dancing with a transvestite beneath electric candlelight in a club down in old Soho. The song caused a bit of a stir at the time, but for me it was a tale of everyday life that was going on all around me.

The Colony's pedigree as a top-notch standard bearer from Soho's boho past was enhanced by the fact that the club's licence was held by just three people throughout the 60 years of its existence – Belcher, Ian Board and Michael Wojas, the last at the helm – and was handed down as an aristocrat might his estate and jewels. However, those jewels have lost their sparkle and now that the club has gone many ex-patrons have said that Soho won't be what it used to be. But, perhaps, as Ian Board once said in typically dyspeptic fashion, 'It never was what it f*****g used to be!'

The Colony's future had come under threat in the past of course but they had somehow managed to keep the spirit alive and flowing at the bar. After Soho began to shed its sleazy image in the mid-1980s, a new generation of restaurants and members' clubs appeared and the district became the favoured haunt of the media and arts brigade. The swankiest new club on the block was the Groucho which opened in 1985 next door but one to the Colony. Although close in proximity, the two clubs couldn't have been further apart in terms of style, size and comfort. If you ordered a vodka and tonic at the Groucho, not only was it served with ice and a slice, it would also be delivered to you on a tray while you perused the menu sitting on a comfy sofa. The Colony didn't do ice until the new millennium, and as for a slice, not a hope in hell. Such sophisticated delicacies were reserved for the manager only. Furthermore, if you had the audacity to ask for crisps you'd be told to bugger off to London Zoo! Nevertheless, the club survived the onslaught from its new rivals and also the introduction of all-day drinking in pubs, which began in the late 1980s. I didn't officially become a member of the Groucho until a few years ago, but that trifling matter didn't stop me from giving the place the benefit of my company from time to time, until I quite literally landed myself in the shit.

You could see the back of the Groucho, including the windows to the ladies', gents' and snooker room, through the green frame of the small window in the toilet of the Colony. I think it was my mum who put the idea in my head. She noted, during a long, hot summer, that one or more of the Groucho's windows were left ajar of an evening. Fired with a certain feeling of discontent at not having been invited as an inaugural member and a natural inquisitiveness about what they were getting up to in this flash new kid on the block, I decided that an exploration in the greatest British tradition of these things was a matter of some urgency. A delegation led by myself and Anne, my wife, sallied forth. After much scrambling over duct pipes and air-conditioning units and up and down various flat roofs adorned by single plimsoles and bicycle frames – the universal furniture of flat roofs – we reached our destination: the open window of the ladies'.

This was all done, I hasten to add, without ropes or crampons and with the help only of a broken school chair. Being the chivalrous chap I am, I gave Anne a leg up, so she went in first. A few seconds passed before she popped her head out and gave me the all clear. I scrambled up the short drainpipe after her, into the Groucho's plush, red ladies' powder room.

Somewhat dishevelled and covered in smut, we stood brushing ourselves down and getting our breath back. Ha ha! We made it! What jolly japes!

Now the only issue was how to get a drink. In the Groucho only members can buy refreshments, so a spurious celebrity would have to be invoked at the bar, with a 'Yeah, we're with Neil Tennant/Janet Street-Porter/Stephen Fry . . .'. Leaving the others to their own devices, we both took a deep breath and strode boldly to the door, ready to enter the fray, only to bump straight into one of our daughters' teachers coming the other way. Miss Terry. Here she was, faced with Mr and Mrs McPherson emerging from the ladies' lavatory together, red-faced and slightly out of breath. My mind raced. Even the most plausible explanation was implausible, including the truth. There was absolutely no way round this Ayckbourn-esque scenario. So we simply smiled positively and strode off with our noses in the air. Now where is that Keith Allen?

By 2001 my Groucho trick had become something of a party piece. But in that long, hot summer, as I celebrated my fortieth year, it became more of a space odyssey. Having partaken of a particularly generous luncheon with some pals I'd been working with on a show called *Night Fever* – c'mon, who can forget Pop Monkey? – I was perched, in a Lewis *'The Professionals'* Collins style, on the sill of the Colony's toilet window. This was not somewhere, I hasten to add, that I spent my whole life but it was a manoeuvre I must have successfully performed a dozen times. A gaggle of excitable onlookers crowded in behind me, weighing up the odds as to whether it would be advisable to follow.

I went to leap the small gap to a flat roof opposite, but things didn't exactly go to plan, and I found myself dangling in mid-air. What a turn-up, literally, as the turn-up of my jeans was caught in the window catch and that was about all that was keeping me from plummeting to certain death on the roof of a Chinese restaurant below.

I was now hanging upside down, mentally thanking Mr Levis and all the generations of his family for the consistent sturdiness of their denim, when I heard a ripping noise. Face down, I frantically grabbed the drainpipe in front of me, just as my turn-up gave way. I got hold of it and clung on for dear life, praise the Lord. Then I began to slide – the pipe had been given a good coating of anti-burglar paint, a by-product of axle grease.

I was gaining momentum on my slow downwards trajectory, but I seemed to be moving quite smoothly and, with my legs now firmly locked on, I looked down. The flat roof below appeared to be approaching quite gently and I must have been about halfway down when I became aware of a kind of disembodied cheering, echoing down the small space between the buildings. My confidence was growing: hey, I'm gonna do this! And then, an ominous silence. Followed by a loud creaking sound.

The drainpipe was coming away from the wall. My world was, quite literally, turning upside down. Water – at least I hope that's what it was – cascaded down the wall, up my trouser legs and reappeared down my neck and up my nose. I started to fall backwards in slow motion and flopped on my back into a huge puddle of pigeon droppings.

When I came round after landing on my head, I looked like I'd taken a dip in a Victorian sewer in need of renovation. I also noticed, perhaps unsurprisingly, that my loyal friends had done a runner. Miraculously, I managed to sneak out of Soho without attracting any accusatory glances or pinched nostrils and felt certain I'd managed to escape justice. The only stain on my person or character was the bloody great big one that seemed to be covering every inch of my gladrags, or so I thought. The next morning Michael Wojas telephoned to say that a Chinese chef had seen the lead singer of Madness jump off the restaurant's kitchen roof seconds before the place was flooded and told me to get round and fix the knackered pipework pronto.

In Daniel Farson's *Soho in the Fifties* he didn't leave the Colony until 4.30 p.m. and not by the same route as me on the occasion of my fortieth. That means he'd have spent a large part of the afternoon in the company of splenetic, gin-soaked friends and acquaintances whose chief amusement was to lob verbal grenades at one another – what Ben Jonson described as 'the leprosy of wit'. The person Farson marks out as being of Champions League standard at this game was the writer Colin MacInnes, who generally entered the Colony by 'pushing the door open abruptly as if it had done him some injustice'. MacInnes chronicled the emergence of the 'mod' scene in his novel *Absolute Beginners* in the late 1950s, with Soho very much the headquarters of this 'un-silent teenage revolution'. The book's jam-packed with references to coffee bars, scooters, jazz, Italian fashions and 'disc shops' which reads like a list of my favourite things minus the raindrops on roses and whiskers on kittens. And speaking of jam, the old 'modfather' himself, Paul Weller, chose it as his book on *Desert Island Discs* not long ago.

Funnily enough, when a movie of the book was being made in the 80s Clive Langer, the producer of Madness's discs, was contracted to do the music and in conversation with Julien Temple, the director, it was suggested I might make a good lead. It was with a mixture of excitement and trepidation, never having acted before, that I approached an audition. I had to do a little scene with the main girl, and considering my inexperience, I thought it went quite well. Seemingly happy, Julien then sent me to meet the choreographer in a dance studio round the corner. Well, if I thought I was an inexperienced actor, nothing could have prepared me for a professional dance audition. I shall spare you the grizzly details but suffice it to say that about an hour in, and on the point of exhaustion, I was being encouraged, again, by the Japanese choreographer and his team to make one more salmon-like leap, just that bit higher.

I don't remember much after that. But when I called Anne to tell her how it had gone, she was terribly amused to hear I was calling from the casualty department of the Middlesex hospital. I had broken my big toe, which I realised may have been a bit of a handicap in performing in an all-singing, all-dancing musical. Surprisingly, I never did get the call. Just think how my life may have changed. Hollywood? I only got as far as Holloway.

It's also funny to think that moody old MacInnes was in his mid-40s when he wrote the novel. It's a triumph that he managed to write anything at all, given the frequency of his visits to the Colony and other Soho clubs. Soho can be the spur but also the killer of creative endeavours.

As the exotically named Meary J. Tambimuttu, editor of *Poetry London* in the 1940s, correctly described it to a friend:

'It's a dangerous place, you must be careful.'

'Fights with knives?'

'No, a worse danger. You might get Soho-itis, you know.'

'No, I don't. What is it?'

'If you get Soho-itis,' Tambi said very seriously, 'you will stay there always, day and night, and never get any work done ever. You have been warned!'

One of MacInnes's other haunts was located bang next door to the Colony and this is where Farson headed next on his daily routine. The Caves de France was a ground-floor drinking club whose clientele was partly made up of Soho habitués who'd been refused membership to the Colony. Apparently, Muriel Belcher knew instinctively whether an aspiring Colony member would be right for the club. You didn't necessarily have to be a great wit, gay, rich, arty or talented to become a member (although any of the above might prevent you from being instantaneously dispatched back down the staircase with a barrage of expletives ringing in your ear), but she had a game hunter's nose for sniffing out a misfit, especially a washed-out, defeated misfit. The Caves was full of such refugees, chronic sufferers of Soho-itis one and all.

Belcher didn't approve of her clientele sneaking off to the Caves de France but many of them did from time to time and Farson describes the place as being 'the closest to Bohemia'. The picture he paints of the majority of Caves dwellers sounds pretty grim, all ravaged faces and musty-smelling clothes, which says much about the spurious glamour of life on the lash in the 50s. Indeed, many of Farson's talented contemporaries failed to live up to their early promise and died young, having resorted to the bottle. Farson himself came close to joining the list of Soho casualties but somehow managed to make it beyond bus-pass age. He died in 1997, aged 70, having retreated to the West Country some years earlier. But despite checking out of Soho, he could never really leave and often came back for a fix of his spiritual home and was enthusiastic about the district's revival. And with the Caves de France long gone, I'm off to the place he described in the 1980s as 'the perfect club for Soho'.

★

Originally conceived as a club for publishers to entertain their clients, the Groucho Club's membership soon extended to people drawn from all fields of the media and the arts; even pop musicians were allowed in, vocalists too! The club's now very much a part of the Soho furniture, but in its early days it was viewed as an interloper by the old brigade, such as Jeffrey Bernard. However, he and other survivors from the good old days gradually acquired a taste for the club's smart but casual charms. By a strange quirk of timely table-turning, a new breed of talented young British artists (YBAs) – the likes of Damien Hirst and Tracey Emin – arrived on the scene in the early 1990s and not only beat a path to the Groucho, but also started to colonise the Colony, and a period of retro-bohemianism took hold. In paying homage to their spiritual antecedents – the post-war 'School of London' painters, including Francis Bacon – the YBAs reinvigorated the Colony's fortunes.

The cross-pollination of 'old' and 'new' Soho meant that for all its swagger, the Groucho was never going to be immune from the occasional bout of dysfunctional behaviour from some of its members. For instance, the biggest star of Brit Art was apparently renowned for imitating his most controversial works of art by getting pickled in real life on more than one occasion.

Daniel Farson spent his time in the Caves de France ginning it up and reminiscing about his 50s pals; he also reflected on 'sinning in Soho'. Not long ago, as part of my intensive research, I had a conversation that touched on these two subjects over a game of snooker at the Groucho Club with Stephen Fry.

Stephen met Daniel Farson's greatest Soho chum, Francis Bacon, on several occasions in the 1980s. Bacon had, of course, gone on to achieve wealth, acclaim and notoriety in equally large measures since his days on a tenner a week at the Colony, and was, like Farson, a Soho survivor on account of being alert to the dangers of falling too far under the district's insidious spell. He'd managed to stay the course, so he told Stephen, because he had a 'little man in his head' who would tell him when he'd had enough to drink and remind him that there was 'work to be done tomorrow'. The reason Bacon felt that many of his fellow artists – like John Minton and the two Roberts, Messrs Colquhoun and MacBryde – had died young was because of the absence of that 'little man'. Looking at the evidence, he certainly has a point. Minton was an extremely talented artist, designer and draughtsman whom Bacon considered his equal. He had a huge lust for life but became booze-dependent and took his own life aged 40 in 1957. Colquhoun and MacBryde met at the Glasgow School of Art and lived and worked together around Soho thereafter. Colquhoun was the more successful artist, yet both succumbed to the sauce: Colquhoun at 48 in 1962; MacBryde four years later aged 52.

Happily for us, Bacon observed that Stephen also appeared to have a 'little man' in his head, having watched him slip away from a party early, politely declining the host's plea to stay for 'just one more'. However, back in the days when Mr Fry lived nearby and the little man in his head used to take regular holidays, Stephen would often leave the Groucho in the wee small hours and walk home along Brewer Street, heading for his flat in St James's.

Walking down Brewer Street at that time in the morning is usually a pretty challenging experience and it's made all the more uncomfortable if you have raw egg running down the back of your neck at the time. This is the fate which befell the noble Mr Fry on one occasion.

Stopping to give a couple of 'les girls' cigarettes one morning, Stephen received a direct hit from the kind of egg you wouldn't want to go to work on. When he inquired of the girls, 'Who in the name of Arnold Bennett just did that?' he was told, 'Oh, it's 'im!' by one of the girls. She continued: 'It's this bloke who's got a weird religious thing about prostitutes and drives around at all hours throwing eggs at our Johns. He obviously thought you were a punter.' Now, I wouldn't normally divulge such information in case 'no smoke without fire' doubts are raised but, as Stephen said himself, 'If anyone were innocent of such a design, then that person is me!'

The resurgence of Soho came as a result of the district shedding its sleazy image, and by the late 1980s the number of sex establishments had dropped from a peak of nearly 200 in the 1970s to around 30. But sex and Soho will always be synonymous because the two have been bedfellows for over 200 years: even Casanova lived here for a while back in the eighteenth century. Had he arrived a little later, and of course if he could have found the time between all his *liaising*, he may well have paid a visit to a certain Mrs Theresa Berkley, who kept a brothel at that time at 28 Charlotte Street – which is not, strictly speaking, in Soho but shares some of Soho's flavour – with a cat o' nine tails, leather straps and birch canes kept flexible in water. Well, thank goodness she kept her birch in water.

When I talked to Peter Stringfellow at his latest club on Wardour Street he was over the moon to have finally got a place in the district because he reckons that just the name 'Soho' arouses the interest of potential punters in a way that Crouch End never could.

Peter will never be more than a small mullet in a big pond compared to Soho's 'King of Erotica', the late Paul Raymond, who died in 2008, but I understand where he's coming from . . . Sheffield, in fact! That's where he used to travel from on excursions to London as a teenager, crammed into a Bedford van with his mates. But, as Peter was keen to emphasise, he and his pals were adamant they weren't travelling to London, oh no, they were heading for *Soho* which was, he says, an 'almost mystical place for Sheffield boys' and where they believed the 'naughty girls' were to be found. Peter remembers being fleeced in one of Soho's many 'clip joints' on that first trip, where the promise of adult entertainment failed to materialise but a large bill for fake champers did. However, it didn't take him long to find a place where the kind of rip-offs he and his mates had come to see were happening in all their naughty, naked glory.

His overriding memory of this trip, which was his starter for ten, is that he saw a dozen or so of the most attractive women he'd ever seen in his life, all of whom wore 'heavy brown make-up'.

While some came to Soho for sex, others came for the music – especially the jazz. I'll let you into a secret. Strictly speaking, my name's not Suggs. I named myself after a jazz flautist called Pete Suggs, not because I liked his stuff – in fact, I'm not sure I've ever heard anything by him – but because when I was a teenager I decided I needed a cool nickname. Who doesn't at that age? So I stuck a pin into an encyclopaedia of jazz musicians and there he was. As I said earlier, my mum was a jazz singer and my dad was a huge jazz enthusiast, so it all seemed to fit together nicely and the name stuck.

Which brings us to the next item on Farson's 1951 itinerary, which he subtitled 'Just a Little Jazz'. He headed to the 100 Club on Oxford Street, which is still going strong, although many decades have passed since it was solely a jazz club. Farson mentions watching George 'Bunny Bum' Melly singing 'Frankie and Johnny' in 1951, which is quite poignant because 'Good Time George' gave his final performance at the club just a few weeks before he died in 2007.

A couple of months before that I met up with George at Ronnie Scott's on Frith Street. This club is a Soho institution of 50 years' standing, and that's where I shall get my jazz fix and reflect on that last chat I had with him. George felt Soho was the right place for jazz from the moment he arrived here in the late 1940s. But it wasn't just the excitement of jazz in

Soho that appealed to him; he fully immersed himself in the whole scene. He told me that, when young, he saw a heading in the *News of the World* that read: 'Soho: City of Sin', and that was it. He immediately put the paper down, headed straight there, and never looked back. He was a Colony Room regular and adored Muriel Belcher, affectionately referring to her as a 'benevolent witch', and he even met his wife, Diana, at the club. George was also a blindingly funny writer and his anecdotes about 1950s Soho are priceless; he describes the men's boutique Vince on Newburgh Street as being the only shop 'where they measured your inside leg even when you bought a tie'.

When we met at Ronnie Scott's it hadn't long been taken over by the theatre impresario Sally Greene, who'd given the place an expensive makeover. She'd bought the place from Ronnie Scott's business partner, Pete King, with whom he co-founded the club in Gerrard Street in 1959 before moving to the current address in 1965. George spoke affectionately of Ronnie Scott, who died in 1996, and made special mention of the deadpan routine he repeated night after night on stage as the club's MC: 'A thousand flies can't be wrong,' said Ronnie of the food being served. George was renowned for the annual gigs he played at the club over Christmas and New Year for many years with John Chilton's Feetwarmers and, having witnessed a few of those ribald, vaudevillian performances in my time, all I can say is we won't see his like again.

We're also unlikely to see many new jazz clubs opening in Soho unless there's a big revival. Trad jazz had its heyday in the

50s and early 60s and the smoky cellar clubs that George remembered are long gone. Ronnie Scott's was, from the beginning, mainly a modern jazz club and over the years has played host to the biggest jazzers of the age and also sprung some non-jazz surprises too. For instance, The Who gave their debut performance of 'Tommy' here and Jimi Hendrix performed live for the last time, jamming with the band War. However, since the takeover at the club there's been criticism over the plethora of non-jazz acts booked to play. Others have suggested that the venue has been sanitised and belongs to 'corporate Soho'. I'm not so sure. To me, it's still a hugely intimate venue and one of the most atmospheric clubs in the world.

Aside from the fact that they've scraped the chewing gum off the carpet and improved the catering, it really hasn't changed that much from the 70s and 80s, when I used to come here to see the likes of Art Blakey and Ella Fitzgerald. But therein lies the nub of the problem: the Art Blakeys, Ella Fitzgeralds, Dizzy Gillespies and Stan Getzs of this world, like George and Ronnie, are no longer of this world. If they were, they'd still be booked to play at the club, but the golden age of modern jazz has passed too. The quota of jazz acts that play the venue has certainly increased in recent years, but whether the club can survive on jazz alone, who knows? Even when Ronnie Scott was around, the club experienced quiet times and often struggled financially and he had a stock joke in his repertoire to emphasise the fact: 'You should have been here last week,' he'd say to the audience. 'We had the bouncers chucking them in!'

★

Having had a few spiced rums and all that jazz, I find that, unlike Louis Armstrong, I don't have all the time in the world if I'm to complete Farson's Soho safari. Back in 1951 he would have hit the pubs next, or rather what he calls the 'Queer Pubs'. The first was the Golden Lion on Dean Street, which is still there today, although no longer full of sailors and guardsmen on leave looking for some action, as in Farson's day. The other pub was the Fitzroy Tavern, which was, and still is, on Charlotte Street. It just goes to show how much things have changed over the decades. Pound for pink pound, there are probably as many gay bars as straight in Soho these days, but whether this means the ratio of straight to gay people has altered I doubt very much. As gay sex was illegal back then, you can bet your dollar bottom there were plenty of closets that remained closed in the 50s, even in Soho. But because everything is so unconcealed in Soho these days, I think the dark ages are gone forever. Part of the reason the gay community was attracted to Soho – aside from the historic openness and 'anything goes' legacy of the district – was boring old economics. The collision of an increasing acknowledge-ment of gay culture and the recession of the late 1980s, which made property in Soho affordable, brought gay businesses to the area in numbers. In a few years bars and cafes offering a bit of glamour and styling were fixtures on Old Compton and Wardour Streets. Straight drinking dens and some high-street chains now copy the clean lines and attention to décor these gay establishments introduced some 20 or more years earlier.

After downing a swift crème de menthe in the Golden Lion without getting the glad eye, I'm heading for the Coach and Horses on Greek Street for a swift one. The Coach doesn't feature in Farson's 50s booze cruise, although he mentions it later in the book because it was the favoured haunt of his friend, Mr Bernard. The Coach and its truculent landlord, Norman Balon, featured in Bernard's weekly 'Low Life' column in the *Spectator* magazine, where he wrote about his sozzled Soho days until his formidable daily intake of alcohol began to take its toll on his health and reliability. Thereafter, the magazine often posted the notice 'Jeffrey Bernard is unwell' in place of his column, which later became the title of a West End play in which he finds himself locked in the Coach for a night. Bernard died in 1997 and Norman Balon, the self-appointed 'rudest landlord in London' (who even barred his mother for being 'past it'), finally retired in 2006, having put in 63 years' service behind the bar.

Norman's departure was greeted with 'another nail in the coffin for bohemian Soho' headlines, but the thing is, he keeps coming back: every time I go to the Coach he's in there watching over things. Having been a fixture at the Coach for so long, I just don't think he can pull himself away from the pumps. Still, it's jolly nice to see the old git every once in a while. I must remember to get hold of his 1991 memoirs, which were charmingly entitled *You're Barred, You Bastards*.

At closing time in 1951 – strictly 11 p.m. back then, of course – Farson headed to the rather grand Gargoyle Club on Dean Street, which dates back to the 1920s 'Bright Young

Things' era. No expense was spared on the décor here, with Edwin Lutyens hired as architect and Henri Matisse as designer. By the early 1950s the glamour was beginning to fade, although a big band was hired to play most nights and the champagne still flowed freely. I remember that traces of the Gargoyle's art deco splendour still remained here in the late 1970s when the place was transformed into a different venue every night of the week, including the Comedy Store and a 60s soul club. There's still a nightclub at the address but I prefer to take my nightcaps in more intimate familiar surroundings these days, which is why I'm off to Gerry's Club on Dean Street. I've been ending my Soho nights here for as long as I can remember.

Gerry's dark cellar bar is the place where I encountered my first avocado many years ago. It wasn't an immediate success. They don't do food here any more, and looking at the place today it's amazing that they ever did food at all. However, back in the 50s, having no food on the premises was not an option because Gerry's owner had a reputation for his huge appetite. His name was Gerald Campion and he was better known as TV's Billy Bunter. Apparently, he used to run the club from 6 p.m. till 2 a.m. and was at Lime Grove Studios in Shepherd's Bush rehearsing Bunter by 8 a.m. I've seen a film called *The Guinea Pig* in which a 26-year-old Richard Attenborough played a 13-year-old schoolboy, but using an actor in his mid-30s to play a lad of similar age really takes the biscuit. Or, in Billy Bunter's case, the whole packet. He appeared in 120 episodes of the live show between 1953 and 1961 and was almost 40 by the time the series was finally cancelled.

Under his stewardship, the club became the favourite haunt of the showbiz set of the early 60s and still gets its fair share of well-known names falling down the staircase in pursuit of one or two for the road. My mum used to work here in the 70s and it was through her contacts at the club that I managed to get a job in my mid-teens working as a butcher's delivery boy, for which I got paid £3 a week with unlimited use of the company push bike thrown in. I've had many memorable nights at Gerry's that I can't remember. And it is always 'nights' there – it's one of those places that it is just impossible to find during daylight hours.

Gerry's belongs to the holy trinity of Soho drinking establishments which have kept old boho tradition alive (the others being the French and the now lost Colony, of course) and I hope it's still here when I'm as grey as its owner, the old silver-haired fox himself, Michael Dillon. So without further ado, I'll see the night off here with a few brandies and dazzle my fellow drinkers with tales of my day's derring-do.

With my legs no longer able to do what my head is instructing them to do, it's time to turn my collar up against the cold and damp and say goodnight to Soho, the beating heart of London. I could have written a whole book on this most wonderful lattice of streets but at least there's one last hurrah to be had if I'm to strictly adhere to Daniel Farson's 1951 timetable. When he and his pals staggered out of the Gargoyle at 2 a.m. they finished the night off at Mrs Bill's coffee stall, situated on the bombsite by St Anne's church. The church took a direct hit at the height of the Blitz in 1940, leaving only the tower intact. I remember the bombsite because the church wasn't rebuilt until 1991, but I don't recall a coffee stall, or indeed Mrs Bill.

Still, being a twenty-first-century boy does have its compensations because, unlike Dan the Man, I can head back to the place where my day began. Bar Italia is open round the clock, so I'll take my coffee there – just as soon as I've worked out where I left my helicopter and taken an incoming call from my 'little man'.

1 The Windsor Castle
2 The Roundhouse
3 The Falcon*
4 The Dublin Castle
5 The Caernarvon Castle*
6 The Electric Ballroom
7 The Edinboro Castle
8 The Tally Ho*
9 The Hope and Anchor

Greater London

250 metres

* No longer operating as described in text

CHAPTER TWO

From Back Rooms
to Ballrooms

Over the years I've played some pretty big venues with Madness: from the capacious O_2 Arena on the banks of the Thames, huge American stadiums and the fabulous bedlam of Madstock, to the compact Whisky a Go-Go on the Sunset Strip in West Hollywood, where legends such as the Doors and Janis Joplin made their name.

But some of my favourite memories are of the gigs we played in humbler venues back in the early days. I have a particular soft spot for two pubs and a ballroom – all still going strong – which sped us on our way back in 1979. If it wasn't for places like these, I'd probably still be delivering sausages on my butcher's bike. So this is my chance to say thank you to them for saving me – not to mention the carnivores of north London – from a terrible fate.

When I first joined Madness or, to be more precise, the Invaders, as the band was then called, one of our main difficulties was getting a gig, any gig. The best bet was to try to get the landlord of a local boozer to give you a break, as pubs were a long way off going gastro back then, or going full stop, as is the current trend. Of course, not all pubs put on live entertainment, but the pub rock movement, which began in the early 1970s, and the punk boom that followed encouraged licensees to open up their back rooms and cellars to mop up the extra beer sales that live bands generated. But, unless you managed to find a gig supporting an established band, it was a hard road getting any joy on the bookings front: publicans wanted acts that already had a following in order to guarantee pulling in punters who required pulling of pints. So we found ourselves in a catch-22 situation: it was impossible to build a following unless gigs were in the offing and, because we hadn't got a fan base, no gigs were in the effing offing. There was only one way out of this concert-free conundrum as far as we were concerned – being a little creative where our CV was concerned.

Having trudged round just about every pub in Camden Town during the winter of 1978–9 in search of a gig, it was with the echo of rejections still ringing in our ears that we entered the Dublin Castle on Parkway with its red-and-cream exterior and hanging baskets dripping water on to the pavement. The Dublin was – and still is – a friendly Irish boozer where you can sometimes find a bit of live music at the weekends.

'What's your act then, lads?' enquired the genial Irish guv'nor, Alo Conlon. 'Erm, we do jazz and a bit of country and western,' I replied. It was pretty weighty stuff for a bunch of seventeen-year-olds to be claiming, I'll grant you, but we were hoping both styles of music might be right up Alo's, and his clientele's, alley.

The man who held the keys to our future had come to England as a stowaway in 1956 and worked as a labourer digging tunnels in London, which perhaps explains how he later managed to unearth some major underground talent, but more on that in a moment. Alo's labouring background chimes precisely with the Dublin Castle's early history, which is why the two seemed made for one another. Back in the nineteenth century thousands of immigrant labourers headed for Camden to work on the construction of Euston, King's Cross and St Pancras railway stations along with their extensive goods yards and sidings. The enormity of their achievements can really be appreciated from the window of a train pulling out of one of those stations. Although the British Rail TV adverts fronted by Jimmy Savile during my childhood would have you believe otherwise, the nineteenth century, and not the 1970s, was truly 'the age of the train'.

The work was all by hand and unremittingly hard and dangerous yet this was no deterrent to the groups of Irish, Welsh, Scots and English navvies who, after a hard day's graft, liked nothing better than to take out their differences in the streets of Camden over which group was getting the best jobs. In one recorded incident – defined as a riot in legal terms – a group of Irish and English clashed over a trivial incident, which quickly escalated and lasted three days, paralysing three police forces.

Eventually, the powers that be sought to keep the tribes of the British Isles apart of an evening by building each group its own pub as far away from one another as possible. So, up went the Windsor, Dublin, Caernarvon and Edinboro Castles on the four corners of Camden Town. Unfortunately, the Caernarvon Castle went down in the Camden Lock conflagration in 2008, which (to quote Her Maj after one's own Windsor Castle suffered a right royal fire in 1992) was Camden's 'annus horribilis'. The other three pubs are still going strong, each with their own loyal following.

The Irish community was still thriving in Camden during the 70s and I well remember blokes gathering outside the tube station waiting for the Murphys Builders' van each morning which, on arrival, would spark an *On the Waterfront*-style scrum for work. Boozers like the Dublin didn't just serve as Guinness-pumping stations, they were also places where regulars went to catch up on the latest news from back home, rather like the village post office of yore. And in the days when 'packing plastic' was a job description and the only cash dispenser known to Camden man was a fruit machine which paid out once in a blue moon, local landlords cashed regulars' cheques after the banks had shut. The Dublin was – and still is – a cog in the local community, so Alo was understandably protective of his domain. He didn't hand over the stage to any old Tom, Dick or Harry.

Our slightly less than 100 per cent accurate description of our musical tastes seemed to have done the trick because Alo took us through the Dublin's red-lit, mock-Tudor bar to the back room, which was used for functions and the occasional bit of live Irish music. I remember thinking it was pretty damn impressive, especially the stage, which was made up of sheets of hardboard laid across stacks of beer crates. Up to this point, we'd really only played a few private parties and this room felt like the real deal.

Alo and his wife, Peggy, like many other Irish couples in the area, held their wedding reception in this very room back in 1966 and, when they took over the pub eight years later, it was a tradition they continued. The venue looked as if it could hold about 150 people at a pinch, which felt like Wembley to us at the time. 'Well, what d'you think, lads?' asked Alo. 'Yeah, it's OK,' we replied, trying to look nonchalant. We had, at last, fallen on our feet, we thought, but there was still one difficulty to overcome to prevent this breakthrough from being 'for one night only': our repertoire.

The spectre of the embellishment of our playlist that we'd fed Alo haunted me somewhat, given that our act owed more to Prince Buster and the Skatalites than to Kenny Ball and his Jazzmen. And as for country and western, well, I'd only heard of Tammy Wynette, and I certainly didn't sound anything like her. Moreover, I wasn't convinced the Dublin Castle was the right place to attempt a cover of her most famous song.

I doubt I'd have got much further than 'Sometimes it's hard to be a . . .' before the locals would have made their views all too clear.

It was obviously a worry and reminded me of a story I'd heard Mike Harding, the Yorkshire comic and folk-cum-country-and-western singer (who once graced the charts with a track containing the immortal lyric 'It's hard being a cowboy in Rochdale'), tell about Bernard Manning who thought he'd booked a Native American sword-throwing act called the Cherokees to appear at his Manchester club in the 1960s, only to discover too late that they were, in fact, a five-piece beat band from Leeds. The second the band took to the stage and started blasting out their latest (minor) hit, an incensed Manning dashed to the fuse box and switched their amps off. When the group's leader remonstrated with Manning, demanding that he turn the power back on because they were the 'famous' Cherokees, big bad Bernard said, 'Oh yeah? Well, Custer's just come back, so you and your mates can booger off!' Would our act provoke a similar response from Alo Conlon, I wondered?

Fortunately, our fears were unfounded: we may not have been jazzers, and we weren't remotely country and western, but Alo knew he was on to a winner and thankfully decided to stand by our band. A couple of months later he gave us a Friday night residency on the strength of that first gig, which had packed the place out.

A little way into that residency we got what I think was our first review. It was in *Melody Maker* on 1 June 1979 and it describes the audience as being made up of 'England's entire phalanx of pop culture during the last 25 years . . . huddled together in a room the size of your average khazi.' The reviewer then proceeds to list the band members and I'm described as 'a big lad called Suggs who sings'. Give the writer a Pulitzer Prize, I thought after reading such an articulate and fulsome appraisal of my good self. All of us are said to look 'vaguely threatening' but, as the commentator astutely observes, 'this proves not to be the case'. Later, the journalist correctly adjudges me 'a natural showman' ('show-off' some might say) and ends on the following note: 'By the third encore, half the punters were jumping on tables waving clenched fists, and the other half were reeling about the glass-strewn floor, jolly pissed.' It is a great social document of a time it is very hard to remember clearly.

Alo Conlon played an important (if inadvertent) role in launching our career and once he'd got a taste for putting on new bands there was no stopping him, because over the years the Dublin Castle has become one of the most influential venues on the circuit and a regular haunt of the A&R brigade on the lookout for new talent. I doubt whether anyone would've been more surprised back in the day by the pub's cutting-edge reputation for music than the man himself.

Sadly, as I sit here tapping away on my Remington Royal during the coldest, wettest January I can remember since the last, news has reached me of John Aloysius Conlon's death. Just a few months ago he was given a lifetime achievement award at the London Irish Centre in Camden Square and deservedly so. I'll be raising a few Guinnesses to the man from Mayo in a few days, as I gather a big send-off is being planned in his beloved Camden Parkway. But in the meantime, here's to you, Alo.

Having taken the Dublin Castle by storm, it was time to give some other venues the benefit of our company, we thought, the first of which was a particularly memorable bash at the celebrated Hope and Anchor pub in Islington at 207 Upper Street. It's a four-storey, red-brick Victorian boozer with elegant arched windows and columns, but it's remarkable for its role as a launch pad for the careers of many bands rather than its architecture.

Although the venue in the pub's basement was even smaller than the Dublin Castle's function room, the Hope and Anchor was London's leading pub rock venue in the mid-70s. Pub rock came to be mocked somewhat in the music press, which, looking back now, seems strange because it was really just an umbrella term for a huge variety of groups who'd taken music back to grass-roots venues. There was no discernible musical genre as such, but the one thing the pubs did have in common was that they were giving an opportunity to bands who were an antidote to the mega-bore groups of the day. Some notable live acts such as Dr Feelgood and Ian Dury's Kilburn and the High Roads were among the pioneering pubsters who paved the way for the punk explosion that followed.

The origins of Stiff Records can also be traced to the Hope and Anchor. Stiff's co-founders, Jake Riviera and Dave Robinson, formed the label in a small recording studio the latter had built in a room above the pub in 1976. Both were movers and shakers on the pub rock circuit and bands and performers such as the Damned and Elvis Costello, who were associated with Stiff, began playing at the Hope as punk started to take off.

Putting on punk bands could be a risky undertaking and forced the Hope's management to batten down the hatches. At the height of punk the basement bar was a lot more spit than sawdust, and chicken wire had to be tacked up to protect staff from flying bottles. Any ego you might've had as a performer had to be left well and truly in the van because the backstage facilities at the Hope made the Cavern Club look like the Palladium. The dressing room was filled with a load of kegs and buckets of beer slops, which gave it the exact appearance of a dray room, which, funnily enough, it was, and our equipment had to be lowered through a trap door in the ceiling. The primitiveness of the Hope was perfect for the pioneers of punk and the Clash, the Sex Pistols and the Stranglers played many of their earliest gigs in that tiny basement bar. The heyday of punk was pretty much over by the time we first played the venue in 1979, but the Hope's legendary status remained undimmed.

The Hope was run by a bloke called John Eichler who took a bit of a shine to us despite us being a bunch of kids to whom the application of the term 'rough and ready' would've been bordering on kindness. As I've said, the basement bar was smaller than the Dublin and held no more than 50 people, I reckon, and this was in the days before half the population was clinically obese. We'd been going to the Hope long before we made a ripple on the local scene because – being the very discerning jukebox jury we felt we were – the choice of music on the old Wurlitzer was the best in town. In contrast to a bottle of Lambrusco, over time that jukebox got even better, as John allowed us to put our own selection of ska and Motown on it, and the Hope became our unofficial HQ.

So, having begun our ascent up pop's greasy pole, we decided the time had come to return John's kindness by doing a gig at the Hope – for a fee, of course. I must confess I was slightly taken aback by the fact that he wanted to hear some of our material first and was downright shocked when the selection of dodgy rehearsal tapes we gave him failed to light his fire. He relented eventually, however, and gave us a gig. The fee he offered was 40 quid – a lottery-winning sum for us back then. Of equal importance was the fact that every band worth their rock salt had played here at one time or another; even stadium-fillers Dire Straits had graced its tiny stage the year before, playing to an audience of six plus a dog according to legend.

We played the Hope and Anchor on 3 May 1979, which by some strange and unwished for coincidence was the very night Margaret Thatcher led the Conservatives to victory in the General Election. As we all know, this turn of events eventually led to unemployment and recession. In our case, that very scenario almost hit us with immediate effect following our debut at the Hope.

The gig itself was great but, in a moment of madness,

I happened to put my foot through a monitor on the stage which had a value of 40 quid or, as the rest of the band politely informed me, our fee to the last penny. But John, being the person he was, not only refrained from telling us to never darken his basement again, he also gave us an extra tenner so we had something to go home with. The Hope still puts on live music to this day, though John pulled up anchor long ago and now runs the fantastic Three Kings in Clerkenwell.

Without having had the opportunity to play the pub venues, we certainly wouldn't have made it, nor, I suggest, would just about any of the bands that made the charts in the 1980s. Henry Conlon (Alo's son, who's run the Dublin Castle for the past few years) made this point during a meeting with Tessa Jowell when she was Secretary of State for Culture. Henry went to Westminster as a representative of Camden's licensees to discuss the onerous new licensing laws that had been proposed for live-music venues. While he was in the culture secretary's office, Henry noticed a gold disc on her wall that had been awarded to Coldplay, whose first ever live gig had been at the Dublin and who had also graced the Hope. Henry thought he'd make a bit of a stand, given that his livelihood was being threatened by the new laws, so he pointed to the disc and asked her where she thought Coldplay and legions of other bands who'd contributed greatly to Britain's culture and economy had started out. The answer was, of course, the music pubs. Many are facing last orders through redevelopment and, for some, time has already been called, such as the Tally Ho and the Falcon in my neck of the woods.

★

During the summer of 1979 things really began to take off for the band and we signed to Stiff Records. But only after we played at a wedding reception at the Clarendon Ballroom in Hammersmith.

The wedding in question was Dave Robinson's, who was head of Stiff. He had expressed an interest in the band but had been too busy to come and see us perform – so he booked us to come to him instead. As a rule, I don't suffer from stage fright but I must admit to getting a bout of nerves that night when I spied a few familiar faces in the audience, most notably those of Elvis Costello and our great hero, Ian Dury, who'd both become massive stars through their recordings on the Stiff label. A few days later we became Stiff artists ourselves, so we obviously did the business at the wedding, and the icing on the cake for us was the advance we got in exchange for signing on the dotted line. Trouble was, being strictly 'cash only' up until this point in our lives, none of the banks in Camden appeared willing to let us open an account and the cheque was burning a hole in our pockets.

No doubt unimpressed by our appearance, most of the bank managers in the vicinity refused to give us an interview and weren't remotely interested in taking care of our hardly earned cash. However, we finally got lucky with a friendly manager at Williams & Glyn's Bank in Camden (I can't remember whether it was Williams or Glyn we saw, but he was a jolly decent bloke) and it wasn't long before we opened our account in the singles chart too, with 'The Prince'. Things were looking up.

Now, if the Dublin Castle started putting new bands on the musical map from 1979 onwards, the Electric Ballroom was the place to go and see established groups or those on the cusp of the big time. The venue had already given Camden a bit of a shove up the rock and pop ladder by the time we set foot on its capacious stage, and playing there was a real step up for us. It's not much to look at from its entrance on Camden High Street, just a small blue shop front with a neon sign. Blink and you might well miss it. But inside it's a Tardis of a place and stretches as far as Kentish Town Road to the rear.

The Electric is a great venue, although it does have its drawbacks for those of a fastidious nature. For instance, when you come off the stage you have to exit the building and walk down a small alley in order to get to the dressing rooms, which in winter, in a sweat-sodden suit, is a less-than-pleasant experience. And if you wear sunglasses on stage, which I've been known to do, they instantly steam up as you enter the fresh air and render you blind. Which can make it tricky to find where you are meant to be going.

In spite of these small inconveniences, the show must go on, and on 12 October 1979 we appeared as the headline act on a bill featuring Echo and The Bunnymen. What a confusion of haircuts there must have been that night! A month later we played three consecutive nights at the Electric and each one of them was wild. We were in that crossover period between punk and 2 Tone, and it is fair to say that the crowds could get a little lively. They certainly did at those three gigs. We might not have been the cup of tea of choice for everyone in the audiences but the energy that was sparking throughout the place was incredible and we loved it.

When the going's good at the Electric, it's very, very good indeed. You can't beat the atmosphere when the whole place bounces up and down as one and condensation drips from the ceiling, causing sparks to fly off the lighting rigs, or when you stand on the PA stack as it sways with the crowd, making you feel like you're on the prow of a ship. The absence of Kate Winslet does not diminish this experience in the slightest.

Not only is the Electric a great gig to play, it's also the perfect place to watch a band. As with all the best venues, it holds about 2,000 people and is long and wide, allowing good visibility all round. That sounds like an advert for a Chelsea tractor, I know, but it happens to be a fact. I've had a perfect view of some greats at the Electric in my time, including the Pretenders, Iggy Pop, the Clash, Ian Dury and the Blockheads, the B52s and many, many more. If a venue makes the crowd feel good, as the Electric does, inevitably the band will too. Rough and ready certainly, but perfect for its function, the Electric is a temple for the working man and woman to let off a bit of steam jumping up and down to whoever happens to be the current obsession.

Before its reinvention as a rock venue in 1978, the Electric was a rather more sedate rendezvous for residents new to the area and looking for lurve. And as such it's an important staging post in the career of a local entrepreneur called Bill Fuller, who set the Electric's glitter ball spinning back in the 1930s during a long and illustrious career in music venues.

Fuller was an Irish immigrant who arrived in London as a teenager and worked on building sites, like most others, before starting his own construction business. In 1938, aged just 20, he branched out into entertainment, buying a rough Irish dance hall on Camden High Street called the Buffalo Club, which had recently been closed by the police. This was the place which was later to reinvent itself as the Electric Ballroom. Bill Fuller must have kissed the old Blarney Stone because he managed to convince the authorities to let him reopen the joint, promising there'd be no more trouble while he was at the helm. He was quite handy as a boxer, which might have swayed the judge to declare in his favour when it came to who was sorting out the door.

Fuller transformed the Buffalo's fortunes by turning it into a venue where Irish couples could meet and hopefully waltz their way to romance. Such was the success of the Buffalo that he opened a string of ballrooms across London and the UK before branching out to the United States. Fuller became a figure of legendary status in Camden before moving to the States in the 1950s where he diversified his business empire with interests in gold mining, management and promotions, and property. He bought two of the most iconic venues in rock-music history: the Fillmore East in New York and the Fillmore West in San Francisco. However, in spite of his worldly wealth, he never fell out of love with the Camden club that helped propel him to those riches.

Even when he began selling off his ballrooms in the 1970s, when he was in his 60s, by which time the road to romance no longer led to the local dance hall, he couldn't bear to part with the Buffalo. So in 1978 he renovated the club and renamed it the Electric Ballroom. He vowed to keep the place until the day he died and would travel from the States to watch his favourite bands, including U2 and the Pogues, performing at his beloved venue. Bill remained true to his word and still held the keys to the place when he died in 2008, aged 91.

His family have vowed to keep the old traditions going, although they face a tough task to avoid a ballroom blitz, as London Underground have proposed a redevelopment scheme on the site – a new tube station and a shopping complex – which will probably pull the plug on the Electric after all these years. The future of this major player in the community's social history hangs very much in the balance and Fuller's family will have to punch well above their weight to see off such a heavyweight opponent.

Twenty-five years on from making our mark on the wonderful world of popular music (and I'm not talking about our appearance on *Cheggers Plays Pop*), Madness once again played Camden in a project we'd cryptically named 'The Dangermen'. The plan was to go back to our musical roots and play ska and reggae covers in the venues where we made our name all those years ago. It was an undercover operation, hence the title of the project, which heralded from the 1960s spy series.

We played four consecutive nights at the Dublin but our career as musical secret agents didn't last very long. A fair-sized crowd of curious punters had already gathered in the back room by the time we took to the stage that first night and it didn't take us long to get into our stride. By the time we'd played a few numbers, the place was stuffed to the gunnels and our cover was well and truly blown. Word soon got around that the Dangermen were, in fact, Madness and by the second night the Dublin was packed out, with queues down the street. It was a warm summer and on one particularly hot evening I asked Henry Conlon if he might consider turning on the air conditioning, to which he replied (only half joking, I'm sure): 'Air conditioning? I'm turning the heating up.' Oh yes, he's Alo's son all right.

We ended our Dangermen days in this country with a return to the Electric Ballroom, which brought the memories flooding back. Earlier this year we made another 'surprise' return to the Dublin as part of the fabulous Camden Crawl. This time it was the location, not the identity of the band, which was supposed to be secret. But again, word must have leaked because when we were led into the pub by a bagpiper bellowing out 'When the Saints Go Marching In' we received a rousing reception. Considering our advanced years, I think we gave a pretty good account of ourselves.

The great thing about the Crawl is that it's not all about people like us, who have been around forever. Far from it. Throughout the weekend virtually every available venue in Camden is host to a new young band, who are given the opportunity to show what they can do in front of a live (and lively) audience. There's such a buzz about the place, and it's inspiring to see and hear all the talent that's out there, desperate to perform. The Crawl offers that opportunity. It took me back to when we were starting out – in those days bands had options as to where they could play, but today it is so much harder. That's why those three north London venues are so important.

500 metres

* No longer operating as described in text

1 The Hippodrome
2 The Bedford Theatre*
3 The Camden Palace
4 Hoxton Hall
5 Wilton's Music Hall
6 The Hackney Empire
7 The Clapham Grand

Greater London

CHAPTER THREE

Let Me Entertain You

Music hall was the most popular form of entertainment for Londoners through most of the nineteenth century and right up until the 1920s, when cinema began to eat into the audiences. At the height of the craze, in the 1870s, there were 78 so-called Grand Music Halls dotted around London and more than 300 smaller venues, which makes it all the more surprising, as well as rather sad, that so few of these palaces of working-class entertainment still survive today. The great halls that housed the entertainments vanished before their historical importance had been evaluated.

Early on, Madness were described as being 'intrinsically' music hall and 'quintessentially' English. Once I realised what those words meant, that description came as something of a surprise. Back in the 60s and 70s, when I was growing up, any mention of music hall would immediately conjure up images of the rather bizarre BBC TV show *The Good Old Days*, which seemed to mainly involve handlebar-moustachioed fellas in stripy blazers pushing ladies on flower-festooned swings singing 'Daisy, Daisy'. Not much competition for my TV favourites at the time, *The Avengers* and *Batman*. Bish, bash, bosh! Holy alliteration! Over the years, though, I've come to realise that there's no disgrace whatsoever in being associated with the tradition that gave us greats like Marie Lloyd, Max Miller or Little Tich.

Lloyd was christened 'Queen of the Music Hall' and her risqué act included bawdy songs such as 'I Sits among the Cabbages and Peas' and 'She'd Never Had Her Ticket Punched Before', which got Edwardian moralists all hot under the collar yet had audiences rolling in the aisles. If Marie Lloyd was the mistress of the double entendre, then Max Miller became the master of the same from the 1930s to the 1950s. Nicknamed 'the Cheeky Chappie', Miller was renowned for taking his comedy to the limits. He dressed in outlandish flower-patterned suits with plus-fours, matching shoes and a trilby hat and was pretty much Britain's first alternative comedian. Now, I've also ended up playing in a fair few venues which were linked, one way or another, with the musical halls but I have drawn the line at flower-patterned suits.

Although music hall wasn't foremost in our thoughts when Madness formed, it was definitely lurking in the wings. Chris Foreman, our guitarist and founder member of the band (age unknown, details kept in a vault in the Bank of England), had it in his blood. His dad, John, was reviving a lot of these old music-hall songs and performing them on the pub and club circuit when we were starting out.

So how did it come to pass that Madness became linked with the music-hall tradition, given that our tastes when growing up were contemporary rather than retro? It certainly wasn't intentional. We were heavily into Bowie, Roxy Music, ska and reggae. Indeed, Chris Foreman's teenage ambition was to be in Mott the Hoople, who made it big in the glam rock era with songs like 'All the Young Dudes' and 'All the Way from Memphis', and that seems a mighty long way from the music hall. Or is it?

Perhaps the 1970s glam rockers were really only a few platform-booted strides away from the music-hall performers of the past, as this article from a weekly, London-based journal called *The Tomahawk* entitled 'An Opinion of Music Halls' (1867) appears to show:

> A man appears on the platform, dressed in outlandish clothes with whiskers of ferocious length and hideous hue, and proceeds to sing verse after verse of pointless twaddle interspersed with a blatant 'chorus', in which the audience is requested to join.

Now I knew my old mate Noddy Holder was getting on a bit, but I didn't realise he was *that* old. Seriously, this review, though clearly written by a journalist with an anti-music-hall agenda, says much about the way the popular song was viewed by a certain class. It also shows how it was evolving and how important a distinctive 'look' was in putting it across.

We were also big fans of Ian Dury and ultimately joined the same record label as the great man. Maybe this is where the music hall really begins to kick in for Madness and me. Ian was another artist closely linked to the music-hall tradition, an interest reinforced by the artist Peter Blake, who was his mentor and lecturer at Canterbury art college. Blake was a big fan and collector of the eccentricities of the music hall, and even owns a pair of Max Miller's shoes. Also in that continuum are the Kinks, another big influence on us. Ray Davies cites Max Miller's *Max at the Met* as featuring in the soundtrack of his life. Ian didn't make any attempt to hide his musical sympathies: not only did he name-check some of the stars of the halls in his songs, but his act and repertoire had clear links with the past. He wrote one of the first singles released on Stiff Records, called 'England's Glory', which was recorded by the veteran music-hall performer Max Wall. In the song he lists 'all the jewels in the crown of England's glory', including stars who made their names in music hall, such as Gracie Fields, Little Tich, Max Miller, Frankie Howerd and George Formby. The song also contains the immortal line 'Winkles, Woodbines, Walnut Whips, Vera Lynn and Stafford Cripps'. The record wasn't a hit, but it's an infectious little number and really does go some way to invoking the sound of old London. I think you may still be able to get it on a Stiff Records compilation. The B-side is called 'Dream Tobacco' but that, my friends, is for another time . . . The song also reminds us that 'Englishness' is an essential component of the music-hall tradition. Putting on one of our albums I don't think you could really mistake Madness for an American band, could you? To be fair, that cuts both ways. I don't recall hearing much tell of Walnut Whips or Woodbines in any Aerosmith numbers.

Looking back at our early videos – something I regularly do when there's nothing good on the telly – it's easy to see the influence of music hall in our dance routines, although once again this was more by accident than design. For instance, the sand dance in 'Night Boat to Cairo' owes much to the off-the-wall music-hall act Wilson, Keppel and Betty, who specialised in Egyptian dance routines. However, I seem to remember we got the inspiration from two blokes who regularly used to perform the dance outside the Odeon in Leicester Square. They were clearly copying the old-time trio I now realise. And so the echoes of these funny old routines continue.

As far as I've been able to discover, only a couple of old stages from the early days of music hall are still standing in the modern city. I'll be calling in on both halves of this architectural double act later on, but first let's take a rummage in the history drawer to discover when and why the music halls were born.

The great-grannies of music hall were the district tea gardens. These were all the rage in the late eighteenth century, open spaces on the edge of town for Londoners to enjoy a stroll, some refreshment and a spot of entertainment too.

Games of cricket, bowls and Dutch pins were all on the bill, along with performing poets, ballad and comic singers, actors, organists and orchestras, who entertained patrons in pavilions, ballrooms or in the open air. The gardens were located all over the suburbs, in places like Islington, Highbury, Stepney, Bayswater and Hackney. We think of these as being inner-city areas today, but back then they were villages on the edge of the city, until they began to be swallowed up when Victorian London started to expand.

It's hard to get your head round the fact that the crowded districts that make up the modern metropolis were once rural hamlets, but there are a few reminders of this history in London today. If you ever find yourself at a loose end in Brixton, for example, you could head up Brixton Hill and take a right into Blenheim Gardens where you'll discover, tucked away behind some industrial buildings, a windmill – yes, a windmill – which first turned its sails here in 1816 when even this bustling part of south London was all green fields.

Despite their genteel name, the tea gardens served more than cuppas; many had taverns too and it was the bar takings on which the gardens' prosperity came increasingly to depend. The quality of entertainment on offer in these places was described by one commentator of the time as being 'lowbrow', which, I imagine, one should read as 'pretty good and not too fancy'; in fact, probably the sort of entertainment that would eventually make up the repertoire of early music hall.

So the tea gardens were all eventually swallowed up by urban development, and the taverns, which once stood in open fields, were left stranded among the new streets of housing and commercial premises, beacons of hope and refreshment in the urban wilderness. It was from these taverns that the music halls evolved. The man who made it happen was called Charles Morton, the so-called 'Father of the Halls'.

Morton obviously enjoyed a good night out and was a regular at the 'song and supper rooms' that sprung up in the West End in the early nineteenth century, places such as Evans's in Covent Garden and the Coal Hole in the Strand. The Coal Hole (not to be confused with the pub of the same name which is still to be found on the Strand today) sounds like a fine old place, the hangout of the great Victorian actor Edmund Kean among others. Inside places like this, well-heeled gents (women weren't allowed) sat at long tables next to a stage and wined and dined while an endless procession of singers and comics struggled to hold their attention. Morton saw an opportunity to do something similar in a pub environment and purchased the Canterbury Arms on Westminster Bridge Road in Lambeth, south London.

He was obviously doing something right at the Canterbury because it wasn't long before he needed more space. In 1852 he set about extending his entertainment empire by building a hall for musical entertainment at the rear of the pub on the site of an old skittle alley. A couple of years after that he extended again, building a larger hall over the top of the original. This, the New Canterbury Music Hall as it was called, was the very first proper music hall in London, with room for 1,500 punters. Morton was so keen not to lose the custom he'd built up over two years that he decided to construct it without stopping the performances. The original hall was demolished on a Saturday night (I've drunk at a few places where that sort of thing happens) and the new one was up and running by Monday.

Morton's hall had painted walls, luxury fittings, a balcony, tables and chairs for dining and a stage with a piano. An entrance fee of sixpence was charged and – unlike the song and supper rooms – women were welcome too. Each act was introduced by a chairman who sat at a table to the side of the stage, and – hey presto, what do you know? – the music hall had been born. Morton's successful recipe, which saw the Canterbury pulling in the crowds until it finally closed in 1912, was soon copied by others, and similar set-ups were built in every corner of town. Just over a century ago, the writer and theatre critic Henry Chance Newton said that 'without its Palaces of Variety and its Music Halls living London would only be half alive'. All of which makes it rather surprising that today just a handful of these places survive, including just two of the original music halls. The first is on Hoxton Street, east London, and is imaginatively known as Hoxton Hall. It has a white, elegant exterior and is part of a modest terrace that narrowly avoided bombing during the Blitz. It began life as McDonald's Music Hall – named after the man who built it – and while I'd like to report that the burghers of Hoxton took to it with relish, unfortunately they didn't have much time to sample its delights. It closed in 1871 due to complaints from the police – obviously no laughing policemen on that particular London beat. Ironically, the hall became a temperance mission in 1879 and several years later passed on to a Quaker organisation, a fate which lowered the curtain on its time as a den of iniquity and excess but which probably also saved it from the demolition squad. It has now renewed its acquaintance with the glamour of showbiz, however, leading an interesting double life as a community centre by day and a performance space by night. With its two-tiered, galleried auditorium seating around 200 punters, it's a lovely, intimate space to enjoy a night's entertainment but it's not quite on the same grand scale as the only other survivor from the nineteenth-century heyday of the music hall.

Wilton's Music Hall stands on Grace's Alley, off Ensign Street, in Wapping. In the eighteenth century this little cut-through was just around the corner from a rather chic residential spot called Wellclose Square, which was a favoured residence of rich seagoing types – captains, merchants, ship owners and the like – who needed to be close to the river, but not so close that they would have to mingle with the dodgier types who worked on their vessels. When I paid a visit recently, in search of Wilton's, I first strolled through this once salubrious area, but could find very little evidence of what it had once been like. Most of it was wiped away by wartime bombs and later slum clearance in the 1960s, and the only memento of its more glamorous days is a cluster of bollards on Ensign Street. These were originally installed as hitching posts for horses and marked the spot which was once a parking lot for horse-drawn carriages used by patrons of the Royal

Brunswick Theatre, which opened its doors here in 1828. These bollards still bear the monogrammed 'RBT' of the theatre with a crown over the top. However, audiences didn't get the chance to catch many performances at the grand new theatre because it collapsed just a couple of days after opening. Talk about bringing the house down.

By the late 1840s, when John Wilton pitched up in the neighbourhood to take up ownership of the Prince of Denmark pub on Grace's Alley, the whole area had undergone something of a sea-change. The development of the London and St Katharine Docks, just a mile or so south, brought an influx of new arrivals and the area soon became infamous as one of London's most disreputable. Nicknamed 'Sailortown' by the locals, it swarmed with rough naval types who, having sometimes spent years at sea, were eager to make the most of their shore leave and were on the lookout for a suitable watering hole to kick off the night's adventures.

Many of them would have beaten a path to Wilton's pub on Grace's Alley, which sat snugly in the centre of a terrace of Georgian houses. It was out of this drinking den that one of the grandest music halls in London grew, a place which has miraculously survived more or less intact, and which still stages entertainment today, just as it has done, on and off, for more than 150 years.

Walking down the Alley, it's possible to almost miss the entrance to Wilton's altogether. The front of the building gives very little clue as to what's going on behind the modest facade, but it's a very different story once you push through the oxidised red front door and step inside to explore what really is one of London entertainment's hidden gems.

On closing the door behind you, you find yourself in a paved lobby with a staircase heading upwards and doorways leading off to rooms on the right and left. The walls are mostly unplastered – unlike most of Wilton's original clientele – and the exposed brickwork gives the place the look of a large Victorian house 'affording an excellent refurbishment opportunity', in modern estate-agent speak. Take a turn to the right and there's the bar. Always a magical discovery.

Like many of the best showbiz tales, the story of Wilton's Music Hall really begins in the bar. When John Wilton was the boss, it was known as the Mahogany Bar because it was the first place in London to have fittings and counters made of, you guessed it, mahogany. It was considered quite swanky for its time and was obviously one of the selling points that brought people here in the first place. I can imagine later Victorians getting all steamed up about stained glass and marble pub interiors in the same way that we might get excited by a sleek, new, modernist bar with intimate, minimalist, leather-upholstered booths and futuristic lighting, but I find it hard to imagine a time when people thought a place was cool because of the type of wood that was used to make the fittings. I doubt most people would even know one specimen of wood from another these days, but a century and a half ago it was obviously a big deal.

So did the latest timber to hit town dictate where people chose to spend their evenings? 'Cor, mate, have you seen that new plywood place up at the docks, yeah lovely, it's got a very light atmosphere. The pine bar, nah mate, that's all finished, too many splinters. You want to get up to that Prince of Denmark, it's all teak! It's a bit dark, but beautifully smooth.' Makes you wonder how they would've reacted to linoleum and Formica.

You can still buy a drink in the Mahogany Bar today before taking your seat for the show, although the room has changed a lot since the old days. The only trace of its original ritzy past is to be found on the ceiling where a few pieces of elaborate plaster moulding cling on tenaciously. A fitting symbol of the precarious nature of the business we call show.

John Wilton began staging entertainment in the Mahogany Bar in 1850 and before long his singing and comedy evenings became a huge success. When you have a big hit on your hands you need to act on it quickly before you become yesterday's papers, so, to accommodate more punters, Wilton knocked through the back wall and extended the bar back towards Cable Street, which ran parallel with Grace's Alley. A short while later he did the same thing again, and again, until he could extend no further.

Business was booming, and Wilton knew a good opportunity when he saw one. He wanted to follow Morton's lead and turn his pub into a fully fledged music hall. It was a great location for a bigger venue, with plenty of passing trade, but he didn't have the free space to build it within the narrow confines of this terraced street. After much head-scratching he came up with a grand design: John Boy Wilton hit on the idea of buying several of the adjoining terrace properties (complete with sitting tenants) in order to slap up a huge great music hall across their collective back yards.

What makes Wilton's such an astonishing time capsule is the fact that if you call in today to have a nose around, you can still see the evidence of how the great man realised his vision. Stepping out of the bar, you head back across the entrance lobby and into the rooms on the other side. These were once ground-floor shops run by Wilton's neighbours and later his tenants. They remained operational even after he began to knock the terraces around. Records show that back in the 1850s a bootmaker plied his trade in one of them, a baker in another. I don't know if Wilton bled them dry with the rent he charged but, if not, the proprietor of the other shop – an importer of leeches – could have done the job for him.

Upstairs there's even more evidence of how he must have re-jigged the buildings in order to realise his glittering vision. The upper floors are labyrinthine and somewhat disconcerting, not least because, at first sight, the windows which once gave a view out on to the back gardens appear to have been painted black. Closer up, I realise this was an optical illusion – a result of Wilton's eagerness not to waste an inch of space when he built the hall across the back yards of the terrace. The blank, black space seen from the back windows is actually the side wall of the hall itself and, because the window frames have lost their glass, you can actually reach out your hand and touch it.

Deprived of access to their rear yards, the only route out of the building for the tenants who rented these rooms above the ground-floor shops was through the front door of the bar. The cumulative comings and goings of shopkeepers, tenants and customers must have been something to behold.

But that's enough about the rest of the building. Top of the bill at Wilton's is the music hall itself, which you enter through a doorway no bigger than an average-sized front door in the downstairs lobby. The minute you walk into the auditorium itself, prepare for your socks to be blown off – not a risk that future generations entering the ExCeL arena in Docklands are going to have to guard against, I suspect. The place needs a fair bit of TLC, and some serious structural work to boot, but to see it in its faded grandeur somehow makes it all the more special and gives you a real and delightfully eerie feel of what it was like in its heyday. I'm not going to bamboozle you with technical data relating to the interior such as the balcony's 'bombe carton Pierre front, supported on unusual helical-twist cast-iron columns' or its 'elliptical vaulted ceiling with ornamental fretted ribs' because that would make it sound like I knew what I was talking about. Seeing is believing in my book, and if you haven't seen Wilton's yet, then you'd better have a word with yourself and resolve to pay it a visit.

Of course a music hall is much more than bricks, mortar and some impressive plasterwork. It's a place to perform. So it was a great pleasure to take a turn around the place in the company of the president of the Music Hall Society

and fabulous entertainer, the irrepressibly iridescent, indefati-
gable, irresistible, individual and indispensable Mr Roy Hudd,
who reckoned playing Wilton's would've been rather like
performing in the working men's clubs up north during
the 70s (i.e. tough).

The majority of the audience would've been made up of
sailors who, back on dry land after months at sea, turned up for
the show with pockets full of money ready to spend on birds,
booze and banter. Rumour has it, according to the venerable
Mr Hudd, that there was once a trap door beneath a bench at
the back of the hall from which some 'heavy' would
intermittently pull a lever, sending a group of well-oiled jolly
jack tars into the cellar, where they would be relieved of their
chattels, via the cosh, and the next thing they knew upon
waking was that they were back aboard ship.

Those who managed to avoid a coshing had the chance to
see stars of a different kind because many of the brightest lights
of early music hall would have played Wilton's – such
legendary names as Sam Cowell, the comic vocalist who's
considered to be one of the country's first singer-songwriters.
As far as I know, Cowell was no relation to he of the high-
hitched trousers and centre parting, although by all accounts
he very much had the 'X' factor back in his day and was
renowned for folksy ballads such as the perennial crowd-
pleaser 'The Ratcatcher's Daughter'.

Another man who graced the stage at Wilton's on many
occasions was 'the idol of the barmaids' himself, George
Leybourne, the nattily dressed swell also known as

'Champagne Charlie', because of the song that made him famous:

Champagne Charlie is my name.
Champagne drinking is my game.
There's no drink as good as fizz! fizz! fizz!
I'll drink ev'ry drop there is, is, is!
All round the town it is the same.
By Pop! Pop! Pop! I rose to fame.
I'm the idol of the barmaids
And Champagne Charlie is my name.

Leybourne was supposedly in the pocket of Moët et Chandon who paid him to promote their champagne, although I'm not certain if this was on a 'drink-as-much-as-you-like' basis. I'd have quite fancied the job myself if this was the deal, though I doubt whether Moët would have been able to afford me! Having said that, apparently champagne was more of a working man's drink back then, and was even available on draught at music halls. Can you imagine the devastation? 'I'm just off for a pint at the local, dear. See you in three days!'

Wilton's also became home to a new breed of singing performers from the 1860s to the 1880s, like Harry Clifton who became famous for his 'motto' songs, offering advice to audiences whose lives had altered dramatically through industrialisation and urbanisation. Roy Hudd told me that Clifton was paid by factory owners to come up with songs that would reconcile workers in the audience to their lot and at the same time induce them to put in maximum effort at the workplace. Now there's a cue for a verse of one of Clifton's finest!

Work, boys, work and be contented.
So long as you've enough to buy a meal.
For if you will but try, you'll be wealthy by and by,
If you'll only put your shoulder to the wheel.

Talking to Roy while soaking up the wonderful atmosphere of this unique survivor makes me reflect on Madness songs and connections with the repertoire of the music hall. Although I am not one to blow our own 76 trombones like the Victorian showmen, we've always had an interest in singing about the woes of the common man and have never been averse to a spot of ribaldry or entering into the vernacular, which is all part and parcel of the songs of the music hall. And what a parcel it is. In his great book, *London: A Literary Companion*, Peter Vansittart describes what he sees as being the stuff of music-hall songwriting:

songs about beer, the lodger, about being up before the beak, about the missus, outsize wives, and timid or erring husbands, the rent collector, mothers in law, in a smoky boozy haze, with rumbustious double-entendres, sly winks, robust sexuality, gallows humour, with the incongruous and absurd demolishing the stuffy and rigid.

Well, that sounds just about the perfect description of all the things I look for in a well-constructed pop song.

It's not only us who've been influenced by that tradition. Though the music halls may have disappeared, the 'lowbrow' street music which they nurtured has adapted and survived, and what a lively little beggar it turned out to be. In my opinion, some of the more bawdy current crop of young artists would have no problem plying their trade in the music halls.

John Wilton died in 1880, at the age of 60, by which time the hall was under new management, having been rebuilt following a serious fire three years earlier. But its days as an entertainment venue were numbered. By now, many of the smaller halls were struggling to survive. They had become infamous for the rowdy, drunken behaviour of audiences and the bawdy songs and 'provocative dancing' they had come to enjoy. That all sounds bloody marvellous to me, but it obviously didn't go down too well with the temperance movement, whose path I keep crossing as I wander through stories of disappearing Victorian London and who blamed society's ills on excessive alcohol consumption.

They brought pressure to bear on the authorities to clean up the halls and new health and safety laws were passed which squeezed out the smaller venues, whose proprietors couldn't afford to comply with them. Many simply returned to being pubs, others were demolished. Those that decided to soldier on soon found themselves under threat from fresh competitors as new-style 'deluxe' music halls or 'variety' theatres started going up in the 1880s, mainly in the West End to begin with, such as the Tivoli in the Strand and the London Pavilion on Piccadilly Circus.

Wilton's finally went dark in the late 1880s. But miraculously, unlike all the other original London music halls bar Hoxton, it survived against all the odds. There were several reasons why it managed to dodge the wrecking ball. As with Hoxton Hall, the first is to do with having a bit of help from above. In 1888, the hall became a Methodist mission and remained so until 1956. Apparently, during the first dock strike of 1889, 2,000 meals a day were served at the hall to striking dockers – that's an awful lot of covers. The fact that the hall was fulfilling an important role in what was now an extremely run-down and impoverished area of the East End probably saved it from demolition. It was also lucky to survive the Blitz, somehow managing to keep its head down when many other buildings in the district were losing theirs. After Wilton's days as a mission came to an end in 1956, it became a rag warehouse and was earmarked for slum clearance, but it received an eleventh hour reprieve in 1964, thanks to a campaign led by the former Poet Laureate and all-round good egg John Betjeman.

I wish I could say that things turned sunnier for the place after 1964, but sadly the future of this unique and incredibly atmospheric old place is still not fully secure. Despite the sterling efforts of the charity which currently runs Wilton's, this Victorian monument to music, merriment and mirth still awaits restoration and requires urgent repairs to prevent it from collapse. There is hope though: Wilton's cultural and architectural importance was recently identified by the World Monuments Fund, who added the building to their list of the world's 100 most endangered sites, alongside such exotic places as the Inca city of Machu Picchu.

The variety theatres themselves were later edged out by the arrival of cinema, and cinema – for a period – was then edged out by TV, but for a few glorious decades variety theatres ruled the roost in London. It was this transfer of music hall into deluxe theatres that ushered in the 'golden age of variety'. This was essentially an exercise in rebranding, to make the genre appear more respectable, as the entertainment on offer changed very little. The requirement to secure licences from a magistrate and the pressure brought to bear by moral reform groups was behind this upmarket shift.

The layout of the new halls was more in keeping with traditional theatres, with fixed seating throughout, thus removing all evidence of variety's pub origins. Eventually, drink was banned from the auditorium altogether and music hall's acceptance as a respectable form of entertainment, albeit in a new guise, appeared to be sealed by the first Royal Variety Performance at the Palace Theatre on Cambridge Circus in 1912. It was a bit of a sham though, given that the biggest star of the day, Marie Lloyd, wasn't invited to sing. Her material was deemed too saucy for royalty. A bit rich, considering the recently deceased Edward VII had given one or two actresses and singers more than his personal seal of approval during the course of his marriage.

The golden age of variety was a bit before my time, but I've heard plenty of stories about that period. Some of the best were told by my mother-in-law, Christina. She's sadly no longer with us, but in their youth Christina and her two sisters used to have a dance act and appeared in many of London's great variety theatres in the 40s and 50s, such as the London Hippodrome just by Leicester Square. It's a place that has been knocked about a bit inside over the years but is currently undergoing an intensive programme of redevelopment as a casino. Restoration and preservation of the original features (many of which have been hidden for decades) of this Frank Matcham-designed building are planned.

Christina regaled me with wonderful stories about her time as one third of the Martin Sisters. Part of their routine involved performing Russian dances on roller skates, which was fraught with danger, given that all theatre stages are gently raked, so they had to really battle to stop themselves drifting helplessly towards the footlights. Their musical accompaniment was provided by a blind pianist whose skill on the ivories was matched by his highly developed sense of spatial awareness. This proved invaluable when it came to walking the girls to and from the theatre during wartime blackouts. The sisters performed six nights a week, including matinees on the weekends: bloody hard work. They often shared the bill with the Crazy Gang, a collection of comedy double acts whose most famous members were Bud Flanagan (aka Ruben Weintrop) and Chesney Allen, whose big number was 'Underneath the Arches'.

As if the raked stages weren't enough of a hazard, the

Martin Sisters' act was often made all the more dangerous and thrilling by interventions from members of the Crazy Gang. Serving that demanding mistress Comedy, they took to opening and closing the stage trap doors, or turning on the wind machine and sending the girls' skirts flying as they tried to descend a flight of stairs – on roller-skates, mind you – during their entrance.

The ownership of many variety theatres in this period was concentrated in nationwide chains (although London was still very much the industry hub) and the Martin Sisters ended up touring the circuit of theatres owned by Moss Empires, having got the contract through their agent, the famous impresario and World Charleston Champion of 1926, Lew Grade. The sisters travelled around the country on trains specially commissioned by Moss Empires, with each compartment occupied by different acts. There was a hierarchy on the train which determined who travelled where. The band went in the first compartment, dancers in the second, the Crazy Gang next, followed by assorted compartments of snake charmers, magicians, and a fella whose act consisted of meticulously winding up a series of clocks, stitched inside his coat, which would go off simultaneously as he reached his punch line and threw his garment open. Presumably to illustrate the secret of good comedy: timing. The bigger solo performers would have a compartment to themselves. What a scene it must have been as that train pulled away from King's Cross.

Years later, in 1978, our record company, Stiff Records, adopted a similar 'package tour' idea and sent artists like

Wreckless Eric, Rachel Sweet and Lena Lovich around the country on the 'Be Stiff' tour train. Variety was clearly alive and kicking in the late 70s.

The larger variety halls which Anne's mum and aunts played during the 1940s and 1950s were far removed from the original pub halls, but it didn't make them less charismatic. By all accounts, most of them were pretty spectacular, which makes it all the more galling that nearly all of them had disappeared by the 1960s.

Variety entertainment began to die a slow death following the arrival of the talkies in the late 1920s and was finally finished off by TV in the 1950s. The main problem for music halls and variety was that in their heyday most of the acts had one signature turn, routine or song, for which they were synonymous, and so doing the rounds of all the venues meant performing in front of a new crowd each night. Unless, that is, the audience followed the act around, which some did. Victorian groupies, screaming and throwing their bloomers and long-johns on stage.

By the time an act came back round, it would have regained some of its novelty and audiences would turn up again. You see those old films of six fellas doing the most intricate dance routine, in complete unison, that they would have perfected over years up and down the country. Pre-TV there was always another town, always another crowd. In the TV era, if an act was showcasing its routine to the nation, that would be it. Everyone who had wanted to see the renowned bird imitator, for instance, just had. There was no new audience to reach out to the next evening. People no longer needed to go to the theatre to watch performers. Once the audiences stopped turning up, it was only a matter of time before the theatres themselves faced extinction. Some of them managed to survive by adapting to new uses. One of the most famous variety theatres outside the West End, which once wowed audiences, stood close to home in Camden.

The Bedford Theatre on Camden High Street was demolished in 1969 after standing empty for ten years, thus bringing to an end a colourful showbiz career which had begun 80 years earlier when the theatre was built on the site of a former music hall. The office building that today stands in its place is still called Bedford House and I used to hear people ask bus drivers to drop them off at 'the Bedford' up until a few years ago. It's like a lot of London landmarks that become embedded in the psyche of the local community, even after they are gone. The Nag's Head in Holloway, just around the corner from me, is another one – the area is still referred to as that even though the pub from which the name came has now disappeared.

Although the Bedford is long gone, and I never saw it in its pomp, for me it lives on for two reasons. The first is because it features in the pictures of Walter Sickert, who headed the so-called Camden Town Group of artists and immortalised Victorian and Edwardian Camden in his paintings. The second reason is that the Bedford appeared, just a couple of years before its demolition, in a cult 1967 documentary entitled *The London Nobody Knows*.

I first saw this 45-minute film on TV in the late 70s, and if it ever finds its way to an art-house cinema near you, I urge you to go and see it. It's based on a book of the same name by the artist and art critic Geoffrey Scowcroft Fletcher, written in 1962. Fletcher had a particular penchant for what he termed 'off-beat' London, and his book is a celebration of the quirky, unusual and downright bizarre places which make the city so special. Sound familiar? The film, inspired by Fletcher's example, attempts a similar job.

The London it depicts is decrepit and ramshackle; what's more, the post-war construction work that's going on all around appears to be making things worse. The streets of this London certainly aren't those which feature in the clichéd images of the swinging 60s. Instead, they're filled with ragamuffin children, winos, vagrants and half-crazed street entertainers. And there are bombsites round just about every corner. I was talking with a friend recently about this and reminiscing about how we used to play on bombsites when we were little – this must have been in the late 60s or early 70s. 'We're going up the bombsite,' we'd say, as if it was a purpose-built playground created specially for us. As kids we had no real notion of what had actually created these spaces of adventure.

The documentary is given a sinister edge by its presenter, former matinee idol and Hollywood A-lister James Mason. No one in the history of cinema has done 'sinister' quite like him. Highlights of the lugubrious Mason's wanderings in *The London Nobody Knows* include visits to Chapel Market, squalid tenements, a gents' loo in Holborn where goldfish swim in the glass cisterns, an egg-breaking plant and several run-down Georgian and Victorian terraced streets.

But the thing that stands out in this documentary is the sight of him skulking moodily about inside the derelict Bedford music hall. He points out the once-fancy scrollwork and the plaster decorations of nymphs and shepherds that lie in ruins on the floor. Then it really gets going when he talks about the 'Queen of the Halls', Marie Lloyd, who was a favourite performer at the Bedford. A scratched 78rpm recording of Lloyd singing the music-hall classic 'The Boy I Love Is Up in the Gallery' provides the background sound-track to the scene of desolation that Mason finds in the auditorium. All rather spooky, and compelling.

The film gives a glimpse of the Bedford in a very sorry state, but in the book on which it's based, author Geoffrey Fletcher suggests what it was like before its slow decline, describing the fusion of audience, architecture, decoration, mirrors and lighting which resulted in what he called 'the true baroque of the music hall'. I never experienced the Bedford in all its baroque pomp, but I share Fletcher's conclusion that its loss 'as a living music hall can only be described as a tragic loss to London life'.

Interestingly, Fletcher contrasts the sad fate of the Bedford to that of another Camden theatre which managed to weather the end of the music-hall and variety era. Known today as the Camden Palace, on Camden High Street, it was designed by the prolific theatre architect W. G. R. Sprague in 1900. Although it's lost some statues of classical figures that used to adorn its exterior, the ivory-coloured stone facade of this building is still impressive and is dominated by a large, oxidised copper dome on its roof.

The Palace has gone through several incarnations and name changes since it first opened its doors. Today, along with the Grand in Clapham and the Hackney Empire, it's one of the three surviving variety theatres outside the West End that date from the turn of the last century. The reason it's still here is because it was adaptable, being put to different uses as fads came and went. It began life as a straight theatre but swapped to variety after nine years, and just before the First World War it became a cinema. After the Second World War had ended, it was all change again, as the Palace became a BBC radio theatre where programmes such as *The Goon Show* were recorded. Finally, it opened its doors to musicians in 1972.

It's quite a striking building, despite having lost some of the twiddly, fancy late-Victorian ornamentation that once adorned its exterior. I had an opportunity to experience the magnificent copper dome at close quarters during an excursion to the Palace in the mid-70s, long before I ever appeared there as a performer.

Back then the Palace was called the Music Machine and was a popular rock venue. I can't recall what year it was when my friend and Madness's future sax player Lee Thompson first showed me the circuitous route up the fire escape that led to the Palace's rooftop dome, or even what band was playing that night, but I do remember the reason we were climbing up there: the celebrated dome had a hole in it and this was our way in. We took the precaution of striking a few matches and throwing them through the gaping rusty hole into the total darkness to ensure there was a floor to land on, but that was the extent of our risk assessment. Satisfied that we weren't leaping into a bottomless pit, we went for it. We were risking our necks to avoid paying the admission fee. After dusting ourselves off in the dark, we entered the Palace through a fire exit which led straight to a VIP bar area. Congratulating ourselves on the daring of our enterprise, we sauntered into the room whereupon it was immediately clear that many of the other guests present were somewhat startled by our appearance. Not surprising really because when I looked at Lee and he at me, we realised we were covered in pigeon dung. Not an auspicious entry into such a fine building. But it did rather open my eyes to the curious delight of risking life and limb to bunk into places without the bother of paying. But beware, it can become a bit of a habit.

In 1979 I entered the Camden Palace again, not through the dome this time, nor by the front entrance for that matter, but by the stage door. I'm so glad this place didn't vanish when it looked as if demolition was on the cards because, besides being a fantastic venue, it is the scene of the most momentous occasion in my life, one certainly worthy of a blue plaque if you ask me. It is where I met my wife, Anne.

It wasn't in the Palace that I first set eyes on her, mind you. That would be the Roundhouse, where I'd seen her on stage. She was in a group called Deaf School and while it was them as a band that had a big influence on Madness, it was the singer, Anne, who had the bigger influence on me. Yes, the Palace holds a lot of happy memories for me, but none better than when I saw Anne's green eyes sparkle across that dance floor.

In addition to sheltering Cupid somewhere in its rafters, the Palace was, and is, a great venue to play. Unlike most theatres, whose balconies are staggered further and further backwards, here they seem to be closer to the stage the higher up they go. It gives the place a real feeling of intimacy, despite its 2,000-plus capacity and, acoustically, it's near perfect, as stars ranging from Charlie Chaplin to Madonna must have discovered when they played here. It changed hands again a few years ago and is now a nightclub and music venue called Koko. During the latest refurbishment, many original features that were hidden during the Palace's new romantic interior makeover of the 1980s were uncovered and brought back to life, although rumours that Spandau Ballet were found lurking behind five baroque-style pillars have proved unfounded.

The Grand in Clapham was built in 1900 for a consortium headed by legendary music-hall stars Dan Leno and Herbert Campbell, and once had a capacity of 3,000. Since then it has served as everything from a theatre to a cinema to a bingo hall, before reinventing itself once more in 2005 as a nightclub. In spite of its chequered history, the Grand is in pretty good nick and has retained much of its original décor.

The Hackney Empire goes one better and not only retains most of its original features, it also functions as a popular theatre today, just like in the good old days. It's had a few inevitable ups and downs along the way, but has successfully held going dark at bay. No mean feat.

This is another venue I'm pleased to say I've played with the band, although that only happened after I'd admired it from afar for many years. The minute you walk into the Hackney Empire you know you're in a building of real pedigree. The rococo-, gothic- and Moorish-influenced theatre was designed by Frank Matcham, who is regarded as the doyen of theatre architects. Matcham set new standards in theatre design and built over 200 around the country, including the Palladium, Coliseum and Hippodrome in the West End. Unfortunately, the genius of his work wasn't really appreciated until long after his death in 1920, by which time fewer than 25 of his theatres remained following the great cull between 1950 and 1975 when no use could be found any longer for so many of them. What a relief the Hackney Empire wasn't one of them.

When the theatre was built in 1901 it was a real state-of-the-art pleasure palace and boasted the most advanced features of the day, including central heating and electric lights. Pure luxury. I finally got to play the Empire in 2008, to launch our new album *The Liberty of Norton Folgate* (have I already mentioned that?). We'd worked out a more theatrical show with which to display our new wares with the help of Luke Cresswell (*Stomp* choreographer and performer) and art collective Le Gun, who were doing the graphics, and we knew it had to be staged somewhere special. You don't get many places as special as the Empire.

It was all shaping up beautifully in the short rehearsal period but unfortunately, in the great tradition of these things – a tradition which may, for all I know, stretch back to the days of music hall itself – the album wasn't quite finished by the time the date of the show arrived. Despite this minor setback, we had three great nights there and the notices were terrific. They culminated in my old celebrity-stalker mate and splendiferous broadcaster Robert Elms, who has always been selfless and unstinting in his unflinchingly optimistic explorations into the nooks and crannies of this old town, describing it as the best show he'd ever seen, and not a trap door in sight! It really felt like a privilege, almost like coming home, to be treading the very boards that had been graced by the likes of Charlie Chaplin, W. C. Fields, Stan Laurel, Marie Lloyd and old Max Miller himself. The great stand-up comics of the 80s and 90s probably felt the same way when they first played the Empire, which is why so many of them lent their support to Griff Rhys Jones's restoration project that raised £17 million a few years ago, and effectively saved the theatre from going dark or, worse, being demolished entirely like so many others.

On which note, with the curtain about to fall on my whistle-stop tour of London's music-hall survivors, I leave you with this question. Why is it that, while so many highbrow art forms have been preserved and protected in their government-funded palaces, the fate of the entertainment venues dedicated to the working man and woman have been largely left to their own devices, only to be saved – if saved at all – by a handful of dedicated enthusiasts battling away at street level? I have no problem with the government giving cash to opera and theatre – in fact, I'm all in favour of it – but it does seem a shame, to say the least, that more effort and funding has not gone into saving some of this enormously important and influential popular music legacy for London. Because, for sure, the vibrant tradition of making songs about everyday life on the streets of the capital that started in the halls is still alive and thriving. Thank you and goodnight, ladies and gentlemen!

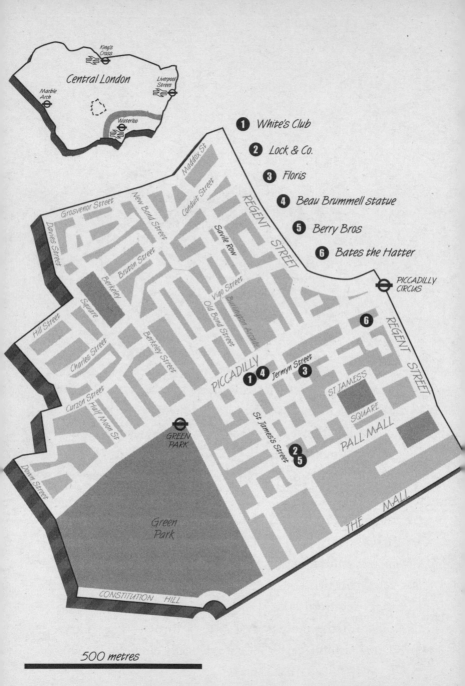

1 White's Club

2 Lock & Co.

3 Floris

4 Beau Brummell statue

5 Berry Bros

6 Bates the Hatter

500 metres

CHAPTER FOUR

Man about Town

G rowing up in the 1970s was pretty tough. I'm not talking about the three-day week and candlelit evenings with no TV during the power cuts. I'm not talking about football hooliganism. I'm not talking about the draconian pub-opening hours or even the Wombles. No, the thing that really made this such a painful decade for a style-conscious young chap like me was the fashion: cheesecloth, tank tops, big hair and even bigger flares.

Maybe it's the traumatic experience of growing up in the 70s – a ten-year winter of discontent for the dedicated follower of straight-leg trousers – that explains my long-standing preference for the more classic style: a throwback to a time when being fashionable didn't automatically entail looking like

Kevin Keegan. It all began when I was a teenager, 15 or 16 years old. Along with a few friends from school, I'd taken to wearing my hair short and sporting clothes from the 50s and 60s, which weren't easy to come by. That may not sound radical, but it certainly made us stand out back then, and would sometimes engender aggro for nothing more than just looking a bit different.

At that time, Avalon for us was a wonderful emporium of second-hand menswear – sadly long-since disappeared – called Alfred Kemp's. 'We fit anybody,' it proudly said above its double-fronted exterior on Camden High Street. By the time I started to frequent this treasure trove of menswear, Kemp's had been going for years. Back then, every London man worth his salt had a couple of suits in his wardrobe – a tradition which I'm doing my best to keep alive – and Kemp's main customer base was local Irish working men on the hunt for something two-piece, smart and affordable to wear in church or the dance hall.

Window displays in the 1970s were often incongruous mixtures of wheelbarrows and cartwheels and odd-looking mannequins draped in fabric and wearing gangster hats: anything but clothes. Kemp's was a more no-nonsense affair, with suits, shirts, coats and jackets hung one above the other all along the windows of its double-fronted exterior. That meant you could get a good look at the stuff before you summoned the courage to go in.

Once you stepped inside, the first thing you noticed was the smell, or lack of it. Instead of that peculiar mixture of sweat and urine (and dare I say death) that accompanied most second-hand shops, there was just a faint and rather pleasant whiff of floor polish. The place was light and airy and the clothes were arranged in size and colour. Suits and shirts on one side of the shop, coats and shoes on the other. The whole place was run more like a Savile Row tailor's than a second-hand shop in Camden Town.

Its highly attentive staff flitted to and fro with tape measures round their necks and eyes in the back of their heads. You could nick stuff from Oxfam, but not here: you'd never have got out of the place alive. Surveying the whole affair from a narrow booth next to the cash desk was the all-seeing Mr Kemp himself. He could judge the value of a pile of clothes just by looking at them and correctly guess your measurements at 50 paces. He could detect the slightest thought of thievery before it had properly formulated in your own head. They said every trader in Camden High Street would be roused if you tried to pinch one of Mr Kemp's suits, but I never saw anyone try.

The clothes were beautifully cleaned and presented, well cut and made to last. Looking back now, I realise that many of the second-hand suits in Kemp's were probably made in the 40s, 50s and 60s – what would be called vintage today and very expensive. You could find the most marvellous treasures there, from velvet-collared camel-hair coats to spats and a truly wondrous selection of suits. You could walk in a scruffy teenager and leave dressed like a king. I did in 1977.

I know it was 1977 for two reasons. First, because it was the year of the Queen's Silver Jubilee – street parties and all the rest. Second, and most important for me, because 1977 was also the year of my first visit to the Roxy.

The Roxy was a club, the hotbed of a new movement they called punk. I was 16 years old the first time I descended the dark stairs that led to this wonderland, hidden away in a dingy Covent Garden basement at 41–43 Neal Street, only a short hop from where I lived in north London. As my eyes adjusted to the light, I had trouble believing them, for there before me I saw a crowd all about my age, and all wearing stuff that wasn't the status quo – or indeed worn by Status Quo. This was before the stuff that Malcolm McLaren and Vivienne Westwood were making was in any way affordable to the average punk, so everyone had done their own thing with whatever they had found or pinched from charity shops – everything from white dinner jackets to customised boiler suits.

The Roxy provided visible – and audible – proof that change was in the air, not just in fashion, but in music too. For me, and the rest of the crowd who gathered here, the overriding sensation was one of vitality, and – as simple as it sounds – youth. Just as I had grown tired of the mainstream fashions of the 70s, I'd become bored with most of the music – old men in capes playing concept albums with solos that went on for days or gangs of fellas who looked like brickies wearing make-up and stomping up and down in glitter and stack-heel boots. It was time to liven things up a bit, and the Roxy was the place to start.

It was the creation of a visionary promoter called Andy Czezowski, and it proved that a new, vibrant and – importantly – young scene was bursting forth, full of do-it-yourself vigour, where anyone could join in. It launched bands like the Clash, Siouxsie and the Banshees and the Buzzcocks, as well as numerous fanzines, filmmakers and DJs, but don't go looking for it today. The whole escapade only lasted 100 glorious days, and now there's just a rather dreary boutique on the site of this 70s fashion and music explosion.

I was making sausages and burgers in a butcher's, which believe me is the lowest rung of the ladder, in the summer of 1977 and the Saturday afternoon before my next evening foray to the Roxy saw me scouring the window of Kemp's clutching my wages, the princely sum of £11. I needed something spectacular but inexpensive, something that would cut a dash but still leave me with a few extra quid for the weekend. I stepped inside and spotted my quarry almost immediately. A shimmering aquamarine tonic suit. I swear there was a beam of sunlight directed right at it.

It was unlikely I'd have to fight off any of the old geezers who frequented Kemp's to claim my elegant prize. The suit was mine for the taking, if it fitted. No sooner had I reached a tremulous hand to the fabric than an assistant appeared at my side, quick as a flash. Is sir interested? Would sir like to try it on? Close up it looked even better, a lovely three-button 60s number. But what if it didn't fit? That was always likely for a skinny 16-year-old in a shop full of men's suits. I knew what would happen next if that were the case: the excess fabric would be grasped from behind in front of a full-length mirror to show me what it would look like if altered, which they could do on the premises. But that act of transformation would cost another quid, which I could ill afford. And even if I had the readies, I didn't have the time. This baby had to fit straight off the peg. I needed it now. I had places to go and people to see, special people. My man held the jacket by the shoulders as I slipped it on with trepidation and – bingo! – perfect. Would you have a look at that? I nearly tore it out of his hands as I swirled round to get the full effect in the mirror. If the jacket fits, the strides normally do too, goes the second-hand seeker's adage, and sure enough they did. A red hanky and matching socks and a pair of Bass Weejuns completed the outfit and I was ready for the Roxy.

Five quid lighter, but with six still to go, I was very much looking the part, bowling down Tottenham Court Road, shimmering in the late-afternoon sunshine. In my mind I was a cross between one of the Four Tops and Johnny Reggae. But this was still the fashion dark ages – the Queen's Jubilee, the NF on the rise and the foul-mouthed Sex Pistols were all over the front pages. Just walking down the road dressed like this was a statement of degeneracy and anti-patriotism as far as many people were concerned. Impervious to the jibes and jeers of the locals and with an abstracted air, I strode south for the Roxy.

I'd arranged to meet a few pals in The Angel round the corner and on arrival was met by a crowd of proto punks and kids in a mixture of skinhead and mod gear. Pubs that didn't ask too many questions about age were at a premium. This one was normally half empty, even on a Saturday, so no questions were being asked, even if the governor was far from friendly as he stared witheringly at us while polishing glasses and chatting to a few old darzers at the bar. Much merriment and appreciation greeted my new outfit; a great night was in store. But no sooner had I ordered a pint at the bar than the door flew open and 20 Charlton fans appeared, swaying in the doorway and obviously up for it. Bumping into disparate bands of football hooligans was an occupational hazard on a Saturday night out in the 70s, so we weren't overly shocked at their sudden appearance. Word had got around that the Roxy was a hotbed of punks and weirdos, and football hooligans of the more conservative type were coming up to town, post match, for a spot of recreational aggro. Within seconds, a Wild West scenario ensued, bottles and bar stools going in all directions. We were well outnumbered and started to make a tactical retreat towards the far end of the pub and the side exit. All except my mate Andrew who, having swiped three pints of lager off the bar, was going in the other direction, backing into the ladies' loo – any port in a storm. I turned to see a fist coming straight for my nose. I ducked and it missed, only to be met by a Dr Marten boot right between the eyes. I went down and the back of my beautiful aquamarine jacket flipped over my head. Oh Lord, let no beer go over it!

Pretending I was dead, while the smashing of glass and stamping of feet reverberated through the floorboards around me, I peeped out from underneath my jacket to see my mates scattered, apart from Andrew, who was successfully disappearing into the ladies', still clutching the beer. I don't know exactly how long all the mayhem lasted, but it felt like a lifetime, as I did my level best to lie still and silent on the floor. Finally, just as I was beginning to think I'd never make it out of the pub, never mind to the Roxy, the boot boys tired of their sport and moved on to pastures new.

One by one we emerged from our various hiding places and reconvened at the bar, remarkably unscathed considering the state of the pub. Camaraderie confirmed and stories exaggerated, we downed what was left of our drinks, headed out into the sodium-yellow night and were soon piling down the dingy stairwell into the Roxy.

As far as I can remember, a certain Johnny Rotten was working behind the bar that day (whatever happened to him?) and a band called Eater – average age about 14 – were leaping around like lemmings on the stage. Looking the part, feeling the part and, most importantly, taking part, I was hit by the intoxicating feeling that this was our time and anything and everything was possible.

Of course, striving to look the part as a teenager in the great street theatre of London goes back much further than the 1970s. A constant in this city, and arguably the country as a whole, has always been the need of each generation to look and behave so very differently to the last. That short-haired young chap stepping out in all his aquamarine magnificence was tagging along behind a very long line of others who'd walked the same road before him: teddy boys, mods, rockers, skinheads, hippies, soul boys and punks – and those are just the cultural tribes from my lifetime. It's a tradition stretching back right through the centuries, to the time when London was still in the first flush of youth.

And for every fashion-conscious London male there's one man above all the rest who serves as an inspiration and a role model. A legendary dandy, wit, and style guru. A sartorial showman who turned heads and caused commotion by simply strolling down the street. No, not me, you fool – I'm talking about Beau Brummell.

Brummell, born in London in 1778, was a fascinating fellow who became one of the Prince Regent's closest pals. But his story doesn't have a happy ending, unfortunately: a fall-out with the Prince plus an extravagant spending habit saw him finish his life in France in 1840, penniless and insane. But in his heyday, by all accounts, he was quite the thing.

There's a rather charming statue of Beau on Jermyn Street in the West End. There he stands, all bronzed, bequiffed and beautiful, gazing imperiously down the tunnel of the Piccadilly Arcade – a glittering passageway full of high-class shops and boutiques. Top hat and cane in his right hand, left hand on his hip, he looks for all the world as if he's just about to spring elegantly from his pedestal and skip off down the Arcade, drawing gasps of awe from the shoppers as he parades the latest gear. He's easy to miss as you window-shop your way past the delights of Jermyn Street, but he is the perfect figure to represent a street in which you can still find handmade shirts, shoes and even perfumes.

At the base of Beau's statue, there's a surprise. An engraved inscription of a quotation, attributed to the great man himself, a line which sums up his fashion creed: 'To be truly elegant, one should not be noticed.' Reading that inscription for the first time brought me up short. This wasn't the Beau Brummell I'd imagined. The raffish dandy portrayed by Stewart Granger in the 1950s movie would surely never have uttered those words. In fact, it seemed to contradict everything I thought I knew about the man. I'd always assumed Beau was the quintessential English dandy – a peacock who delighted in parading himself in the latest and most daring fashions, the more outrageous the better; a man who craved attention, taking the timeless urge to be noticed and turning it into performance art. This, however, does not appear to be the case at all, according to a fascinating book, *Beau Brummell: The Ultimate Dandy*, written by a chap called Ian Kelly.

Beau was the man who invented understated cool. A dandy, certainly, but also the inventor of the style which still characterises up-market British fashion to this day – sober colours, nice cuts, definitely no flares. Without Beau, we wouldn't have the suit as we know it, or lots of the other beautifully made items you see on display in so many of the shop windows around Jermyn Street. Nor, according to Cecil Beaton – the Queen's favourite designer in days gone by – would we have the lovely double-breasted overcoats the guards wear outside Buckingham Palace. It is Beau's influence, according to Beaton, which keeps London at the centre of masculine elegance, and who am I to argue? Even those second-hand suits hanging in the window of Kemp's were, it seems, the great-great-grandchildren of the Regency outfits which Beau commissioned from the posh tailors of Piccadilly. Who knows, he might even have given my tonic suit the thumbs up, but perhaps not the red socks.

For Beau, it seems, the devil was always in the detail. According to another of his biographers, Lewis Melville (*Beau Brummell: His Life and Letters*, 1924), one of Brummell's greatest triumphs was his neckcloth.

The neckcloth was then a huge, clinging wrap, worn without stiffening of any kind and so bagging out the front. Brummell, in a moment of inspiration such as rarely comes to a man in a lifetime, decided to have his starched. The conception was, indeed, a stroke of genius. But genius, in this case, had to be backed by infinite pains. What labour must Brummell and his valet, Robinson, have expended on experiments to discover the exact amount of stiffening to produce the best result!

The sensation that Brummell made when he first appeared in his starched neckcloth was tremendous. It must have rewarded him amply for all the toil and moil. What was a shoe buckle five inches wide to a stiffened cravat? Nothing else was talked about for a few days in polite circles. The clubs were sparsely occupied, as all the members were at home practising before the looking-glass.

It's been a while since I toiled, or indeed moiled, with my neckcloth, but I wanted to look the part on my sartorial voyage of discovery. Which is why I climbed into my nattiest two-piece and a crisp white shirt before setting out to investigate how much survives of the London that Beau once knew. If he were to leap from his Jermyn Street perch today and join me on a stroll through his old stamping ground, how many old friends might he recognise in the modern streets of Piccadilly?

In Beau's day, as now, Piccadilly was the place to come and shop if you were a city gent with an eye for fine tailoring and a wallet fat enough to pay for it. In fact, its very name is proof that this neck of the woods has been linked to the rag trade for centuries. A 'piccadill', I'm reliably informed, was a stiff collar, like a ruff, worn by high-ranking gentlemen in the days before Rolexes were widely available as a statement of style and distinction. Sometime in the early 1600s a tailor called Robert Baker set out his stall in these parts and began flogging piccadills to the great and good. Quite what made his ruffs such a must-have item is not recorded but he was obviously doing something right, because over the years he made a fortune from them. He used the profits to build himself a grand house, which obviously became something of a local landmark in these parts. Within a few years it had become known as Piccadilly Hall, which some historians suggest was a derisive nickname bestowed upon a successful tailor's new house. But it was Baker who had the last laugh. The nickname stuck and lived on, long after the house itself had been demolished. Over the years, it became a shorthand way of describing the neighbourhood which once stood around the house. Which is why Piccadilly, this most fashionable and swanky part of London, still has a name which recalls its long-standing links with the rag trade.

Standing among the crowds beneath the statue of Eros in Piccadilly Circus, it's almost impossible to imagine what the area must have looked like when Baker built his house. The history books tell us it consisted of a small handful of green and no doubt very pleasant estates belonging to the super-rich, a slice of the country in what is, today, the heart of the city. Baker's new pad must have stood out like a sore thumb, but it also represented the shape of things to come. By the late 1600s the builders were descending on the area in ever-growing numbers, parking the seventeenth-century equivalent of white vans and cement mixers on the grassy parkland of the aristo-crats. The Great Plague and Fire of London had devastated large areas of the city further east, so many wealthy Londoners were moving west to set up shop in new developments here. Another major attraction, of course, was the fact that the area was within spitting distance of the royal court at St James's Palace, the home of the royal family until Victoria upped sticks and moved into Buckingham Palace in 1837. Not that any of the locals around here would ever have been caught doing anything as common as spitting. They paid people to do that sort of thing for them.

By the time Beau swaggered on to the scene in the late 1700s, this was rapidly becoming the place to be seen if you were a well-heeled eighteenth-century gent. And there weren't many who sported fancier footwear than Beau: according to legend, he polished his boots with champagne.

Being seen wasn't difficult as far as Beau was concerned, because people were usually looking. He may have advocated understated dress but, according to his biographers, that didn't stop an audience from gathering every morning at his house in Chesterfield Street to watch him get into it. As a style icon, his opinion was keenly sought on matters of taste and fashion, and he would hold court to the great and good of London – including the Prince Regent himself – while his valet, Robinson, scurried backwards and forwards with selections of cravats and such-like for the great man to choose from. I'm not sure I'd fancy a crowd of spectators oohing and aahing as I get dressed in the morning, although a bit of help finding a matching pair of socks wouldn't necessarily go amiss, but Beau was cut from a different – and no doubt very expensive – cloth. It's said that the daily performance could last anything up to five hours, not least because he was also a pioneer of the new-fangled habit of getting washed and shaved every day – not a very common practice in those days.

Once he was finally washed and scrubbed, Beau might have headed out for a spot of retail therapy. There are some London streets whose names are inextricably tangled up with the trades that have been practised there over the years: from hacks in Fleet Street to quacks in Harley Street to slacks in Savile Row. It's largely thanks to the sterling efforts of Beau Brummell and his chums that Savile Row became known as the spiritual home of British tailoring. Like Jermyn Street, it was born during that late seventeenth-century building boom, when so many people left the East End to set up shop in the newly fashionable West End, and quickly became a popular haunt for high-ranking army officers. The first tailor arrived in the street in 1806 and Beau – an officer in the Hussars – was one of those who immediately beat a path to his door.

That original shop has long since disappeared, but others have fared better, and Beau would definitely have recognised some of the names above the doors here, including Henry Poole and Gieves & Hawkes, although in his day they were based at premises on Piccadilly. I don't know if Beau ever patronised Gieves & Hawkes, but if he did he would have bumped into some pretty distinguished military men in the changing rooms, including Nelson and Wellington. From the early days, the firm was linked to the military, a tradition which continued into the nineteenth century, when they supplied suits and headgear for all those empire-building Brits who travelled far and wide to conquer the world wearing fine British tailoring. When Livingstone and Stanley doffed their hats to each other in the middle of the African jungle, an eagle-eyed observer might have spotted that both their pith helmets carried Gieves & Hawkes labels. The firm's services to the military didn't end there: in the Second World War they helped develop a range of James Bond-style gadgets, such as hollow buttons used to hide explosives or poison and stitched on to the outfits of undercover agents in occupied France or Germany. Sadly, that clothing line has since been discontinued, although they still do a jolly nice line in dinner jackets.

Once he'd done his shopping, Beau – like any self-respecting London male – would probably have fancied a sit-down and a cup of something warming while he enjoyed some me time. At this point I must ask you to risk a dizzying leap of the imagination and picture a world before Starbucks and Costa Coffee. That may be harder for modern Londoners to swallow than a scalding Americano (without milk), but I should add that this did not mean Beau could not have enjoyed a cup of coffee. Coffee houses were all the rage then, as now, and he would have been spoiled for choice.

If he craved something milky, he could have found it at another place which is still going strong today: White's, at 37–38 St James's Street. These days White's is known as Britain's oldest and most prestigious gentlemen's club, a status which it has somehow managed to cling on to despite the fact that it does not boast me among its membership. But it started life in the 1690s as a chocolate house, at a time when drinking chocolate – a rare luxury which only the rich could afford – was the latest craze to hit London. Back then it was known as Mrs White's Chocolate House and was based not at its current address, but on nearby Chesterfield Street, a five-minute stroll to the north. If you're wondering who Mrs White was, the answer is that she didn't actually exist: this quintessentially English establishment was founded by an Italian called Francesco Bianco. My grasp of Italian may not stretch to Dante in the original, but I think I can follow the logic that leads from Bianco to White. I hope Francesco didn't break the bank for that piece of rebranding advice.

Mrs White's soon acquired a racy reputation as 'the common rendezvous of infamous sharpers and noble cullies'. A cully, my dictionary informs me, was someone 'easily deceived, tricked or imposed on'. The sharpers, we can presume, were undertaking the deceiving and tricking. It was a meeting place for men of the world to swap stories and debate politics, or to buy tickets for the nearby Royal Drury Lane Theatre. Over the years it evolved into a fully fledged gentlemen's club, before moving to its current premises in 1778, the very year that Brummell was born.

The members of White's weren't only there for the chocolate. They also came to gossip, read the papers, smoke their pipes and partake of a little light lunch. As a matter of pure research, you understand, and not at all because of White's extremely extensive wine cellar, I recently arranged to have lunch at this venerable institution with my brother-in-law, Keith, and an old pal, Rupert, who is a member, in order to experience an environment that has barely changed since Beau and chums came in for their afternoon constitutionals.

I would have done well to have spent a little time moiling with my neckcloth, as my first faux pas as I enter the mahogany-lined portals is a lack of tie, a problem that's hastily attended to as two wooden boxes are politely proffered by the doorman, each containing an array of ties carefully graded through a rainbow of colour to suit any outfit. I select a suitable navy-blue tie to set off my Prince of Wales two-piece, and we make our way up the stairs and into the impressive dining room. It has huge windows running along St James's that give the room a lovely and rather magical light which reflects evenly from an enormous arched ceiling running the length of the room, which was apparently the template for all future gentlemen's clubs.

We are a little late and the place is already packed with other diners. As a consequence, we miss out on the best tables lining the windows and have to take our place at the members' table towards the back of the dining room instead. This consists of a long table of 14 place settings and we arrange ourselves at one end. We have barely started our first course, smoked eel in my case (not a wobble of jelly in sight), and are taking inaugural and appreciative sips of the house Macon, when a rather jolly-looking gentleman in a pink bow tie makes a beeline for our end of the table and proceeds to sit down next to us. Given the generous dimensions of the dining table, this feels rather like it does on the top deck of an empty bus when a stranger makes it his business to sit right next to you. But this is the form on the members' table. If a lone member feels like a chat, he can sit right next to you, if not he'll leave a place or two between. Our companion's body language suggests he's definitely in a Michael Parkinson mood.

Halfway through a bottle of superior claret and the second course underway (a plump roast grouse with bread sauce), conviviality is soaring. Not least at the sight of Keith nearly falling off his chair at the length and affordability of the wine list. The light is fading as we reach the cheese course, and a group of octogenarian dukes opposite are finishing a bottle of port in silhouetted silence. Bill settled and feeling replete, we are heading back down the grand stairs and out into Piccadilly. But I can't leave without having a little peek at White's famous bow window. This was installed sometime around 1811, when Beau was in his pomp, and it rapidly became a prime spot for the club's top dogs to sit and display themselves for the delight and titillation of the passing public – and Beau hogged it more than most. And although I doubt you would have seen any 14-year-old punk bands in Beau's club of choice, there was certainly plenty of youthful recklessness among the sharpers and cullies in his company.

According to club legend, a good friend of Brummell, a certain Lord Alvanley, once bet three grand on which of two raindrops would roll down a pane of the bow window first. For sheer scale and recklessness, his bet certainly beats my occasional flutters on the horses. When you realise that back in the early 1800s three grand was roughly the equivalent of £200,000 in today's money, you can see why he was more than a little disappointed when the two competing raindrops conspired to merge halfway through their descent, thus making the bet null and void.

In Beau's day, it's said that Londoners in search of some free entertainment would gather outside the bow window hoping to catch a glimpse of him or his pals in all their elegant finery. I stand there for some time and can only conclude that a little light drizzle has deterred the crowds from gathering to check out the cut of my strides.

If Beau fancied something a little stronger than hot chocolate, he could have given White's a miss and headed further down the street to Berry Bros, another remarkable eighteenth-century survivor, based at 3 St James's Street. Berry Bros & Rudd, to give it its full name, must be one of the oldest shops anywhere in the world, with a lineage which they can trace back all the way to 1698, when a grocer's shop called the Coffee Mill was opened here by a certain Widow Bourne. The front of the shop today – with its row of elegantly glazed windows, dark paintwork and rich golden lettering – can hardly have changed since the early years. The sign which hangs above the entrance, depicting an old-fashioned coffee-bean grinder, is a reminder that this place was once more famous for its coffee than its claret. But all that had changed by 1810 when, having passed through a succession of proprietors, the shop changed its name to reflect a change of owner. George Berry – son of a wine merchant from Exeter – was the first of eight generations of the Berry family to work in the shop, a tradition which continues to this day. George would have been the man who welcomed Beau into the premises when he first came calling.

I don't know if he bought his boot-polishing champagne from here, but if he did he would have been spoilt for choice: Berry Bros stocks some of the finest wines known to man, all stored in a network of underground cellars which stretches right up to the precincts of St James's Palace. It's said that there was once a secret passageway linking the palace itself to the shop, making it possible for lascivious royals to slip out of the palace and indulge in whatever they fancied without fear of detection. I'm assured this passageway has long since been bricked up, not that I can imagine any of the present-day Windsors ever feeling the urge to use such a cut-through in any case. Perish the thought. You don't need to descend to the cellars to see another of Berry Bros' most famous objects, a huge set of scales which were once used to weigh coffee, but which have also traditionally been used to weigh the customers. Just think how useful it would be to have a speak-your-weight machine in your local off-licence, right next to the crisps and peanuts. You'd save a fortune on snacks.

My wife Anne very kindly bought me and my mate Tony two places at a wine-tasting at Berry Bros as a birthday present last year. Yes, brothers and sisters, all once again in the name of research, I went just so that you too can share the experience without actually having to suffer the ghastly ordeal.

We descended to the first level of cellar, to be greeted by five or six rows of trestle tables facing a small desk and an audio-visual set up. Each place-setting had arranged before it eight glasses of red wine in two rows of four, from the relatively affordable to the fabulous and enormously expensive, going from left to right. A jolly and extremely knowledgeable wine merchant from the firm then proceeded, very entertainingly, to take us through the finer points of Bordeaux wine. It was all going swimmingly. Tony and I eschewed the spittoon and were savouring some very fine wines. Judging by the level of questions coming from the floor, there were some serious people in the room. What wines to lay down, the different *terroir* and the effect of close proximity to water – you name it, we covered it. As the various geographical and topographical charts were flashed across the screen, Tony and I were holding our own and keeping up with the notes in our information pack.

About halfway through the event, while we were discussing the subject of gravel, I think, Tony noticed that the two people either side of us hadn't turned up and that their gleaming rows of glasses were unattended. Checking his notes, he realised we were heading towards some very marvellous – and in some cases thousand-pound-a-bottle – glasses of wine. He decided it would be a waste if he didn't swap one of his slightly inferior glasses for one of the top-end glasses belonging to his vacant neighbour. These were the wines that even the merchant wasn't spitting out.

I followed suit and soon we were slightly out of kilter with the rest of the class. While subtlety of nose and notes in the flavour were being discussed, we were three or four wines ahead and, needless to say, my notes were getting in a bit of a tangle, as was my head. I looked down to see the word 'GRAVEL' written on my pad in capital letters, and that was the last serious contribution to my information pack.

The lecture wound down and as we had a 15-minute break before lunch, I took it upon myself to head for the surface and some fresh air. Feeling more than slightly light-headed, I checked my phone for messages and – ping! ping! ping! – three from my agent. 'You haven't forgotten your voiceover in an hour . . . half an hour . . . fifteen minutes?' Voiceover? What voiceover? I called her. 'Are you OK?' she asked. 'Er, no,' was all I could reply. I had ten minutes to get to Soho: this was a serious bit of business and I couldn't get out of it. Striding swiftly, albeit with a slight weave, I headed up Piccadilly, talking loudly to myself. Fortunately this is not an unusual sight in Piccadilly Circus.

Equally fortunately, when I arrived at the recording studio, I discovered there were no huge tracts of information to recite – just a few words to replace something I had recorded earlier. Even that was a struggle. Job done, I headed back to meet my mate Tony just as they were tipping out after lunch. Always impeccably dressed, he looked remarkably unscathed and could have passed for the soberest of judges, were it not for one button in the wrong buttonhole on his jacket. At which point, I could have sent him, had he still been around, to one of Brummell's many Piccadilly tailors, a certain Mr Weston, described by Beau as 'an inimitable little fellow – a little defective, perhaps, in his linings, but irreproachable for principle and buttonholes'.

If you turn right after leaving Berry Bros and head down St James's Street to number six, you find yourself at the door of yet another emporium that Beau would have recognised at once. Even in Beau's day, Lock & Co., Hatters was already a distinguished elder statesman in this neck of the woods. There'd been Locks on St James's Street since the 1670s, when the family joined the exodus from the east following the Great Fire and bought up the leases of seven houses here. They soon joined forces with a hat-maker called Davis, who also owned premises on the street. When he died, James Lock inherited the business which bears his name to this day. There can't be many shops that still trade from the same premises they set up in three centuries ago, but this grand old place is one of them, and it remains one of London's top hatters to this day. Don't take my word for it, ask the Post Office. It's said they once delivered a postcard from overseas which was simply addressed to 'the best hatters in the world, London'.

From the outside, the shop is all understated elegance. Its three-storey Georgian facade is rather dwarfed by the two buildings on either side, underlining the sense of this place as a dignified survivor from an earlier age, when style wasn't something you needed to shout about. Over the years, a hatful of famous customers have stepped through the green front door of Lock's, including Admiral Nelson, who was clearly a model client. One of his last acts before setting sail on the *Victory* in 1805 was to settle his bill here.

I don't know if Beau was ever a customer, but you can still buy top hats at Lock's, just like the one our statuesque pal is brandishing on Jermyn Street. I imagine you'd cause quite a stir if you strolled round Piccadilly sporting one today, but then, if the legend is to be believed, there's nothing new there. It's said that the chap who invented the topper – John Hetherington – first wore one in public in 1797 and promptly started a riot. When he was later brought before the Lord Mayor on a 'breach of the peace' charge, the officers of the crown reported that 'several women fainted at the unusual sight, while children screamed, dogs yelped, and a younger son of Cordwainer Thomas was thrown down by the crowd which collected and had his right arm broken'.

I have no idea who Cordwainer Thomas was, or what his young son may have been up to when he was trampled by the terrified throng, but the fact remains that Hetherington was hit with a whopping £50 fine for his crime of fashion – wearing 'a tall structure having a shining lustre and calculated to frighten timid people'. And you thought Amy Winehouse got there first.

Quite what a respectable company like Lock's is doing openly selling such scandalous headwear today is beyond me, but for those of you who wish to meddle in such territory, the last time I checked prices start as low as £340 – although a vintage example in silk could set you back thousands. Beware, though. After the Hetherington debacle a law was passed which banned the wearing of top hats on the streets of London and, as far as I have been able to ascertain, it has never been repealed. Maybe that's why you don't see many toppers around today – we're a law-abiding bunch, us Londoners.

I have always admired Lock's and that admiration only grew greater when I discovered that it was here that my favourite style of hat was born. A hat that has never, to my knowledge, caused riots on the streets and only occasionally filled timid Londoners with fear and terror; a hat that became an integral part of the London city gent's uniform for decades, alongside the briefcase and the brolly; a hat that starred in movies with screen legends like Chaplin, Laurel and Hardy and Oddjob; a hat sported by the dashing John Steed in *The Avengers* and the bumbling Captain Mainwaring in *Dad's Army*; a hat made sinister in *A Clockwork Orange* and cool by Louis Armstrong; a hat that's appeared in more than one Madness video over the years; a hat that transcends the class divide; a hat that's known and loved around the world; a hat they call the 'coke'. What do you mean, you've never heard of it?

You thought I was talking about the bowler, didn't you? Which is, of course, the name by which the hat became widely known over the years. But at Lock's they called it a coke and they still do to this day (and they are the best hatters in the world – just ask the Post Office).

It all started in 1849 with a customer called William Coke. He was a member of a rich landowning family in Norfolk who commissioned Lock's to design a new style of hat for his gamekeepers – something strong enough to protect them while they were out and about in the wilds of East Anglia keeping his game. Among the many hazards he wanted to protect them from were low-hanging branches and ruthless poachers. The hatters put their heads together and came up with the design we recognise today. Before they put it into full production, they needed the thumbs-up from the customer himself. At this stage, most of us might have been content to examine the prototype hat and perhaps give it a stiff rap with the knuckles to test its suitability for the job. Mr Coke, it seems, was rather more thorough. Having given the hat the once-over, he exited the shop and placed the hat on the pavement outside. Then he jumped on it. Several times. I don't know what weight the scales at Berry Bros would have recorded for the country gentleman, but I think we can safely assume that he'd enjoyed his fair share of hearty dinners over

the years, plus the odd glass of port with his stilton. As his
bulky frame descended towards the hat, the unfortunate staff
might have been forgiven for harbouring mild anxiety as to
how the test might turn out. Had things gone wrong at this
stage, this might have been the parallel story of how the flat cap
was invented. Happily, as it turned out, any anxieties they may
have had were unfounded. The hat survived the impact of the
aristo and sat there, gloriously unscathed in all its black
rotundity. Mr Coke was satisfied and gave the go-ahead for
production to begin, and within a few weeks the gamekeepers
of his family seat, Holkham Hall in Norfolk, were all equipped
with their new headgear. There's a photo of some of them,
taken a good while later, which shows them seated on a huge
pile of hay, tucking into their lunch with bowler-hatted relish.
They're all looking towards the camera in a vaguely menacing
fashion, as if daring the poachers of the world to come to
Norfolk and have a go if they think they're hard enough.

At Lock's there's a tradition that new hat designs are called
after the original customer who commissioned them, which is
why even to this day the hat is known as a coke. It's known as
a bowler to the rest of us because once the prototype had been
given the thumbs-up by the great man himself, production of
the hats was farmed out by Lock's to a firm south of the river,
Southwark to be precise, run by Thomas and William Bowler.

Those of you with an appreciation of fine music may be
aware that Madness have often been proud wearers of headgear, and most of us have sported a bowler at one time or
another. The feel of a real bowler is a tremendous thing, denser

and heavier than you'd imagine if you've only ever come across one of those plastic Laurel and Hardy jobs from a fancy dress shop that only seem to come in size small. If that is the case, I suggest you get down to Lock's whenever you can and have a feel of the real thing. Marvellous. I still have vague memories of hordes of bowler-hatted gents streaming out of Liverpool Street station swinging their rolled-up brollies, like a pinstriped army, and it was as an ironic reference to this that I first took to wearing one in about 1982, on the cover of our album *Complete Madness*.

I expect you're thinking that back then, at the heady height of my musical fame, I was living a shallow and incredibly decadent show-biz life and that rather than stepping out to buy the hat myself, I despatched one of my style consultants to do the deed for me. Well, if that was the impression beginning to form in your mind, then you would be way off the mark. Like generations of London men before me, I simply decided I wanted a bowler and headed off to the shops to buy one.

It would be jolly convenient at this stage in proceedings if I could report that I bought the hat at one of Beau's old Piccadilly haunts or, failing that, that I stumbled across it during a nostalgic fumble through the second-hand stock of Alfred Kemp's in Camden. If only life unfolded with such pleasing symmetry. The fact is, I did neither of those. I picked mine up just round the corner from Lock's at another old hatters which is also still going strong today. Which brings me back to Jermyn Street, where Beau still stands sentry over his former domain.

Bates, at 21a Jermyn Street, may not have a history quite as long as Lock's, but it's hardly a Johnny-come-lately. It opened for business in 1902, the year Edward VII came to the throne, Norwich City Football Club was formed and Theodore Roosevelt became the first US president to ride in a car. None of which facts are directly relevant to the story other than that you can bet your bottom dollar all of them – the king, the president and the fans and footballers of Norwich – wore hats, because every man did back then.

I had been advised that Bates was the place to go to buy a bowler, but had not been warned about what the purchase might entail. I realised it wouldn't be quite as straightforward as I had anticipated when, having announced the purpose of my visit, I was approached by the manager who was wielding a circular metal device which looked like either an instrument of torture or an inverted piano and gloried in the name of a 'conformature'.

It soon became clear that rather than simply taking a hat from the shelf and trying it on for size, the selection of a suitable bowler can only take place once the contours of one's cranium have been accurately mapped, as the hats are so solid and the head comes in many shapes. After the conformature was secured to my skull – and strangely dashing it looked too – a series of pins were carefully adjusted to gauge its exact dimensions. At this point, I half expected him to plug it in and send a current coursing through my temples. Fortunately, I avoided this shocking fate and he simply lifted the strange contraption off my head and placed it on the counter. Only after this ritual has been completed can a bowler be selected and tried on for size. It fit like a glove, if you know what I mean. I paid my money and made my escape.

That bowler was my first purchase of an item of traditional English headgear (I have subsequently bought others but I don't have a coke habit) and my only foray into the world of that traditional London hatter. So you can imagine how surprised and pleased I am when I return – a quarter of a century later – to have a look around the old place, only to discover how little has changed during the intervening years. Bates is still a treasure trove of hats in all shapes and sizes. Alongside the bowler, I see other endangered species, like the fez, deerstalker and top hat still flourishing in the rarefied atmosphere. Like exotic survivors from a more elegant age, they are living out their happy, sheltered existences and waiting for a kind-hearted and sartorially adventurous customer to pluck them from the shelf and release them into the wild.

It isn't only the merchandise which is familiar at Bates. As I'm shown around the premises by the current owner, Timothy Boucher, I immediately spot an old friend, the diabolic conformature. Resisting the pull to feel the weight of it on my head once again, I move away and spot another familiar face across the shop floor – a member of the Bates family I'd been introduced to on my previous visit all those years ago. His name, I remember, is Binks, and I am pleased to see that he hasn't changed, or indeed aged, in all that time. In fact, he hasn't even moved in all that time. Hardly surprising, I suppose, since Binks is dead and has been for more than 80 years. Not only dead but stuffed as well, and displayed in a glass case attached to the wall above the till: a stationary tribute to the taxidermist's art. I should add at this point that Binks is not an unfortunate shop assistant cut down in the service of hatting, but a cat.

According to Mr Boucher, Binks first ventured on to the premises in the 1920s – in the halcyon age when every London man worth his salt wore a hat from breakfast through till bedtime, and sometimes beyond. Whether Binks came in quest of a mouse or some headgear is unclear, but he was immediately adopted by the shop staff and has been a part of the furniture here ever since – metaphorically at first, but now quite literally. From the lofty vantage point of his glass case on the wall, he surveys his former domain with haughty insouciance, a silk top hat tipped at a suitably raffish angle on his head, and a cigarette lodged in his mouth to complete this tableau of feline contentment. He looks like the cat who got the cream, or in his case, the Player's Navy Cut. And because he cannot move from his perch, he remains blissfully ignorant of the fact that beyond the doors of Bates the Hatters is an utterly changed world where all the old certainties have disappeared, a world where the deerstalker and bowler have given way to the baseball cap or – worse still – the simple, unadorned head of the human male, in all its unconformatured nakedness.

Saying goodbye to Bates, I'm back on Jermyn Street, and there's one last place I want to visit before I head for home. A turn to the right carries me past the fragrant pong of the fancy cheese shop where the Queen buys her mature Cheddar and on towards another old friend that Beau would have recognised at once.

Did I mention that Beau was famous for washing every day – another habit we have in common, although it's unusual for me to allocate three hours to the process? It's said that he was so scrupulous in his ablutions that he never had the need to use scent or cologne to cover his traces. Beau may have been a stranger to BO, but the same boast could not be made by most of the other Regency bucks in eighteenth-century London, most of whom must have stunk like skunks. Unless, that is, they had an account at Floris & Co., 89 Jermyn Street.

Remarkably, this wonderfully fragrant survivor is still run today by descendants of the man who started the whole thing in 1730. That was the year when Juan Floris, a native of Menorca, arrived in London to seek his fortune. He began as a barber, but soon realised there was a market for selling the scents he squirted on his freshly cropped clients before they left the premises. Within a few years of buying his shop on Jermyn Street, he had a client list to die for, and had earned the first of many royal warrants as the king's favoured 'smooth-pointed comb-maker'. (History does not record who supplied the king's rough-pointed combs, but whoever they were, they've long since bitten the dust.) They used to make all their fragrances in the basement of number 89, a tradition which only ended in the 1960s, when production was moved to a larger site outside London. You can still catch a glimpse of the basement through the blue grille on the pavement in front of the shop, but these days the interesting stuff is all above ground.

Pausing only to glance up at the rather impressive plaster-work of the royal warrant, which perches on a lintel above the front window of the shop, I step inside. The hustle and bustle of Piccadilly quickly recedes and I feel as though I've entered a world which I thought had vanished centuries ago, a world where banknotes are ironed and coins washed before they're returned to the customer on a mahogany change-tray (a tradition that's recently been phased out at my local Lidl). This sense of connection with the past is no doubt enhanced on my visit by the fact that the man who greets me as I step through the door is Juan Floris's great-great-great-great-great-great-great-grandson (that's seven greats, if you weren't counting).

As John Bodenham shows me round this wonderful time capsule of a place – all mirrors, mahogany and musk – I can almost imagine myself back in the eighteenth century. Flush from a reckless wager at White's, I'd park up the sedan chair outside (no traffic cameras in those days, although I do notice a suspicious-looking chap with an easel) and nip in to pick up a fresh bottle of my favourite pong before setting off for a debauched night of carousing in the company of my dandified cronies. And even if Beau himself was unlikely to appear round the corner to greet me, at least the mirrored display cabinets that line the walls are the very ones he might have peered into two centuries ago as he checked to see that his cravat was still as shipshape and elegant as it was when he put it on that morning before an audience of admiring fashionistas.

Sadly, this fragrant flight of fancy is abruptly halted when John explains that the mahogany cabinets which grace the shop today aren't original, as I've assumed. Worse still, they've been acquired second-hand – hardly fitting fittings, I suggest, for a shop with such grand associations. But it turns out that I am wrong on that score. They may not be original, but these display cases still have a pretty distinguished pedigree: before they graced the Floris HQ, they'd been used to show off precious objects at the celebrated Great Exhibition in Hyde Park. In 1851, after the show was over, they were snapped up by Floris and installed in the shop. If they'd been good enough for Queen Victoria, I decide, they are good enough for me. I withdraw my complaint and move quickly on towards a room at the back of the shop, where I've spotted a white-coated lady seated at a table covered in a glittering array of glass bottles. What, I wonder, is a chemist doing here?

The vision in white – Sheila is her name – is Floris's resident perfumier. If you don't fancy any of the many tried-and-tested scents on sale in the front of the shop, you can, for a price, step into Sheila's fragrance factory and work with her to create one of your very own. The bottles on the table contain some of the 4,000 different scents she mixes and matches to create her unique blends, their labels announcing such exotic ingredients as tonka bean and galbanum oil. It takes several months of consultations and experimentation to finalise a bespoke scent, so, fighting the urge to carve my own niche in the pantheon of perfumiers, I decide to opt for something prêt-a-snorter instead and head back out front to make my selection.

The Floris order books are a veritable compendium of famous names, and a quick flick through the pages reveal that I am just the latest in a long line of sophisticated fashion icons to come calling. Besides the great Beau himself, who regularly stopped in for a chat, the list of clients includes more royals than even the most rabid revolutionary would want to shake a stick at, some redoubtable women (Eva Peron and Florence Nightingale to name but two) and a couple of legendary writers – Oscar Wilde and James Bond creator Ian Fleming. Oscar's favourite scent was a concoction called Malmaison, named after the Malmaison carnation, apparently the buttonhole of choice for elegant Victorians. Fleming's choice, named after the street number of the Floris shop itself, was No. 89, a taste he shared with his own fictional hero. When he wasn't saving the world, the great Bond took baths in water fragranced with Floris Lime Bath Essence – a pleasing example of early product placement for which I hope the author was appropriately rewarded. (Note to editor: please don't cut this bit, we'll split any kickbacks 50–50.)

Having made my selection – a bottle of Bond's favourite No. 89 as it happens – I leave Floris's feeling fragrant and refreshed. I almost expect a total stranger to walk up and hand me a bouquet of flowers just like they do in the adverts, but the closest I get is a guy with a flyer for Golf World. Even that affront (do I look like a golfer?) doesn't dash my spirits as I wander down the street and back towards Beau.

My travels in his bubbly-bright bootsteps have thrown up a few surprises, not least the discovery that the greatest dandy of them all was not quite the peacock I'd thought him to be. As I walk past the statue of the great man himself, still perched on his pedestal and surveying his domain, I take it as a compliment that he doesn't turn to watch me as I go. I know you'll tell me it's because he's made of bronze, but I prefer to think it's his way of giving me the thumbs up for my understated style and classy deportment. Thank goodness I left the red socks and hanky combo in the wardrobe today.

1 Elvaston Mews Livery*
2 Royal Albert Hall
3 Bathurst Mews Livery
4 Taxi tea hut, Warwick Avenue
5 Orderly boy statue
6 Regent's Canal
7 The Roundhouse
8 Camden Lock
9 Camden Stables Market
10 The Village Garage*
11 Kingsway Tunnel*
12 Bunhill Fields non-conformist cemetery
13 Bank of England
14 T. Cribb and Sons

Greater London

1000 metres

* No longer operating as described in text

CHAPTER FIVE

From A to B

Listen, boys and girls, I'm gonna tell you a story... If you are old enough, you'll read that in the voice of Max Bygraves, a variety performer of yesteryear. This particular story is about a long-ago city whose streets were full of horses. No, it's not My Little Ponyville. It's London Town.

I never thought I would be interested in horses except as vehicles carrying hopes of a big win. I didn't think the equine community and I shared much in common until I realised – and I confess the realisation came only recently – that I had actually shared my first adult home with a horse. Before I go much further and alarm friends and family, let me clarify.

The first house I bought was a mews house and there was probably a gap of 80 years or so between my residence and the departure of its equine inhabitants. Actually, Anne and I bought it from a potter who was sleeping upstairs and using the cobbled stalls as her studio, kiln and all. I suppose the potter's residence threw me off the scent a bit, but I don't think much of the internal structure had really changed since its horsey beginnings. And, of course, mews houses are dotted all over London because, along with London's potters and musicians, the city was once full of horses needing homes. So I thought I would try to follow the trail that takes us from a transport system dominated by the nag to the glorious mess brought about by the combustion engine that we currently enjoy. Musing on our mews took me back to my first experience of parking a car in our cobbled stall in December 1981. It's not primarily why I remember that month more vividly than others from the 1980s, but it is a contributory factor.

December 1981 was a month of momentous events in my life, parking aside. As that old French crooner Maurice Chevalier sang, 'Ah yes, I remember it well.' 'It Must Be Love', our ninth top-ten single in a row or something, was flying up the charts; we'd just bought our first house, the mews house in question; and I was about to marry Anne. I was 21 years old and it was nearly Christmas.

The group had been so busy touring and recording that there was a window of just a few days to get married and have a honeymoon. We got married on 21 December. It snowed and we had the whitest of white weddings in a church in Kentish Town. It was a beautiful affair and family and friends galore retired to Lauderdale House in Highgate for drinks and music and dance. After which Anne and I were whisked off to spend our two-day honeymoon in the Ritz in Piccadilly before I was off on the road again.

What Anne didn't know was that I had also organised to buy her a car as a wedding and Christmas present. I'd managed to track down Anne's favourite, a Karmann Ghia. These beauties were designed by Mr Porsche but have a VW engine. A perfect mixture of style and reliability, a bit like me.

The only problem was that the car was in Luton. Which even those with a poor grasp of geography will know is not actually in London. So on the first morning of married life, and on the pretext of sorting something out at our mews cottage in Camden, I left Anne at the Ritz having breakfast and struck north for Bedfordshire.

I roped in Lee Thompson, mate and Madness sax player, to join me as co-driver/pilot. We arrived in Luton to find the car was in beautiful nick, British racing-green with black-leather interior. Lee did all the tutting and sucking air between his teeth, while kicking the tyres and stroking the paintwork. It's an ancient ritual men in these situations do, just like builders when they come through the front door of a possible new job. Hands were shaken and a deal was done. I was anxious to get back to my bride at the Ritz, but the words speed and haste could not be used to describe our journey back to London.

After half an hour of scraping the ice off the windscreen, and that was just on the inside, we were off. Wahey! We lurched forward, leaping and skidding on the slippery road, the previous owner's smile rapidly evaporating as he leapt out of the way. We were heading back into town, albeit in first gear.

Though the car was a thing of beauty, it was not luxurious. It was built in the mid-70s and was functionally pretty basic. Because it was so cold, the windows were constantly steaming up. The heating consisted of a lever you slid from left to right, blue to red, cold to warm. Unfortunately, it took the length of the journey back to London before anything approaching warm air was coming out.

The journey took a good few hours. Lee had politely declined to help with the driving and was preoccupied with window-scraping duties. My abiding memory of that perilous journey back was of the car skating across empty London streets and a navigation error that took us kangaroo-leaping over a snow-covered London Bridge, the beautiful sights of the city barely visible through the steamed-up windscreen.

I finally made it back to Camden in pitch darkness. It must have been around four-ish. Never mind – at least I was home now. As I carefully navigated the car into the cobbled lane on which our new home stood, I felt a surge of relief – surely the worst was over? All I had to do now was park Anne's new motor and nip back to the Ritz and wedded bliss. I'd been away all day – that would take some explaining. I had to consider the possibility of ruining the surprise and actually telling the truth.

Like snooker, parking is all about angles. I was tired and am no Pythagoras. As beads of perspiration pricked my forehead, and gears crashed, I edged forward and back hundreds of times, and began to question the point not only of cars, but also of life itself. I wondered why I had bought the house without considering practicalities like parking. Roger Moore – the Saint – never had a problem with his mews pad and his motor. Maybe it was the car, or maybe it was me? I settled on it being the car.

I did eventually get the car into the stall and once it was perfectly tethered with a giant bow around it I headed back to Anne. When I finally arrived at the Ritz it was well into the evening, and I had told my new wife I was just popping out for a couple of hours. She hadn't called all the hospitals in London and no search party had been sent out for me, but I think it's fair to say that when you have only two days together for your honeymoon, disappearing for one of them is not ideal. I think the car and the bow and Anne's knowledge of my driving skills was explanation enough. It must have been, because if you fast-forward to the present we are still together, with two lovely daughters.

Back to that cobbled street. With the benefit of hindsight, perhaps I shouldn't have been so hard on myself. While I wasn't exactly James Hunt (another fellow mews dweller in his time), the truth was that the street was very narrow and the stall tiny. Our lovely new mews pad hadn't, after all, been designed to accommodate people like us who wanted somewhere to park their car, though it seemed perfectly suited to that purpose, and cheap into the bargain. It was, as I now know, built for horses. And horses have a very tight turning circle.

By all accounts, Victorian mews quarters were cramped, smelly and unsanitary, and, remembering the layout of our house, I wouldn't have wanted to share it with a horse. It's one thing to live cosy with your Karmann Ghia, as we did – we could keep an eye on ours through an internal window, while sitting in front of a fire – it's quite another to sleep above a stable. The idea was to keep grooms and carriages close to the big house so that its inhabitants could make that impromptu trip across town for a game of cribbage. The horses were effectively lodged at the end of the garden, hidden from public view and – crucially – down-wind from the nostrils of the rich folks.

We could only get sight of the big house that would once have owned our little hovel if we clambered up on to our roof, which, of course, being young, lithe and athletic things, we often did. Up on the roof (I've started humming along with the Drifters) we had a view of the world as it was 100 years before: the backs of vast houses, five or six storeys high, loomed at the end of long gardens. Most of the big houses had been turned into flats and their gardens parcelled up, while our little house was pretty much as it always had been, cobbles and all.

I am not a horse-rider. I tried once and I fell off. I had sort of assumed that, apart from the mounted police, royalty and the military, no one goes riding in London and that the mews houses, like my own first home, have for many years all been fitted out for human rather than equine habitation. But, in the spirit of adventure, I was curious to find out what our place would have looked like when Dobbin and co were in situ.

So to find out more I headed for Elvaston Mews in west London, to check out a mews stable that was still operating as originally intended, one of London's last livery yards. It is just a brisk walk from Hyde Park, which at over 350 acres is the largest area of open land in central London and a place where generations of fashionable Londoners have come to exercise their horses. Heading south from the park's fading red gates, I strode down Queen's Gate and passed one of London's many statues of men on horseback. This one is of the obscure Lord Napier of Magdala, a Victorian military man who in 1868 captured a fortress called Magdala in Abyssinia, modern-day Ethiopia. A final-year student at the nearby Royal College of Art, Eleonora Aguiari, wrapped Lord Napier, horse, plinth and all in bright-red duct tape as part of her end-of-year show in 2004, her aim to bring public attention to the obscure and ignored topics of the past, like Lord Napier's imperial campaign.

Once you stop and take notice of these features of our streets, it is a never-ending source of fascination. The stories they have to tell of the past and present are part of what makes living in this vast and ancient city such a joy. On this occasion I had no artistic or political agenda to pursue – I had other matters in mind and I'd left my duct tape at home – so I used the man on horseback as a handy and fitting signpost and strolled on down the wide tree-lined street in search of the turning on my right that would take me to my mews.

Turning into the mews itself, which is tucked away behind the big houses at the front, I was greeted by a sight which must once have been commonplace in these parts: a pair of horses tethered to the wall of the corner building, and both on the receiving end of a little light grooming. I'm no expert on these things, but judging by the swish of their tails, they looked like they were enjoying themselves. The woman wielding the brush was Jenny Dickinson, who had been running the stables here for the past ten years, offering her clients what's known as a full livery service – bed, board and daily exercise. On this particular day she had six guests in residence, although she told me there was actually room for nine horses.

I was surprised to see how far back the building seemed to stretch. It felt much larger than my old mews house, with three stalls off to the right of the cobbled corridor, each still boasting the original white ceramic tiles that were put in when the place was first built 200 years before. I know a saddle when I see one, and there were several hanging from the walls, together with other paraphernalia which no doubt served equally useful horse-related purposes – although quite what they might be was well beyond my understanding.

The whole place had a pleasing farmyard pong – a comforting blend of horseflesh, straw and polish. All in all, it was easy to imagine that crossing the threshold from street to stalls had whisked me away from the modern city and set me down in a country stables far from the madding crowd. I could almost imagine the sound of hammer on anvil as the local blacksmith bashes away at his metalwork next door. It was only when I emerged blinking into the autumn sunlight that I realised I hadn't imagined that sound at all: as if stage-managed to complete this illusion of rural bliss, there really was a blacksmith hard at work, shoeing one of Jenny's trusty steeds. As he took a breather between hooves, he explained to me that by day he works as a farrier to the Household Cavalry, but he also offers a mobile service to civilians like Jenny. He carries his portable forge and anvil around in the back of an estate car, the equine equivalent of the AA man, always there in an emergency to help put your transport back on the road.

As it turns out, I was fortunate to make my visit when I did. Since then not only has the yard closed, but a planning application has just been approved to convert this fabulous mews into a two-million-quid luxury home. I think that there must surely be enough two-million-quid homes in London to go round. What we have lost here is one of central London's last working stables. As far as I've been able to discover, there's only the one in Bathurst Mews in nearby Knightsbridge left. There is something sort of life-enhancing to think of people trotting out in Hyde Park at 6.30 on a summer's morning, just as they have for the last 250 years. Added to that, it's something that's traditional but vibrant and it generally adds to the mix of old and new in London as a living, breathing city. To lose all that for the sake of yet another tasteless home for a multi-millionaire seems to be a very bad turn of events. Before I get too worked up someone throw a blanket over me and give me a sugar lump, and I'll rein myself in. (Boom, boom!)

As I watched Jenny weave her way on horseback through the busy traffic of Queen's Gate and head off for a trot around Hyde Park, I tried to imagine what the streets around

Kensington would have looked like in the heyday of the horse. I realise that the images I conjured up are based on Hollywood versions of Dickens and George Bernard Shaw – London as a dark-brown, foggy city of narrow streets full of drunks and urchins, which I'm sure is completely wrong for Brompton Road and Knightsbridge, which feel too posh even for smog. Then I tried to picture something more suited to my surroundings – a tree-lined square and a gentleman with hat and cane escorting a lady with parasol and wide-skirted dress, the kind of scene that is straight out of *My Fair Lady* or perhaps *Oliver!* when things started looking up for Mark Lester. Then I realise what's missing from these visions, salvaged from my memory of wet Sunday afternoons spent watching the TV: none of them has any proper traffic on the roads.

I decided to try another experiment, replacing every white van and truck I could see with a cart or horse-drawn wagon, the buses with the horse-drawn omnibus, black cabs with the original 'Hackney carriage'. It wasn't long before my imaginary Knightsbridge was packed full of horses, and that's even before I started adding private transport.

A Victorian journalist by the name of W. J. Gordon (I hesitate to call him a 'hack') wrote the definitive work on this subject – *The Horse-World of London*, published in 1893 – in which he attempted to record for his fellow Londoners, and I include myself in his audience, the role of the horse in Victorian London. Gordon estimated the number of horses in London as 300,000, compared to a human population of about seven million. That would mean that there was about one horse for every 20 Londoners. That's a lot of horseflesh. Even Michael Cimino, the infamous *Heaven's Gate* director, with the film budget of his dreams, might struggle to depict an authentic London of 100 years ago. It was heaving with horses.

Gordon breaks down that figure of 300,000 into a dozen categories of work horses. I won't go into the detail here except to note that brewers' horses are in a class of their own. It's no surprise they justified their own category, given the huge volume of public houses that abounded in London in the nineteenth century, and given my fondness for the London pub, I'm glad they're singled out for attention.

You don't have to think too long and hard before you realise what a huge industry must have revolved around those 300,000 horses: their housing and welfare, food, harnesses, saddles and general horse paraphernalia. Then there were all the related jobs – from the vet to the lowly crossing-sweeper whose job was to dart across busy streets to clear the horse manure so that the gentry could cross from one side of the road to the other without dragging their crinolines in the piles of excrement.

The crossing-sweeper, or 'orderly boy', is remembered in a rather romanticised statue in Paddington Street Gardens, just to the west of Marylebone High Street. There is a cuteness to the figure – his head cocked to one side, his face cherubic and well fed, despite his shoeless feet – that doesn't ring true. Perhaps a more accurate depiction of a crossing-sweeper is the one given by Dickens in the form of the wretched pauper Jo in *Bleak House*. Jo's death causes Dickens to make an impassioned criticism of his own society's hypocrisy and its failures to deal with poverty.

Horse-drawn London also had some pretty appalling traffic and congestion problems. Seems it wasn't very different from today. It was quicker to travel from London to Brighton than it was to cross the city and, judging by early film reels from 1910, pedestrians took their lives in their hands when trying to navigate their way through waves of horse-drawn traffic. My driving instructor would have been appalled at the absence of lane discipline. I suspect that complaining about the roads, other road-users, traffic and pollution is just another continuum of London life. Rickets may have been eradicated, but moaning about pollution, noise and the traffic is, I think, something we may have inherited from the Victorians.

Despite the sheer number of horses on the move in Victorian London, there is not much surviving evidence of their presence. The crossing-sweepers might have cleared up all the dung, but you'd think there'd be something besides a few mews houses to remind us of a third of a million horses wandering the streets of the city. Actually, there is something else after all, and – what's more – it is right on my own doorstep in north London.

It's very easy to mooch around a neighbourhood, feeling totally familiar and comfortable with your surroundings for years, without really looking closely at what lies just beneath the surface. Just a short canter from my own front door is a place where I've whiled away many a weekend morning over the past 20 years or more, without ever really stopping to think about its horsey associations. It's called Camden Stables Market and it's part of the complex known collectively as Camden Market. The use of the word 'stables' will have already alerted the sensitive reader to the fact that this part of the market was once something other than an 'alternative' shopping magnet for self-styled London bohemians in all their rich and colourful variety.

It's not that I didn't clock this fact at the time – simply that I never thought very much about what the name actually said about the history of the place. I suppose you could accuse me of wearing blinkers, but I usually had other things on my mind when I visited. I've been going to the market for years and my two daughters used to run a stall there, selling home-made clothes. When I wasn't giving them a hand, I would happily take a wander along the busy walkways in search of rare vinyl imports or a bite to eat. Uncovering the origins of the place never seemed to feature during any of those leisurely strolls. Until now.

My route to the market takes me north from Camden tube station up Camden High Street towards Camden Lock, and if you head that way you pass the Roundhouse en route. This grand old building – refurbished a few years ago as a performance venue – was built in 1846 as part of an engine-shed complex for the Midland Railway, which ran trains into this part of London from the north. It's a funny old building because it's not square, like I think you'd expect. It is round – see what is happening there with the name again? – and it's round because it contained a turntable to turn engines around.

But it looks more like a temple than part of a train depot. It's a real landmark on the walk up to the market, and we're lucky it survived Victorian demolition because only ten years after it was built it was redundant, as the engines had got bigger and didn't fit inside any more. All that work with a compass consigned to the bin.

Aside from its architectural charm, it's worth noting the Roundhouse on your way up to the market because the railway and all its associated sheds and shunting areas also explain the presence of the stables. They were built by the same people, the Midland Railway Company, in the middle of the nineteenth century, at about the same time that the Round-house went up, at a time when this part of Camden was what we would call a transport hub. Horses were a central part of the set-up, used to unload and transport the goods which had been carried here by rail from the industrial north. Some took to the road and made deliveries to the rest of the capital, others headed for the nearby Regent's Canal.

The Regent's Canal was a major thoroughfare through London, running east to west. It flowed from the Limehouse Basin at the Thames through Islington and then underground in a long tunnel to King's Cross before winding north to Camden. From Camden the canal then stretched out west to join up with the Grand Union Canal and Paddington, the terminus of Brunel's Great Western Railway. So Camden was, as I always instinctively knew, pretty much the epicentre of London's comings and goings one way or another.

On my most recent visit to the market I noticed a few

desultory shoppers around, but most of the stalls were closed as it was midweek. If I'd wanted a kaftan or a piercing I'd have left disappointed, but this time my focus was on something different – I was shopping for atmosphere and insight. As I wandered along the cobbled walkways, I more or less had the place to myself and it didn't take long to see that these must once have been stables on an industrial scale. The whole site is a mishmash of old warehouse buildings and stable blocks where the horses put their hooves up after a busy day at work. It's built on several different levels – above and below ground – and there are ramps round every corner. Stairs and horses don't really mix very well. Besides the architecture itself, I started to spot other remnants from the market's former life, including rings bolted to the grey brick walls which would once have been tethering places for the animals.

There was also once a horse hospital on site, which was much in demand, since working life for these creatures was a hard slog. If you pop your head inside one of the buildings that used to house the hospital, you'll discover that today it's a second-hand furniture warehouse, chock-a-block with merchandise. It's a huge space. At least 20 feet above your head are cast-iron pillars which support the roof. Each of them has deep-set grooves, slots which would once have held in place a series of wooden planks dividing the space into smaller stalls for the horses. In the corners, where wall and ceiling meet, there are the old hatchways which would have been used to shovel in hay for the horses from street level up above. Through the gloom I could see someone crouched over a table, polishing it up to a lovely sheen. A hundred years ago his predecessor might have stood there shodding a horse instead.

There were reminders of the place's former function wherever I looked, and not just above ground level. Beneath this huge site, a network of tunnels – or catacombs, as they are more atmospherically described in the history books – was built by the Midland Railway, linking canal-side warehouses with goods yards and railway depots, going the most direct route underground rather than joining the throng of traffic above ground.

It's actually a bit spooky down there – dark and wet – and as I splashed through the puddles in my brogues, it was easy to imagine how these passageways would once have echoed with the sound of horses' hooves as they shunted railway wagons and carried goods away from the depot to other parts of the capital. Looking up from the catacombs at the beautiful arches of brick (the Victorians loved a brick – I can't help thinking they would never have been so lovingly laid in this century), cast-iron ventilation grilles set in the roof provided the only source of light and fresh air to the beasts of burden below. You can still spot some of these grilles above ground along Chalk Farm Road.

The tunnels have been revamped and there is now quite an extraordinary sculpture of galloping horses protruding above the entrance to this part of the market, with an accompanying history cast in bronze and a rearing beast at ground level which I think is meant to be welcoming rather than off-putting. These beauties are more thoroughbred than beast of burden, so given what we know and can guess about the lives of the horses that lived and worked here, it is probably fair to say a bit of artistic licence has been exercised by the sculptor.

After my visit to the stables at Camden, I had the bit between my teeth, as it were. I started to realise that there were more remnants of horse-drawn London knocking around the place than I'd thought. For example, in certain parts of London, revealed beneath the wearing tarmac, you can see wooden cobbles, such as in Endell Street, which runs south off High Holborn down into Covent Garden. Heading a bit further east towards the Barbican, at Chequer Street, near Bunhill Fields, the nonconformist cemetery and last resting place of one of London's great sons, William Blake, there's another visible stretch of wooden cobbles, about ten paces in length.

Many roads, particularly those that took heavy traffic or which were sited near hospitals or the houses of the well-to-do, were blessed with wooden rather than granite-block cobbled roads. The wooden surface, covered with tar, was considerably quieter but also kinder to the joints of the horses. After the Second World War most of the tar-covered blocks were ripped up and sold off as domestic fuel, but the eagle-eyed can still spot a few lingering survivors here and there.

Another relic from those days is the assortment of granite drinking troughs that are dotted around the city. Most of these were established in the second half of the nineteenth century, as the second phase of a campaign which began with the introduction of public drinking fountains for the city's human inhabitants.

An august body, the Metropolitan Drinking Fountain and Cattle Trough Association, founded by Samuel Gurney MP with support from the Earl of Shaftesbury, the Earl of Carlisle and the Archbishop of Canterbury, no less, started installing fountains around the city in 1859. This was the year after the 'Big Stink', a year when sewerage was at its worst and the city was permeated by a germ-heavy fug. This year of the stink followed two decades marred by cholera outbreaks which caused many deaths. Before the fountains were established, fresh drinking water was a rare commodity and the cheapest and most readily available drink for Londoners of all ages was beer, which I must say does have a certain appeal.

Thanks to Mr Gurney and his friends, all that changed in 1859, and his name still adorns the first fountain, which survives to this day on Holborn Viaduct, outside the Church of the Holy Sepulchre in the City of London, in sight of the Old Bailey. Once they'd sorted out the drinking arrangements for the human population of London, the campaigners – under pressure from the Society for the Prevention of Cruelty to Animals – turned their attention to the needs of the horses. Not more than 200 yards behind the water fountain on Holborn Viaduct is a granite trough for animal refreshment in West Smithfield. The smell of raw meat can hang in the air, reminding me that Smithfield is still a working meat-market to this day. For those vegetarians who wish to forego this particular sightseeing trip, I can report that the trough is surprisingly large – maybe 12 or 14 feet in length – and was planted with winter pansies when I saw it.

Previous page: Soho in the 60s

Above: Venue for the first Madness gig

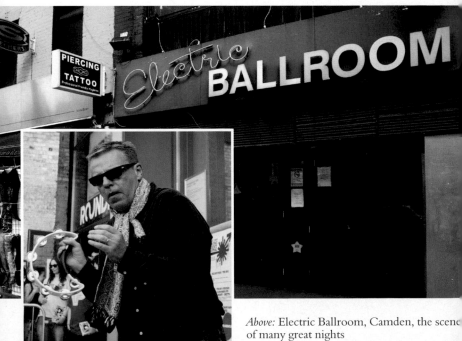

Above: Electric Ballroom, Camden, the scene of many great nights

Inset: Earning beer money outside the Roundhouse on the 2009 Camden Crawl

Previous page: Wilton's Music Hall. 150 years of laughter and still going strong

Inset: Getting the perfect-fitting bowler is important…

Above: …and I think you'll agree, it was worth

Left: Beau Brummell

Below: Graham McPherson (or have I got this wrong…)

bove: The mysterious Kingsway Tunnel

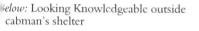

elow: Looking Knowledgeable outside cabman's shelter

Above: Guess where we're all going? You got it. A Routemaster summer holiday

Below: The Beverley Sisters just happened to be walking down Denmark Street in matching macs and bootees, when a film crew appeared from nowhere

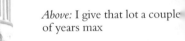

Above: I give that lot a couple of years max

Left: Tin Pan Alley today

Left: My office

Above: The last night's racing at Walthamstow Stadium

Inset: One of the greatest pop songs of a generation

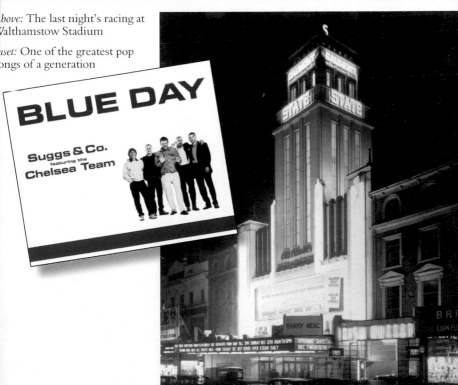

Right: The wonderful Gaumont State Cinema

Above: Dinner at the local iguanodon, of course

Below: Crystal Palace Park. Sure hope he's not ticklish

So, while many of London's horses clearly had a dog's life, some philanthropic groups were looking out for their interests. Although biblical quotations and admonishments on the evils of alcohol were unlikely to be of interest to a parched pair of cab horses, the health value of clean water was vital, a fact which London's alehouses and gin-shops soon cottoned on to. Not to be outdone by the Victorian temperance movement, some publicans put troughs for horses outside their bars, enticing the cab and wagon drivers in for a pint while the horses quenched their thirst outside: an early sort of two-for-one offer. The locations of these drinking troughs were so important that they were included on ordnance survey maps and omnibus drivers had the troughs marked up on their routes, the watery equivalent of modern-day petrol stations.

So what about those original horse-drawn omnibuses? The first service, introduced by George Shillibeer, ran between Paddington Green and 'the Bank', the Bank being the Bank of England. It was launched on 4 July 1829 and offered Londoners their first taste of public transport across the metropolis.

Looking at old engravings, passengers travelled in what resembles a box on wheels pulled by three horses. The box had a rear entrance, which was where the conductor stood, just like on the classic Routemaster. Passengers sat facing each other on long benches. The first services offered by Shillibeer carried middle-class Londoners into the city from the leafy suburbs, and they were quite pricey. But the idea quickly caught on and competition brought the fares down. Sitting on top of a double-decker was, according to Gladstone, four-times British Prime Minister during Victoria's reign, the only way to see London. A sentiment which certainly gets my vote. There aren't many finer ways to enjoy the city than from the front seat on the top deck on a ride down the Strand and Fleet Street.

Aside from his love of bus travel, Gladstone was pretty famous for his devotion to helping the prostitutes of London. By the time Gladstone was spotting fallen women to save from the top of his horse-drawn double-decker, there were a number of different companies touting for business. For instance, if you lived in Putney and worked in the City you might travel to Liverpool Street on a service run by the London General Omnibus Company, which was, according to Gordon, journalist and the fount of all horse wisdom, 'the greatest user of living horse power in London. They have, in round numbers, ten thousand horses, working a thousand omnibuses, travelling twenty million miles in a year, and carrying one hundred and ten million passengers.' I wouldn't have fancied being the crossing-sweeper cleaning up after that lot.

By 1900, the number of London horse-drawn buses had reached 3,736, most of which were double-deckers pulled by two horses, rather than the original three: good news for the accountants, but less so for the horses themselves, I should imagine. They were also bringing in revenue through the medium of advertising for things like good old Sapolio Black Lead.

Mr Gordon takes delight in describing one vast omnibus yard out in the sticks at Farm Lane, Fulham, now, of course, a very desirable area of London and blessed by proximity to London's premier football team.

Farm Lane housed double-decker stables for 700 horses set around a courtyard. Gordon says:

> At Farm Lane, Fulham, the Road Car Company has the finest omnibus yard in Britain. At half-past seven in the morning when the first car comes out, and indeed at any time, it is one of the sights of London. In the central court are over sixty cars which have been washed and examined during the night, the cleaning of each seven being one man's night's work. Around the quadrangle are the stables, on two storeys, and in them are 700 horses. Four of the floors have each about fourteen studs of eleven in a long double line standing in peat, the gas jets down the middle alight in the fading darkness flickering on the double set of harness for each stud, which gleams black and shiny on the posts that make the long lines look longer, while the growing daylight streams in from the high windows on the inner wall and from the ventilators overhead.

It must have been quite a sight and smell, but sadly, unlike the stable yards in Camden, no traces remain of this major depot and the best guess is that it is now probably the site of a trading estate, home to architects, caterers and couriers (the last is, I suppose, at least related to getting something from A to B).

However, one of the ideas pioneered by those early

omnibus owners has survived. They wanted to make it easy for the paying public, many of whom were illiterate, to identify the route of the bus. Eventually, they fixed on numbers as the best way of doing it, but before that they used a colour-coding system, keeping the sides of the omnibuses clear for adverts but painting the route colour on the carriage. For example, if you were travelling with the General Omnibus Company between Putney and Liverpool Street, you'd be on the white line. If you were travelling out of Victoria northwards, you'd use the 'royal blues'. As Gordon says, 'The wheels of a car are a means of its identification. By the colour of the body you tell the line the vehicle travels; by the colour of the wheels you tell the company to which it belongs.' This brilliantly simple idea of using colours to show the route a bus was taking and its destination was ultimately copied by London Underground and showed off to beautiful effect in Harry Beck's London Underground map.

Those old horse-drawn double-deckers also have a direct descendant which itself has almost disappeared completely from London's streets, and that's the old Routemaster bus, which was designed for London Transport. I say 'almost' because the number 9 from the Royal Albert Hall to the Aldwych and the number 15 from Trafalgar Square to Tower Hill were reprieved as 'heritage routes', and you can still hire others for private events. The Routemaster, in particular route 29 (Wood Green to Trafalgar Square via Camden), played an important part in the early life of Madness. It was how we got to rehearsals and how we got around London. It gave us a perspective on the city, and what we saw from the top deck of that bus, and others, then featured in our songs.

These old-style buses had other glories too. I'm sure it was not only me and my friends who enjoyed the occasional ride without a fare on these old wagons. 'Get on a red bus and not pay the fare, get on the red bus and go anywhere,' as I sang in 'Somewhere in London'.

The other delight I associate with the old Routemaster is cigarette smoke, because there was a time when smoking in a public place was not a crime but rather a sign of a convivial atmosphere. When I couldn't afford my own fags, an added pleasure of the bus ride was to go to the top deck – the smoking saloon – and just inhale other people's smoke. And when I did have the cash to buy my own, there was no better feeling as a kid than to sit like a lord at the top of the double-decker with my feet warming on the heater and a smoke on the go. The only time I remember it raining on this particular parade was when once, soon after lighting up, I made the mistake of asking the conductor for a half-fare ticket. As he fixed me with his steely eye, I immediately realised the difficult choice I'd forced upon myself. Either to stub out my fag in acknowledgement that I was still a child (under 14) or carry on puffing manfully and stump up the full adult fare. Economics was the winner on this occasion and the fag was duly extinguished.

The bus will always get my vote ahead of the tube, because I like to see where I'm going and what's going on around me. But since it's such a major part of London's transport story, it seems churlish not to give the Underground a bit of elbow room in my jaunt through London's transport past, though I have to say that's more than it ever seems to give me.

The London Underground is owned by Transport for London, which is part of the Greater London Authority, and was set up to look after the capital's buses, tubes, trains and cabs. But it started life in 1863 as a money-making commercial enterprise, with the same kind of competition for passengers as existed between the rival omnibus companies. It was the Great Western Railway who started the carriages rolling when they opened an underground rail link between their terminus at Paddington and Farringdon Station in the City. It caught on quickly, but I wouldn't have been keen. I'm not sure what would be worse: having your face pressed against some sweaty armpit or inhaling carcinogenic soot blowing back from a steam engine. But, despite these deterrents, the concept obviously appealed to Londoners and as passenger numbers increased, so did the competition between different operators.

One of the consequences of competition was that the different railway companies wanted to take their customers to the same areas of the city. Often they would forge alliances with competitors and integrate stations to accommodate more than one line. But it didn't always work out like that, and in some popular parts of central London different stations would spring up cheek-by-jowl to compete for business. An example of this was a station called British Museum operated by the Central London Railway Company, located about 100 yards from Holborn Station, which was operated by the Great

Northern Piccadilly and Brompton Railway Company (you can see why London Underground eventually shortened that mouthful to 'Piccadilly'). It was not a great surprise that when finally the network was combined under one management board in the 1930s, one of the stations had to go, and on this occasion it was the British Museum station that got the axe.

Sadly, the lovely British Museum station building was demolished. It had the typical red-glazed tiles and arched entrance that echoed the tunnels below ground. I can't help wishing they'd retained its facade, just as they did the former station at Aldwych, which still promises passengers a ride on the defunct Piccadilly Railway and provides, in my opinion, a kind of poetic adornment to the street.

But while you can knock down the building and remove the station from the tube map itself, the task of removing the evidence below ground level is a different matter altogether. Which is why, if you should travel on the Central line between Holborn and Tottenham Court Road, I urge you to look up from your copy of the *Evening Standard* for a moment and stare out of the window really hard, remembering, of course, to avoid any eye-contact with fellow travellers during this risky procedure. If you're lucky, you'll catch sight of the abandoned station, a ghostly glimpse of a vanished world which flits past the window in the blink of an eye. I wouldn't make a special trip for the purpose, as there's not an awful lot left to see – there's no platform and the 'roundel' station sign has been taken from the wall – but if you're passing through this way it's certainly worth a moment of your time. At which point, I feel we should return to ground level for some fresh air before I venture too far down the track which leads to trainspotterdom and unsightly anoraks.

Not too far away from the ghost station of the British Museum is one of the more surprising relics of London's transport system. Travelling south on the top deck of the bus, I've often passed an odd slipway extending under the road at Kingsway and have wondered idly what it is. Finally, in an attempt to solve the question once and for all, I consulted my battered *A–Z* and noticed a series of funny dashes marked along Kingsway and round Aldwych which remain mysteriously unexplained on the key. The mind boggled: what could these curious markings – a long series of morse code 'O's – actually represent? I asked my mum – a long-time London resident who's pretty familiar with that neck of the woods – and it was she who suggested they were probably there to mark the spot where the tram used to run. It turned out she was right. That mysterious opening on Kingsway is the entrance to a purpose-built Edwardian tramway tunnel.

These days the Kingsway Tunnel, as it's called by those in the know, is padlocked and off limits to the casual visitor. But I got a glimpse of what lies behind the gates by hooking up with a chap called Nick Catford, a lover of all things subterranean and a man who seems to have the knack of persuading the powers that be to let him have a nose around all sorts of places that are no-go areas for the rest of us.

With Nick as my companion, we walk down the slope that takes you from street level at Kingsway and into the gloom of the tunnel itself. The noise of traffic recedes and it feels as though you're entering a secret slice of London. The old tram tracks are still visible on the ground in front of us, guiding us forward all the way to the remnants of the former tram station itself, a couple of hundred yards further down the tunnel. Down here the walls are lined with white-glazed bricks and there are even the tattered remains of advertising posters on the walls. We notice the outline mark that had been made by a long-removed London Transport roundel sign, which would have reminded passengers on the top floor of the tram that they'd reached their stop. Light floods down from a flight of steps covered with autumn leaves and the odd crisp packet. That would have been the route taken by prospective passengers from the pavement above to catch the last tram that ran through here more than 50 years ago. As I look around, it occurs to me that it wouldn't take much to return this place to its former glory.

The Kingsway Tunnel was built for what most of us would regard as traditional trams, but there was also such a thing as horse-drawn trams although they didn't operate in the centre of town. Apparently the clatter of hooves combined with the ratcheting noise of the metal wheel which kept the tram attached to the rails was too painful for the sensitive ears of the residents in these parts, who lobbied successfully to keep them out. As a result, horse-drawn trams were confined to the suburbs, plying routes from Brixton to Kennington in the south-west and Blackheath to New Cross in the south-east.

The tunnel at Holborn was the sole preserve of electrified

trams, which took off (not literally, I hasten to add) at the beginning of the twentieth century and were quicker, cleaner and quieter than the horse-drawn variety, not to mention cheaper to run. When the tunnel opened in 1906, a fleet of single-deck tram cars was purchased for the astronomical sum of £750 pounds each, to carry passengers on a route from Angel in Islington south through the tunnel, all the way to its exit on the Embankment at Waterloo Bridge. It was a pretty quick ride, taking only 12 minutes, so no wonder it was so popular.

The route proved such a hit that by the 1930s, this was one of the busiest stations in the capital, and the single-deckers were replaced by two-tier trams – which meant the tunnel roof had to be raised. After the Second World War the popularity of trams went into decline, as the bus became the new boss on London's streets. The Kingsway Tunnel station finally closed in July 1952, after a week of nostalgic farewell celebrations across the capital. Photos from the time show Londoners queuing round the block to secure their seat on the last trams to criss-cross the capital. I can't quite imagine us throwing a similar kind of party for the bendy bus.

After the trams were retired and the tunnel closed, it was used as a storage garage for decommissioned buses that were held in reserve for the Coronation and as a flood control centre. It even starred in a film, when it played the role of a train tunnel in *Bhowani Junction* opposite the lovely Ava Gardner. I am not sure the director George Cukor really did the Kingsway Tunnel justice, and the Kingsway's agent couldn't have been great because the film work dried up. I guess there just aren't that many good roles for tram and train tunnels. Now it is a storage depot for great lengths of pipe, paving slabs and cobbles: a rather gloomy municipal B&Q slowly decaying beneath the streets of Holborn.

I don't think the trams at Holborn took the Oyster card – Londoners' current passport for public transport – but there are other elements of the modern-day system which would have struck a chord with travellers transported forward in time from an earlier age. In the early part of the nineteenth century, for example, there were different travel zones within the city. The drivers of the original horse-drawn Hackney carriages, the ancestors of today's black-cab drivers, had a monopoly on picking up and dropping off customers in the central area of the capital. Alarmed by the threat to their livelihoods posed by the new horse-drawn omnibuses, which offered Londoners a cheaper, if less comfortable, way of getting from A to B, the Hackney carriage drivers lobbied successfully to keep the omnibuses from making stops to pick up and drop off in central London. So a kind of central zone operated in the city for a few years. But you can't stop progress and the buses represented a bit of a transport revolution. The cabbies couldn't stop buses challenging their supremacy, but they did retain their monopoly on picking up fares from the kerbside, which they still jealously guard.

There are some reminders of these original London cabbies and their horses which still survive on the streets of the city today – thanks largely to the efforts of their modern-day counterparts, London's black-cab drivers. They're called cabmen's shelters and in case you're wondering, no, they aren't homes for distressed cab drivers who've lost 'the Knowledge'. To find out more about these mysterious green huts which adorn several street corners around the capital, I hailed a taxi and took my seat behind a man who's done more than his share to keep them going. As Peter Raymond weaved his way expertly through the west London traffic towards Warwick Avenue, he wasn't taking me to the tube station made famous by Duffy, and I wasn't worrying about being chucked by my girlfriend, I was heading for the site of one of the surviving huts.

Peter filled me in on the history of these places. It was not long before a familiar story began to emerge of a worthy philanthropic impulse which concealed a far more sinister agenda: to keep London's cabbies out of the pubs.

The story begins with a gentleman called Captain Armstrong. He'd noticed that whenever the weather was bad – a rare occurrence in London admittedly, but still an occasional hazard – it was almost impossible to find a cab driver (no change there then). Investigating this problem further, he discovered that the elusive cabbies were often to be found taking shelter in cafes and pubs. When they finally emerged into the daylight, they often displayed the inevitable con-sequences of whiling away the long rainy hours in a licensed premises, and were in no fit state to steer a coach and horses from the Coach and Horses and through the streets of the city. Along with like-minded souls, including Lord Shaftesbury, who you'll recall was one of the driving forces behind the drinking-fountain-and-water-trough movement, Armstrong decided to offer cabbies a place of refuge which would be dry in both senses of the word, a series of havens in the shape of sheds scattered around the city, where they could shelter from the storm and enjoy 'good and wholesome refreshments at moderate prices'.

Between 1875 and 1914, 61 of these shelters were erected at a cost of about £200 each. As they were all placed on the public highway, the police specified that they should not take up more space than a parked horse and cab, hence their size and shape. The idea was so successful that it was later adopted in cities as far afield as Melbourne in Australia, where they not only copied Armstrong's idea but even the shed design itself. I'm told they still have one surviving shelter in Melbourne to this day, a tasteful cream rather than the characteristic green of London's originals. I'd have liked to check out the Melbourne version for myself but sadly I couldn't afford the fare Peter demanded to drive me there in his cab, so I had to make do with the Warwick Avenue example instead.

As we pulled up outside this beautiful, oblong, green-panelled hut, it felt for a moment as if we'd arrived at a scaled-down cricket pavilion. There are 13 huts like this across the city, all of them Grade II listed, but this is one of the finest. As I approached the door, I dreamt of entering a Tardis-like structure, with corridors leading off into ballrooms and libraries. Actually, it turned out to be exactly the same size on the inside as the outside, but it still crams a lot into a small package. Though there's no ballroom, there is a compact working kitchen and enough room to accommodate up to 13 cabbies.

There is an air of exclusivity to these places and Peter admitted that he was quite daunted when he stepped inside his first shelter in Clapham in south London. From those first wary steps, he has risen to become the secretary of the Cabmen's Shelter Fund, and an inheritor of the Earl of Shaftesbury's mantle. Before you all rush to take advantage of these charming sheds, the first rule here is you have to be one of the current 25,000 licensed black cab drivers in London to be able to enter. It's probably not the most exclusive members' club in London, but it requires significant dedication to get your foot in the door. I mean, do you know the quickest route between Dalston Lane and Bhowani Junction?

I was lucky enough to have the rules temporarily waived to allow me to sample the atmosphere for a few minutes. Breathing in the enticing aroma of a breakfast being prepared just a few feet away from where we sat, I asked Peter what the draw was. He suggested that one of the great things for cabbies was the opportunity to learn the nuts and bolts of the job from fellow drivers. When to take a cheque. When to ask for the money first. Or, 'When to go south of the river?', I asked. But mostly they were there just to gossip. 'You should have seen who was in the back of my cab last night. And as for what they were doing...' There are some pretty strict rules too: no gambling, drinking or swearing. I imagine that keeps the numbers down, but I guess you have to with a potential 25,000 covers to serve.

As I stepped out of Peter's peaceful haven and waved him off into the mid-morning traffic, I wondered what his horse-driving predecessors would have made of the motorised frenzy of the modern city. But I was forgetting that there was a time before the combustion engine reigned supreme, when horses and cars shared the streets of London. Just over the road from Great Ormond Street Hospital for Children is a little side street called Barbon Close, WC1, where you can still see the painted advertisement for a firm called G. Bailey and Sons, who promoted themselves as both 'horse and motor contractors' – many businesses kept a foot in both camps while the battle between the two forms of transport played itself out on the streets of the city. I can picture the scene in their workshop: someone re-shoeing a van in one corner while his colleague changed the oil on a carthorse.

Horses were phased out eventually, of course. The benefits of motorised transport were recognised pretty early on by the bus and tram companies, and the speed with which they switched to motorised vehicles was phenomenal. Horse-drawn buses had pretty much disappeared from London by 1915 – perhaps not surprising when you think about the cost of running that stable out in Fulham which Gordon described. But for general haulage and goods deliveries, the change was much more gradual. In fact, the horse stayed on the road delivering goods well into the 1950s, hence the darkly comic rag-and-bone men of the 1960s classic television series *Steptoe and Son*, who plied their trade with a cart pulled by a horse called Hercules.

From the sublime to the more ridiculous, in what I imagine to be the suburbs of London, Benny Hill's Ernie drove a horse-drawn milk cart, while his rival Two-Ton Ted from Teddington drove the baker's van, in a song which is a reminder that the world of the milkman and his horse-drawn milk cart was still recognisable to Benny Hill's audience in the 70s. Clearly our sympathies were meant to be with Ernie and his horse Trigger and not the van driver, or maybe I've got that wrong and there is some other deeper message about the moral superiority of dairy produce over baked goods.

These days, people stop and stare at the sight of a horse walking down the road, and when you see one it's usually mounted by a policeman doing a spot of crowd control. But, strangely enough, the horse-drawn funeral – which is, I am sure, how Ernie would have preferred to make his last journey, the hearse pulled by Trigger, of course – is one Victorian tradition which has survived into the twenty-first century.

Horse-drawn funerals were once the only way to go, although these days they're much rarer, and sometimes have more sinister connotations. When Reggie Kray – the last of the infamous gangster brothers – died in 2000 his funeral included a hearse drawn by six black horses. Not surprisingly Bethnal Green Road in the East End came to a standstill for more than an hour as the procession passed by. Wouldn't you stop and stare at the sight of six horses in full funeral regalia drawing a coffin through one of London's inner-city suburbs? Nowadays you'd be forgiven for thinking that such funerals are just the preserve of old-school gangsters. But you'd be wrong, as I recently witnessed in Soho. One family firm in the East End is still harnessing its horses and offering ordinary Londoners of all colours and creeds (no criminal records required) the chance of a more traditional farewell. I thought that the Kray funeral represented a theatrical one-off until I came across T. Cribb & Sons of Beckton.

This firm was established by Thomas Cribb in the 1880s. An advert featuring its founder conveys the kind of in-your-face Ronseal message that today's undertakers might blush at. I particularly like the reassuring statement: 'Always in readiness for the removal of bodies from hospitals and asylums on the shortest notice.' I don't think you'd see that advertising strapline in the *Yellow Pages* these days. Today it's run by Thomas Cribb's great-grandson, John Harris. In my quest to find out a bit more about how and why this firm of undertakers still preserves the horse-drawn tradition, I went to see John and some of his horses dressed in their funereal finery. John told me that these black horses come from the northern part of Holland but were known in the trade as 'Belgian blacks' because they used to be transported overland to Antwerp before coming across in barges to London. These horses would then be taken to the Elephant and Castle, just south of the river in Lambeth, where there was a big horse depository. I could say many unkind things about the Elephant and Castle as it stands now – time has not been kind – but the word 'depository' and the image of a pile of steaming horse dung is lodged uncomfortably in my mind's eye when I conjure it up now, so I'll leave it at that.

John told me that once a month his grandfather would go to the Elephant and Castle to buy and sell horses. That trade lasted until the Second World War, and never picked up again. The car had taken over. Cribb gave up the old ways and converted to four wheels for almost three decades until an old lady gave firm instructions before she departed: 'When I go I want a horse and cart.' In order to oblige, the company hunted around for a pair of horses and got the carriage from a prop supplier to the Hammer Horror film studio. John now admits that this was not a particularly authentic solution, but it gave the old girl the send-off she had desired.

Funnily enough, our friend Mr Shillibeer, who brought London the horse-drawn omnibus, couldn't make a go of his business, so he turned to a more reliable trade where the business is steady. He designed a form of horse-drawn hearse that became the thing to die for. The Hammer Horror carriage was probably a rip-off of one of his designs.

The firm thought the request was a one-off, but demand just grew and, as John said, 'Very quickly we thought, well, we've got to get this sorted out properly.' They tracked down an original hearse carriage and restored it. So having disappeared for a while, horse-drawn funerals were redis-covered and are now, to coin a phrase, back from the dead.

It is slightly odd that of all the journeys made by Londoners 120 years ago – by tram, omnibus or simple horse and cart – it's only the journey to the grave which can still be made much as it once was. The tradition of the funeral procession is to travel slowly and with formality, and perhaps these require- ments – satisfied by the sedate pace of the horse – explain why this tradition has survived. And not only survived but, as I discovered, reinvented itself too.

John Harris's family business now represents the archetypal London mix of old traditions adapting to change. Cribb's now caters for Hindi and Sikh funerals and has a Buddhist prayer room as well as a chapel of rest. Sometimes the firm uses white horses and white hearses because not all cultural traditions they serve in London have black as the colour of mourning. So for that last journey to the cemetery horses still have a place in modern multicultural London, even though they'll never reclaim the streets they once ruled like kings.

We have new kings of the road now and unfortunately, even with my tin lid on and my throttle pulled right back, it isn't me and my scooter. Even with your motor running for a spot of cruising down the highway, the lyrics don't really fit London's windy streets, do they? No. Despite the resurgence of the bicycle and Chris Hoy and his endless thighs, the king of the road is still the car, though its oomph remains measured in horse power.

Back in the very early days of cars on the streets of London some people thought motorists were nothing short of barbarians. Decent people with manners had horses. At least, that is, if you can call the Marquess of Queensberry a decent man. I am not talking about the bloke who invented the rules of boxing or persecuted Oscar Wilde (obviously everyone knows that was the ninth Marquess), no I'm on about number ten, the one who found time to wage a bitter campaign against the motorists of London, following a close encounter in 1905 with a motor car on Hammersmith Road in west London, in which he suffered a graze to his arm. According to the *London Chronicle*'s report of the case, the offending vehicle was 'going at a rate of 25 miles an hour'. I don't think I've *ever* gone down Hammersmith Road so quickly. Queensberry, wanting to clarify the pedestrian's rights in the brave new world of the motor car, asked the local magistrate to confirm if 'I am at liberty to carry a rifle or revolver to protect myself and my family against sudden death on the road?' Could he not, he asked, have permission to shoot at any motorist, or 'motor fiend', who endangered him in future? I have some sympathy with him on this point, while not, of course, advocating the use of firearms. However, the magistrate did not give him the assurance that he sought and the motorists of London slept a little easier in their beds.

At first the private car was not thought to be a serious mode of transport, and the attitude of the Marquess reflected that of many other Londoners, although perhaps there were few who were prepared to pursue their vendetta quite so ruthlessly as he did. The car was considered a menace and a nuisance and the expense of the vehicle itself made it prohibitive for anyone other than the super rich or early petrolheads. But within 30 years of the Marquess's complaint, motorised vehicles were becoming more of a feature. In 1900 there were only 8,000 cars in Britain. In 1927 Ford opened its car plant at Dagenham in Essex to provide cars for the London market and London's streets began to empty of horses. By 1930 over a quarter of a million cars were registered to homes in London alone.

By my calculations, I reckon the best time to drive around central London would have been the 1930s, by which time the Marquess and his gun were safely out of the way but the streets were still pretty clear and open. Sadly this means I've missed the golden age of motoring by a full 80 years.

If I had been motoring back then, I might have refuelled at the Village Garage in Bloomsbury – a legacy from the halcyon days of motoring in London, which only recently pumped its last gallon of petrol. Tucked away off Tottenham Court Road, this beautiful art deco garage was built to supply petrol for vehicles run by the Bloomsbury Estate, the property wing of the Duke of Bedford's family, which over the previous 300 years had acquired and developed most of the property in this part of London. Wouldn't it be nice to have your own garage?

Fortunately, I dropped in on the garage a few months before it finally called time, and was shown round by the proprietor, Tim Curtis. Unlike the petrol stations of today, there was no corporate branding and the garage buildings were painted a beautiful white with pale-blue trim – the sort of scheme you'd expect to find on the bridge of an old liner in an Agatha Christie novel. But there was no mystery about what made this place popular with the locals. If filling up with fuel could ever be an aesthetic experience, this was the place where it might happen. An attendant, often Tim himself, would come to your car and fill up for you, leaving you free to enjoy the scenery. When I arrived, he was attending to a sleek black Bentley, but all Tim's clients, from Bentley to Beetle drivers, were able, just for a minute or two, to experience the same attention and luxury.

Though Tim was diversifying by offering a valet parking service right in the heart of London, there was one factor, which he could do nothing to change, that limited his operation. The garage was on such a small parcel of land, hemmed in by roads and buildings on and around Store Street, that there was no room for expansion. Even though some of the railings had been removed to widen access, I saw Tim's problem with my own eyes when a petrol tanker arrived to make its delivery. The tanker was just too big to get on to the forecourt. Half of it managed to squeeze on and discharge its load of fuel, while the rear end stuck out into the road.

I was glad that no one tossed me the keys and asked me to reverse it. For a brief moment I had visions of parallel parking the thing on Russell Square – another Karmann Ghia moment. It was a graphic reminder that central London's streets were built for traffic of a quite different scale. Forget the talk of Mayor Johnson potentially reintroducing the Routemaster, perhaps I should start a campaign with Boris to bring back the horse.

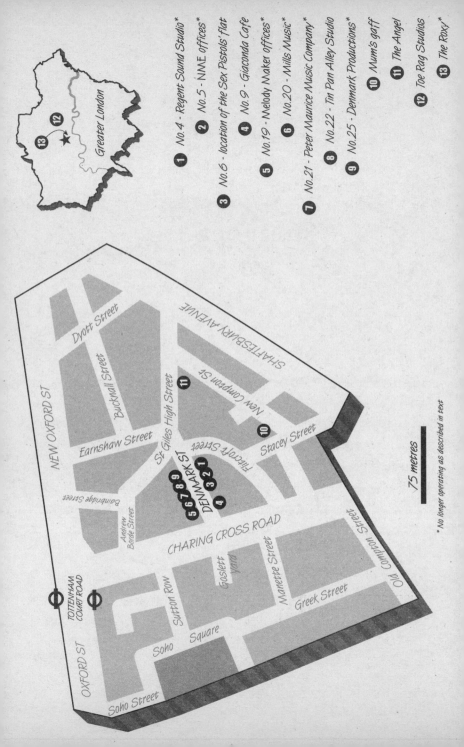

1 — No.4 - Regent Sound Studio *
2 — No.5 - NME offices *
3 — No.6 - location of the Sex Pistols' flat *
4 — No.9 - Giaconda Cafe
5 — No.19 - Melody Maker offices *
6 — No.20 - Mills Music *
7 — No.21 - Peter Maurice Music Company *
8 — No.22 - Tin Pan Alley Studio *
9 — No.25 - Denmark Productions *
10 — Mum's gaff
11 — The Angel
12 — Toe Rag Studios
13 — The Roxy *

75 metres

* No longer operating as described in text

CHAPTER SIX

Street of Song

I'm off at a canter into the heart of central London, specifically to Denmark Street. It's an unassuming thoroughfare located off Charing Cross Road which many a songwriter, me included, consider to be the spiritual home of British popular music. The street's musical heritage dates from the golden age of music hall back in the mid-1800s and continues right on through to rock'n'roll and honest-to-goodness pop. What it doesn't host is a roots folk club, or the earliest recorded set of Morrismen bells. No, I'm talking here about can't-get-you-out-of-my-head popular music, thanks in no small part to the pioneering independent studios that sprang up along this stretch in the 1960s. The list of stars who've beaten a path to this small yet perfectly formed 'street of song' is longer than a prog rock guitar solo.

Walking along Denmark Street today, I wonder whether the street can sustain its association with music up to and beyond the twelfth of never or whether it will soon be a case of 'thanks for the memories'. West End rents have gone up the ladder to the roof in recent times and multiple chains would doubtless love to stake a claim on this prime patch of real estate. Also, the development and cheapness of a home-recording set-up has led to the demise of all bar one of the street's studios. Today, Denmark Street just about retains its musical cred because of the specialist musical instrument shops it hosts, which draw a huge variety of customers from all over the world, from absolute beginners to veritable virtuosos. It would be a big loss to London if the street's association with the sound of music was lost forever, and it only takes a quick trawl through the tracks of its years to discover why. Okay, don't worry, that's enough musical puns for a while.

Music hall and, later on, variety were all the rage between 1850 and 1930. This is the era when popular music started to become divorced from its folk roots, a welcome by-product of the industrial revolution. Forget the Spinning Jenny, Stephenson's Rocket and the Manchester mills, the real legacy of the industrial revolution was that as a result of the rural population moving to live and work in towns, working people had different life experiences and different things to sing about. After a hard day's slog, those with a few pennies in their pockets needed a bit of light relief. Catchy, humorous new songs about the here and now became all the rage in the halls.

Professional songwriters were eventually engaged to

pen hits for particular singers who needed material, the most popular of which became pub songs associated with the typical, and much derided, good old Cockney knees-up. And Denmark Street, right in the middle of theatre land, is where many of those stars' songs were born – by which I mean, written.

Denmark Street's musical origins were forged when music publishers began setting up shop on the street in the late nineteenth century. The publishers sold sheet music to musicians who played in the orchestras of the many theatres and music halls nearby. It became a magnet for tunesmiths with an original song in their heads and a hole in their pockets. They made a beeline for Denmark Street in the hope of flogging their songs to music publishers, who competed for the best songs to offer to music-hall performers, all of whom were constantly on the lookout for a good tune. The acts popularised the songs and the more popular the song, the more money the publishers would make.

Not everyone could afford or wanted to go out night after night to the music halls. But you could bring the songs of the halls back home if you had a piano because you could buy the sheet music for a few pennies. With the arrival of the more affordable mass-produced upright piano around 1880, sales of sheet music from Denmark Street increased greatly. London was soon the centre of the old Joanna manufacturing industry. Apparently, by 1911 there were 136 piano-makers in England and 133 of them were based in London, most of them in or around Islington. It's probably roughly similar to the number of bars there now. Admittedly, the quality of some of these models might've had more in common with Russ Conway than Henry Steinway, but that didn't matter to households who got the benefit of hearing the hits of the halls in the comfort of their own homes.

So if a song in the music hall was a hit, then the sheet music had a mass market. However, the chances of these wannabe Lloyd Webbers earning riches from their rags were not good. In the days when the only king known to Londoners lived at Buck House and not Graceland, songwriters were royally ripped off. Had I been around at the time and been given the thumbs-up by a publisher having given him a couple of verses of 'Baggy Breeches', I would've probably been offered no more than a few quid and a decent lunch in exchange for my masterwork. At best, the publisher might've agreed to give me a share of the writing credit along with A. N. Other. Sharp practice was rife in music publishing during the early days, not just in this country but in the States too, and dealings on the less than sunny side of the street over the pond explain how Denmark Street came by its Tin Pan Alley nickname.

Tin Pan Alley was originally a name given to a group of buildings near Broadway on Manhattan's West 28th Street where scores of music publishers had set up shop. When songwriters came to play publishers their new compositions on the in-house pianos, dodgy hacks would transcribe them as they floated around the street on the New York breeze and then tout them round other publishing houses, passing them off as their own. To prevent the latest lullaby of Broadway from being pilfered, the publishers began to employ people to bash tin pans in the alleys outside while their ivories were being tinkled. I suppose this quirky practice hardened budding songwriters to the harsh realities of the trade if their songs were subsequently panned by the critics. Boom boom. Or should that be bang bang? Or boom bang-a-bang even?

So, in the days before Teflon, the name Tin Pan Alley stuck and was eventually applied to its counterpart in London, Denmark Street, owing to the large concentration of music publishers it hosted.

Things began to look up for songwriters in this country with the passing of the 1911 Copyright Act, which gave them lifetime ownership of their songs plus 50 years in the hereafter. And by the 1920s, many publishers employed in-house composers and arrangers, as revenue from songs was expanded through the arrival of the gramophone, wireless and films. The days of the 'recording artist' had arrived and popular music was set to become very big business indeed.

There was another notable arrival on the street in January 1926: *Melody Maker*. Now here's a rag I have poured over in my time, and in which I once saw an advertisement seeking applications for my own job, which apparently I had forfeited by non-attendance at a particular Saturday afternoon session, of which more to come later.

Melody Maker was a monthly music paper launched from the offices of publisher Lawrence Wright at 19 Denmark Street. It was one of the first music newspapers in the world and went on to become a bit of a wrinkly rocker before being incorporated into the *NME* in 2000. It was supposedly aimed at an audience who were 'directly or indirectly interested in the production of popular music', and Lawrence Wright shamelessly used the paper to promote his own music. Wright composed music under the name Horatio Nicholls, and his composition 'Araby', performed by the Savoy Orpheans, was the first record to be reviewed in the paper. Well, if I ran a music paper I'd review my own songs too, wouldn't you? Wright also made the brazen claim in the paper that the song 'What Did I Tell Ya' by Walter Donaldson and B. G. de Sylva, to which his company owned the UK copyright, 'would be the sensation of 1926'. It wasn't.

February's issue announced the death of the bandleader and saxophonist Bert Ralton, who made his way to the great gig in the sky having been accidentally shot while hunting in South Africa. According to his obituary, 'He died bravely playing the ukulele and singing to his attendant while on the stretcher taking him to hospital.' Musicians obviously knew how to go with dignity in those days.

Shortly before he copped that stray bullet, Bert Ralton had done some experimental demos in London for Columbia Records at a recording speed of 80rpm, but following his death Columbia abandoned the experiment and returned to good old 78rpm. Is this an early incidence of pop one-upmanship, I ask myself? Was Ralton attempting to make records louder than his rivals, which running at 80rpm would surely achieve? Did

Spinal Tap follow Ralton's lead by having amps manufactured that could be turned up to 11? Like the fate of Glenn Miller's plane, or the reason for Michael Bolton's fame, this is likely to remain one of popular music's great mysteries. As for *Melody Maker*, it was bought by Odhams Press three years later, who issued the following statement: 'The passing of central control will not affect the *Melody Maker* in any way except that it will ensure complete editorial independence from vested interests.' Now what could they have been referring to?

From the late 1920s up until the mid-1950s Denmark Street remained pretty much unchanged, with the big singers of the day making regular visits to Tin Pan Alley in search of new tunes or to hear songs that had been especially written for them by a trusted songwriter; performers very rarely wrote their own material in those days. There's an intriguing short film about Denmark Street made by Pathé at the tail end of 1950 that shows the whole process of making a record in those days and I urge you to try to find it online.

In the film, the hottest group on the block, the Beverley Sisters – a sort of Girls Aloud of their day, but more twin-set than fishnet – roll up on Denmark Street in pursuit of a new song. The commentator informs us that Tin Pan Alley is the 'birthplace of melodies which have kept Britain singing in good times and bad'. If my memory of the Beverley Sisters is anything to go by, I imagine times were mainly bad. Publishers, managers and popular songwriters of the day gather on the street for a chinwag to demonstrate what a jolly friendly place it is. What's immediately striking is that most of these men look like wartime spivs. None of them is under the age of 60, by my reckoning, and some look as if they might've been around at the birth of music hall. The old 'Daddy of Tin Pan Alley', Lawrence Wright, looks like Captain Mainwaring's father.

What is also fascinating is the make-up of the street back then. The retail outlets we see today stuffed with more instruments than you can shake a drumstick at have windows full of sheet music. Seemingly every property belongs to a publisher, and their shop fronts appear to be a showcases for the songs that have brought them renown. It all looks strangely drab and office-like, but maybe the fact that the film is in glorious black and white doesn't help matters. Once we go upstairs into the various rehearsal rooms of publishers – like Campbell Connolly, Sun Music and Southern House – you see what a hothouse of musical creativity this little street was back then. At Leeds Music (number 25) the camera goes from one audition room to another, where the likes of Mantovani, Joe Loss, Vera Lynn and Anne Shelton are trying out new songs.

At the Peter Maurice Music Company at number 21, an impossibly young Petula Clark is captured trying out a song called 'Have I Told You Lately That I Love You?' Not only is this the title of a later song by Van Morrison, it has a similar lilt to it too, until Pet tells her pianist to 'make it go a little quicker'. Thereafter, the tune ceases to be a ballad and becomes a roll-out-the-barrel-style singalong. 'That's better!' exclaims Pet. Well, she was young, to be fair. It would be years before she got her act together and went 'Downtown'. The film ends with a group of arrangers writing down musical scores who look as if they've been locked in their cramped office since Champagne Charlie was doing the rounds. It all looks terribly twee, old fashioned and in need of a sharp knee in the crotchet.

Tin Pan Alley continued to be run by venerable old-timers for many years to come, but in 1954 a jazz violinist by the name of Ralph Elman looked to the future, which hadn't yet begun, and opened one of the first independent recording studios in the country at 22 Denmark Street. Up to this point, songs may have been composed, arranged, auditioned, rehearsed and finely tuned in Denmark Street, but it wasn't where music was recorded. This part of the process was pretty much a closed shop, carried out in the studios of the big record companies such as Decca or EMI's Abbey Road.

Of course Abbey Road and its studios are famous because of their link with the Beatles – Sir Paul on the zebra crossing with no shoes and all that. Elman himself later enjoyed 4.44 seconds of fame by playing violin on 'I Am the Walrus'. The Fab Four revolutionised popular music, but Elman's own little studio on Denmark Street was also pretty revolutionary, and a very risky financial venture at the time to boot. All made possible by the invention of magnetic tape, because prior to its arrival, and the accompanying reel-to-reel tape recorders, music was cut direct to disc. Not only were tape recorders cheaper than disc recorders, they were simpler to operate and easier to incorporate into a studio. As technology progressed, multi-track recording on tape liberated producers from the ordeal of having to get a faultless 'live' performance from the assembled musicians in one take. All in all, magnetic recording greatly reduced the start-up costs and logistics of commercial recording and afforded independents the chance to do battle with the big, established companies. Elman's studio opened doors for performers and independent producers that would otherwise have remained tightly shut.

When the 60s began to swing, many more studios opened on the street and could be hired by the hour by anyone wishing to make a record. And over the next couple of decades, an endless procession of nobodies beat a path to the street's studios. Well, they might've been unknown when they arrived, but their anonymity didn't last long. The likes of the Kinks, Small Faces, Elton John, Donovan and Paul Simon recorded in the studios of Tin Pan Alley during the 60s. Even those subversive so-and-sos who'd got Britain all hot under the collar by taking a leak on a garage forecourt – scandalous – hit the street's studios.

The Rolling Stones recorded their first album in Regent Sounds Studio at 4 Denmark Street in January 1964. Regent Sounds first pushed play and record in 1963, and Sir Jumpin' Jack Flash & Co cut a demo at the studio soon after. The group was then snapped up by Decca, who were anxious not to miss out on the next big thing, having turned down the Beatles in 1962 on the grounds that guitar groups were on the way out. Now, as bad decisions go, I'm struggling to come up with one to top that.

However, when the 'Forecourt Five' began recording their first album at Decca, they didn't get on with the strait-laced studio set-up with its tie-wearing producers and engineers. Having decided that Decca's studios were not to their satisfaction, they decamped to Denmark Street where they resolved to record the album at the homely Regent Sounds Studio. The fact that they had the freedom to do this was down to their first manager and guru, Andrew Loog Oldham, who, in turn, had learned a trick or two from his hero, the legendary, now disgraced producer Phil Spector. Picking up a tip from Spector, Oldham negotiated a deal with Decca whereby he and the group retained ownership of the master tapes and leased them to Decca. Being an inveterate hustler and ultra-confident 20-year-old, Oldham also took on the role of producer despite having no experience whatsoever, something that the emergence of independent studios gave him the chance to do. Spector himself turned up at Regent Sounds to lend Oldham a bit of spiritual support during one of the recording sessions, arriving with a few bottles of brandy. Indeed, Spector is listed as playing maracas on the track 'Little by Little', although legend has it that he was actually hitting an empty brandy bottle with a half-crown coin.

The band apparently loved the atmosphere of the cramped Regent Sounds Studio, with its primitive egg-carton sound-proofing and less-than-state-of-the-art recording equipment. Over the years the album, simply called *The Rolling Stones*, has consistently been adjudged one of the greatest debut albums of all time and, to be fair, it's got a fantastic live feel about it.

Today, the former Regent Sounds Studio is a guitar shop called Regent Sounds, so even I can spot it, and if you wander in, after admiring the restored 'Regent Sounds Studio' painted sign above the shop, there are still traces to be found of its former incarnation, most notably the window located at the end of the showroom that used to separate the studio from the producer's mission-control area.

The rise of independent studios and producers, along with artists who were beginning to write increasing proportions of their own material, began to take its toll on the Tin Pan Alley old guard, most of whom were hopelessly out of touch with contemporary music. When a young, London-based Paul Simon tried to flog a handful of songs he'd written to Mills Music at 20 Denmark Street in 1965, he was told his compositions were uncommercial and was sent homeward bound empty-handed. Considering 'Homeward Bound' was one of those songs, along with 'The Sound of Silence', I'd say that was a bit of an oversight, given that both feature on albums that are among the biggest sellers of all time. I think the experience must've deeply traumatised Paul Simon because soon after he formed his own publishing company and called it Charing Cross. To make matters worse for Mills Music, they had an office boy working for them at the time by the name of Reg Dwight who was trying to make his way in the biz. He was paid £5 a week at the time but failed to make an impression. A few years later, having changed his name to Elton John, he was to become responsible for two per cent of the world's entire record sales. I think that puts Mills Music a close number two to Decca in the hotly disputed 'duffest decisions made in music' chart.

The consensus among the whippersnappers of pop that Tin Pan Alley publishers were out of touch and losing the plot is perfectly summed up in the Kinks' song entitled, strangely enough, 'Denmark Street', in which a budding musician takes a journey to the famed road only to have his song and hair criticised by a pen-pusher, but is signed up anyway, just to be on the safe side.

The balance of power increasingly shifted away from Tin Pan Alley's old guard as the 60s became the 70s and the publishing houses began to downsize or moved away from the street altogether. For others it was the last waltz. It's no coincidence that I use that metaphor because it links very nicely to my favourite Tin Pan Alley(ish) story, which features Engelbert Humperdinck's song 'The Last Waltz'.

'Enge', as he was known to his close friends, or Arnold George Dorsey, as he was named at birth, was managed by a successful bloke by the name of Gordon Mills, who worked for Denmark Productions at number 25. Mills also managed the Welsh foghorn Tom Jones. The song was penned by the songwriting partnership of Les Reed and Barry Mason, who wrote tons of hits and were a music publisher's dream in the 60s before pickings became slim.

'The Last Waltz' got to number one in 1967 and Barry Mason tells the story of being so proud of his first-ever chart-topper that while he was having a pee in a hotel urinal, he noticed the bloke next to him was whistling the song and he felt he just had to put him in the picture. He proceeded to tell the stranger that he'd written the song he was whistling, but unfortunately for him, the chap was a fairly knowledgeable record-company executive. 'What's your name then?' the stranger enquired.

'Barry Mason,' came the reply.

'I thought Les Reed wrote "The Last Waltz",' said the disbelieving exec.

'Well, he did,' replied our Barry. 'He wrote the music and I penned the lyrics.'

'Yeah, well, I wasn't whistling the lyrics,' came the response from the still-peeing exec.

Also, somewhere in the windmills of my mind (sorry, couldn't resist that one), I seem to remember a documentary from around 1972 entitled *Whatever Happened to Tin Pan Alley* which looked at how the street had changed since the days when artists looked to publishers to provide them with a hit. At the time, the place was considered a wasteland and its demise was summed up by the songwriter Nick Chinn, who went on to write stacks of glam rock hits with Mike Chapman for producer and RAK Records owner Mickie Most. Chinn said that he and Chapman gave up playing their songs to publishers who didn't understand what they were about and went to RAK Records to seek out someone who was making hit records. It was the end of the road for Tin Pan Alley as a place for music publishing, but the street had reinvented itself as a home for independent studios and, later, instrument shops. In reality, it never really lost its appeal to mad-keen musos.

The street's studios continued to flourish in the 1970s and were a Mecca for artists hoping to lay some tracks on wax for the first time. Some would spend their days hanging out at number 9, otherwise known as the Giaconda Cafe. Legend has it that the Small Faces were sipping coffees at the Giaconda when they decided to turn pro, and it was where David Bowie met the musicians who would later make up his band the Lower Third. The cafe remained the place to tune in, turn on and drop crockery throughout the hippy era, and also became a popular haunt of punk bands such as the Clash and the Sex Pistols, who moved into a flat at number 6 in late 1975. That must have put paid to any quiet nights in for the folk in the next-door flat.

Throughout this time, the Giaconda served as a sort of rock'n'roll job centre as opposed to the real employment exchange that sits at the position all popstars covet, number one. The cafe closed many years ago and has gone through several incarnations, but last year number 9 reopened to great reviews as the Giaconda Dining Room. Just what the rockers of yesteryear would make of their old greasy spoon being reinvented as a classy joint serving up such gastro delights as pumpkin risotto, God only knows.

In time, the musical instrument shops that dominate the street today began to replace the publishing houses and one of the people responsible for that transformation is the founder of the Orange Music Electronic Company, Cliff Cooper. Cliff launched a host of specialist instrument stores in the street in the 1970s, as well as the famous Orange brand of amps, speakers and guitars, whose users over the years have included such luminary rock figures as Jimmy Page, B. B. King, Noel Gallagher and Stevie Wonder. Cliff's a pretty unassuming fella, but like many of the characters you meet in Tin Pan Alley, where Cliff still keeps an office, he has a wealth of stories to tell. The most intriguing of which is that of his association with the brilliant but doomed record producer Joe Meek.

Cliff Cooper was in a band called the Millionaires and recorded with Joe Meek at a small flat-come-studio above a leather shop at 304 Holloway Road, a place which has become a must-see for pop pilgrims on the London rock-heritage trail.

Meek famously wrote and produced the huge instrumental hit 'Telstar' (named after the telecommunications satellite that was launched in the same year) at his 'studio' flat in 1962 and made number one in the US and UK. Meek was a true innovator who recorded thousands of hours of material with a hugely diverse range of artists, some of whom would later become big stars, like Rod 'The Mod' Stewart. Most of these recordings never saw the light of day. The troubled producer died in tragic circumstances, shooting himself after shooting his landlady. He died broke, having never received the royalties from his five-million seller, owing to a protracted lawsuit brought by a French composer accusing him of plagiarism which was resolved in Meek's favour a year after his death.

Meek died when the psychedelic scene was about to explode, by which time his recordings were considered old hat. Moreover, his business affairs were in a mess and creditors needed to be paid. The Official Receiver was called and Meek's recording equipment and 67 tea chests full of master tapes were put up for auction. Cliff bought the tapes for £300 in 1968, on the understanding that the collection wouldn't be broken up or sold and that he wasn't permitted to release any of the music on the tapes because he didn't own the copyright.

Over the years, Meek's legendary status began to grow and grow and a couple of years ago a play based on his life story, entitled *Telstar*, hit the West End. Recently, a film biopic of the same name was released. Increasingly there have been calls by Meek aficionados for the release of the so-called 'Tea-Chest Tapes', which are said to include unreleased recordings by the likes of David Bowie, Gene Vincent, Billy Fury and Jimmy Page. For much of the past 40 years the tapes have allegedly been preserved by Cliff in a Tin Pan Alley basement, but just recently he put them up for auction, where a bid of £170,000 failed to meet the estimate of £250,000. Quite an investment to make on spec, and probably more than the Telstar satellite cost to launch all those years ago.

For a while, Cliff was the landlord of Tin Pan Alley Studio, which is still going after all these years and is the street's sole survivor at number 22. Today, Steve Kent runs the basement studio that Ralph Elman first opened in 1954. Steve was a musician and singer before he moved to the other side of the glass and became a producer, and has worked with some top talent, such as George Michael and Marc Almond. When I visited him at the studio recently, he told me that the place had acted as a sort of training ground for groups such as the Who and the Small Faces in the 1960s before they moved on from what he called 'the Denmark Street stage of their careers'. The studio continued to flourish throughout the following decades, until computers and home-recording equipment began to take business away. As Steve says, in the past artists had no option but to go to a studio if they wanted to cut a record, which meant that Tin Pan Alley was busy 24/7. Today, rent and rates have gone through the roof but studio rates are falling owing to the stiff competition from home recording. But Steve is determined to keep this small, den-like studio going, come what may. Let's hope so, because Denmark Street without a recording studio would be like rock without the roll.

Although the recording technology at Steve's studio is pretty much state-of-the-art today, the atmosphere of the place, with its low ceilings and walls that seem to have absorbed the conversations, chords and crashing cymbals of pop legends, is redolent of the early years of pop. But there is somewhere where musicians can go to get a truly authentic retro experience that replicates the recording experiences of bands of the 60s and early 70s, and that's a studio where Madness recently recorded some tracks for our album *The Liberty of Norton Folgate*. Situated to the rear of a Victorian terrace on Glyn Road, Hackney, Toe Rag Studios is a real blast from the past. It is the brainchild of producer Liam Watson, who has gathered together a large collection of vintage analogue recording equipment from the 1960s and installed it in a studio lovingly created to resemble those from the golden age of pop.

However, Toe Rag isn't a museum: it's a successful working studio that specialises in recording in the old-fashioned manner in vintage surroundings. The floor of the compact 'live room' has a black-and-white chequered, linoleum-style floor and bakelite headphones hang from the green doorframe of this predominantly white, sound-proofed space. A 1965 Ludwig drum kit sits ready for action in one corner of the room and in another stands an old upright piano that just happens to be the same one that we used on our first single, 'The Prince', Liam having picked up the instrument from the now defunct Pathway Studios in Highbury, where Madness recorded the track back in 1979. Behind the glass panel that separates (or protects, in some cases!) the producer from the band is Liam's control room, which is a veritable Aladdin's cave of classic equipment. Reel-to-reel tape recorders vie for space with speakers, mixers, cables and microphones. And to give the place a really authentic retro feel, Liam even wears a white lab coat when at work here, just like the studio technicians of yesteryear (he's drawn the line at smoking a pipe at the same time, though).

Dominating the control room is a mixing console that came from Abbey Road Studios, which, Liam informs me, dates from the period when the Beatles were making musical history there. It's all levers and dials and very Heath Robinson by today's standards, but to Liam, who's been collecting recording kit since he was kid, it's the business. He can't be sure that George Martin, the Beatles' famous producer, ever used the console when recording the group, but, as he pointed out to me, there's no harm in making the assumption that he did. It's a great studio because you have to record mainly live, with all the musicians in the room, and the sound Liam achieves beats the pants off many of the digital recordings of today.

Toe Rag is all very much in the spirit of the studios that used to sit side by side in Denmark Street back in the 60s. Tin Pan Alley might be down to just one studio today, but it's still a colourful, vibrant street with a history to match. Like the remaining music pubs of London, it needs to be cherished because of its glorious association with popular music. Admittedly, in its early years it didn't produce songsmiths of the caliber of Irving Berlin and Cole Porter, who were Tin Pan Alley stalwarts in the USA, but we almost matched them. So putting old Rubber Lips, David Bowie, Reg Dwight, the birth of independent producers and studios, and the continuing invention and reinvention of the sounds of pop music to one side for a minim, consider this. When Americans Frank Silver and Irving Cohn wrote 'Yes, We Have No Bananas' back in 1923, English composer Fred Heatherton trumped them, I feel, with his evergreen and marvelously English standard 'I've Got a Lovely Bunch of Coconuts'. In my songbook, that's reason enough to celebrate Tin Pan Alley. When challenged to come up with a song about exotic fruit, Tin Pan Alley wasn't to be squashed.

Greater London

1000 metres

Former site of
1 Billingsgate Fish Market
2 Manze's Pie and Mash Shop
3 The Fish Plaice
4 Billingsgate Fish Market
5 Eel Pie Island
6 Cooke's Pie and Mash Shop
7 Martyn's

CHAPTER SEVEN

Food, Glorious Food

Music may be the food of love, but you can't spread it on toast, can you? A man has to eat, and London is now one of the food capitals of the world. We have some of the best chefs too, and you can sample almost any of the planet's cuisines right on your own doorstep, though I would generally recommend a plate. Well, who would have thought it? Certainly not me, when I was growing up in a world of Smash and spam. Exotic cuisine consisted of the Happy Garden Chinese takeaway, spaghetti Bolognese and, the London perennial, the humble kebab.

But – shock, horror and hold the front page – as I am about to reflect on the stories behind a few of the tastiest and oddest foods I have encountered in London, as well as some places that feature on my personal food map, the radio is informing me that a new study tells us that kebabs aren't good for us if we eat them regularly. Well whoopi-do, well I never, people who have kebab and chips every night turn out to be less healthy than those who eat a more balanced diet. Don't you love these studies? Who comes up with them? Presumably the same lot who announce red wine is good for you, bad for you, good for you etc.

Anyway, to go some way towards redressing the balance in the interests of public health, let me share with you my personal and exhaustive 40-year study of the late-night kebab. It has proved no more dangerous than a certain repetition of raw onion the following day. Admittedly I couldn't completely vouch for the entire list of ingredients that make up the slowly revolving elephant's leg that is the doner, but having worked making hamburgers in a butcher's, I can guess, and I don't think anyone died from eating one of them, well not as far as I know.

The 'scientists' who sat around watching subjects eat kebab and chips for six months might have been better placed simply to offer the advice that it's better to eat a doner from a shop that's busy, so the meat doesn't get to hang around too long. There, how's that for science. And as for my man the shish, I challenge any scientist on earth to suggest there could be anything remotely unhealthy about a freshly grilled skewer or two of lamb, lashings of mixed salad and a drizzle of chilli sauce, all cosily wrapped in a lightly toasted pitta bread. Leaving aside the six pints of lager, obviously.

I am not going to claim the doner kebab is a London invention first popularised by Samuel Pepys and cooked on the burning embers of the original St Paul's when it was destroyed by the Great Fire of London, though now I've said that, it does have a certain ring of authenticity. After hours of diligent study, I now know that actually the doner was invented in Berlin not London. But what is the London equivalent of this convenient and cheap dish of the working classes of Berlin? A few dishes come to mind. Let's start with eels.

Londoners along the Thames have been catching and eating eels for over 1,000 years, God help them. A smoked eel pâté is a tremendous thing, but when jellied, which is traditionally how generations of Londoners have enjoyed them, eels are not my takeaway dish of choice. However, in the spirit of enquiry, I have tried to follow their snaky trail through London and found it rather electrifying. Let's begin by heading way up west, travelling along the river towards Teddington.

As you get to Twickenham and feel the country breeze ruffle your toupee, you'll find Eel Pie Island, nestling appropriately in a snaking bend in the river. It's a proper island, joined to the northern bank, the Middlesex side, by a gently arching footbridge. It's actually more famous for being part of the music scene in the 1960s than its culinary heritage. The Stones, the Yardbirds, the Small Faces and the Who all played at the Eel Pie Hotel, an extremely grand building with a white-painted front and veranda overlooking the Surrey bank. The hotel became something of a hippy hangout until a police raid in 1967 did for the sex, drugs and rock'n'roll and left the owners with a list of required repairs totalling £200,000. It burnt down in 1971.

The island is now rather an idyllic spot, all leafy tranquillity and boats and not a mosh pit or Marianne Faithfull lookalike in sight. But how did this suburban island come by its curious name? Well, if you were after a bit of traditional London nosh in Tudor times this would have been the spot for you. It was the home of the finest eel pies in London. I can say that with some certainty because apparently that's the view taken by Henry VIII and who am I to argue with one of England's greatest gourmands? The story goes that Henry was given a pie from the island to sample, and liked it so much he asked for the first pie of the season to be made especially for him. Given the size of the man, it must have taken some amount of eels to fill a pie, or indeed pies, to satiate that big appetite. At last the mystery is solved. Who ate all the pies? Henry.

Eel pies and meat pies survived down the centuries and became more associated with the poor than the affluent, as they reduced in size from large dishes fit for a feast to pies you could hold in your hand. In London, they became more closely associated with the East End than the leafy suburbs of the western reaches of the Thames. Hot pies, eel pies and meat pies were sold by street vendors in the eighteenth and nineteenth centuries. By some accounts, at the height of their popularity there were as many as 600 piemen plying their pies around London. After my experience on the mincer in the butcher's, I'm still a bit wary of 'meat' pies and it would seem that even my own scepticism has something of a tradition, because by the middle of the nineteenth century Londoners were obviously concerned about just what exactly lay under the crust of pastry, as an honest-looking pie could hide a multitude of sins.

A Victorian journalist, Henry Mayhew, wrote in his book *London Labour and the London Poor*, published in 1851, that it was generally held that piemen weren't 'too particular' about the meat they bought as they could 'season it up'. Some young wags would return the pie-sellers' cries of 'al 'ot pies' with slightly grisly chants of their own, like 'bow wow' or 'mee-ow'. They weren't wrong to be worried because food and drink was commonly adulterated in nineteenth-century London. Milk had chalk added and coffee was coloured with lead oxide to bulk up the volume and make it look more palatable.

The addition of poisons like lead to food was becoming so big a problem that in the end the Victorians introduced the first food-safety laws to try to regularise what was sold. I guess it's from that perfectly sensible beginning that we have arrived at notices on almost everything warning us about nuts or the possibility of nuts, even on a very nutty snack, like, for example, a bag of nuts. By the time of the Great Exhibition in 1851, it should also have been show time for the piemen of London, what with all the thousands of hungry culture-vultures descending on the capital from all corners of Britain and beyond, but it was to be the last hurrah for the pie boom. Selling hot pies on the streets was becoming a dying trade because as soon as the first pie shops opened their doors around 1850, with stalls outside selling eels and clean marble interiors offering a variety of hot pies straight from their on-site ovens, the poor street vendor couldn't compete on quality or on price and 'cook shops' – shops that cooked food and sold it straight from their premises – began to open up across London, and in particular the East End.

But I have digressed from my eely investigations. What of the origins of a dish of eels? If you were too poor or not drunk enough to buy a pie of dubious origin at a penny a go, then you could buy hot eels at half the price.

Their popularity in London was based on the fact that eels were plentiful in the Thames and appear to be able to survive quite polluted waters. In Victorian times many of the eels that made their way on to London's streets came from Dutch eel boats. They sailed down the Thames and moored at the east of the city, just off Billingsgate fish market, which in those days was sited at the bottom of Lower Thames Street, along the bank of the river. They sold their eels straight off their boats, and they had a monopoly on the trade for a while, which was granted to them for helping to feed Londoners after the Great Fire. Imagine the scene in 1666. There you are, carrying your belongings in your cart, no home, no food, wondering what is going to become of you, when you hear the reassuring drawl of a Dutch eel fisherman: 'Hey, sho you've had a bit of a fire, guys, just relax, no worriesh, have shome eels.' I wonder if they were nicely shmoked?

As we are on the subject of the fire and feeding Londoners, let's not forget that food was behind the fire in the first place. It was caused by a spark from the ovens of Thomas Farriner, a baker on Pudding Lane, at the site now marked by the Monument and not far from old Billingsgate market. Warehouses were crowded around the baker's shop and stored oil, coal and timber, so the whole area went up like a bomb. Before an inquiry into the cause of the fire was completed, a Frenchman, Robert Hubert, confessed to starting the fire as part of a Gallic plot against the capital, though it later transpired that he wasn't even in London until two days after the fire started. He ended up being hanged for arson, convicted on the basis of his own confession, even though the judge doubted his evidence. The inquiry, reporting three months after the fire, concluded that Hubert was 'a poor distracted wretch, weary of his life' and had confessed to a crime he never committed, and that the fire in the Pudding Lane baker's was most likely an accident.

At the top of the Monument is a gold, burning orb. Originally the designer wanted to put a bust of Charles II up there, but the King thought better of it. He was worried that he might be associated with the cause of the fire rather than as the man who saved London from the flames, and given what had happened to his dad, Charles I, who had the misfortune of being beheaded, he was a bit wary of a shift in public opinion.

If you head down to Lower Thames Street today in search of eels you'll be disappointed. The original market is no longer in operation. The Victorian buildings are still there, and are pretty impressive in size and scale, including a huge, grand hall with towering arches and the usual Victorian brickwork and artistry. A cathedral to all things with fins. The old market buildings were refurbished by the architect Richard Rogers when the commercial fish market decamped to West India Docks in Poplar in the 1980s, and they are now elegant, cavernous spaces available for hire for corporate events. The new market is a bit more utilitarian. It has a lot of car park and can't match the beauty of the old market. The smell remains pretty authentic though, and if you feel like getting up at 5.30 a.m. you will be greeted by the most extraordinary array of fish from all over the world.

So, having rowed out to the Dutch eel boat to stock up on eels, what did the Victorian cooked-eel seller do next? Well, there was a lot of skinning, gutting and boiling before they went out on the street with great kettles of stewing eels. I'm already imagining the pong. On the street, hot eels were sold with liquor, the same green liquor you get with pies and mash now, which is a basic parsley sauce, though each pie shop will tell you they have a special ingredient. The other traditional accompaniment was spiced vinegar, which is again a condiment offered at any self-respecting pie shop.

In my devotion to seek out the story behind the great pie and eel story, I took myself off to Broadway Market in east London to meet Robert Cooke, who runs one of the Cooke family's pie and mash shops. The Cookes are one of a small number of families, along with the Kellys and Manzes, who have dominated the pie and mash trade for generations in these parts.

Robert's is not the oldest working pie shop in London. That honour belongs to the Manze shop at 87 Tower Bridge

Road, which opened in 1902 and has been trading there ever since. But it's certainly no new kid on the block. The menu here offers delicacies that haven't changed much in 150 years. Above the shop doorway, the gold letters announce that not only is Cooke's a pie shop, but also an importer of live eels, and in the window another sign promises hot and jellied eels.

Out the back, Robert shows me a kind of water tank with drawers. It has connecting pipes at the back that provide a constant water supply. It looks for all the world like a filing cabinet, only the drawers are for eels, presumably of the 'live, imported' variety. I am guessing you'd have to file a lot in the bottom drawer under 'w' for 'wriggling' and some under 's' for 'slippery'. They can't all be under 'e', surely? This old relic was used to keep live eels on the premises until their moment of destiny came, but now the eels come when their wriggling days are over and there is no need for the eel tank.

If you are in two minds about eels, out in the shop there's a framed excerpt from a report from the Medical Research Council of 1928 extolling the virtues of the eel: 'The body oil of eels, which is almost 30% of their whole substance, contains not only vitamin D, but almost as much vitamin A as cod-liver oil.'

The shop had a makeover in the 1930s. Perhaps the MRC endorsement had boosted sales of eels, who knows? The interior is not glamorous exactly, but the cream tiles and pale-blue and icy-green colours have a charm that you won't find in your local fried chicken shop, which now competes for the closing-time munchies business.

During the day there is a different clientele sitting on the hard wooden benches at the marble tables. Two ladies of a certain age are having lunch when I'm there. One of them, a little twig of a thing, is tucking into a huge plate of pie, mash and liquor while the other is having jellied eels. Mid-afternoon, a couple of large cabbies, whose wives have them on health regimes, come in for a post-salad lunch of double pie and mash. They both admit that it is almost an addiction, and I know quite a few people who suffer from it. My old mate Rob Dickins, the head of Warner Bros records, used to take bemused execs over in London from Burbank, California to Manze's in Tower Bridge. And Steve Jones, erstwhile guitarist of the Sex Pistols, who now lives in LA, was telling me that his first destination when returning to London is the pie and mash shop in Chapel Street. In fact, he admitted to being caught licking the window once, when he arrived to find it shut, much to the astonishment of his American companion.

At the end of the Second World War there used to be 130 pie and mash shops in London, now the numbers rumble around 20 to 30. Many of those that survive, like Robert's family shop, have teetered on the brink, as the food, cheap as it is at £2.50 for pie and mash, has gone out of fashion. Robert is hopeful, though, and he's beginning to get new, younger customers, for whom his brand of takeaway, in contrast with the now familiar flavours of the chicken chow mein or Hawaiian pizza, suddenly seems quaint and exotic. What can't be denied is that nowhere in London can you buy a dish that, in all its essential elements, is just as it was when it was served to Londoners over 150 years ago.

The gourmet eel pies beloved of Henry VIII may have gone out of fashion, as eel flesh is now more expensive, but jellied eels, a rare dish on its own which is still punted out from seafood stalls around the East End, are often offered as a companion to the meat pie and mash. And with the exception of tripe, jellied eels are possibly the only substance on Earth I have put in my mouth and have yet to force down my gullet. And, believe me, as the well-brung-up Londoner what I am, I've tried. Jellied eels may even be a French import, being pretty similar to the French dish of *aspic d'anguille*. There's also a similar Italian version, served with balsamic vinegar. Both of these dishes sound a bit nicer to my ear, but perhaps I am being unpatriotic. Maybe it's the cold fish jelly that surrounds the eel chunks and is not much more than the cooled fat released from the eel flesh and bones during cooking that stops me in my tracks.

The diners out front in Robert's shop are having their eels with chilli vinegar, just as generations of Londoners did before them. I'm all ready to go, satisfied with my research, when Robert pulls me aside and takes me to the engine room of the operation, out at the back. In for a penny pie, in for a pound, I'm thinking, as I put on an apron. I have come to cooking a bit later in life than some, but I know my way around a kitchen, so I'm not fazed by the huge pots of peeled spuds – no surprises there. What catches my eye is the machine for rolling pastry. I wonder if Gordon Ramsay has one of these? It looks like the sort of thing that might have featured in the Great

Exhibition, though it's actually a twentieth-century contraption. It works like this: you put in fist-sized balls of homemade pastry, crank up the machine, which looks like a cross between a lawn mower and a mangle, and out the other end shoot perfectly sized oval pancakes of pastry to line and cover the individual pie cases arranged on the counter beside me.

In this kitchen, this is what passes for mechanisation. The rest is all done by hand. It's not exactly mass production, but it all runs like clockwork. There I am in my pinny, lining the pie dishes with the pastry, for Robert to start filling them up with beef flank and gravy before it's back to me to whack on the lids and then trim back the pastry. With a bit of help from Robert, I make about 16 pies and then we carry them to what looks like a safe in the tiled kitchen wall. Now, I knew these were going to be special pies, hand-crafted by yours truly, but I didn't expect Robert to treat them with such reverence. As it turns out it isn't a safe but a very old oven. In they go and then out they come, golden-brown. Lucky diners.

That's a truly traditional London meal out, though Londoners are as likely to plump for a curry on Brick Lane, not much more than a stone's throw from Broadway Market. I had thought that the curry house was brought to London with a big wave of migration from the subcontinent in the 1950s and 1960s, following Indian independence and then partition, but actually the tradition goes back so much further. The first Indian-run restaurant opened its rather grand doors at 34 George Street, just off Portman Square, about 150 years earlier, in 1809. It was called The Hindostanee Coffee House, and despite its rather odd name, it did serve Indian food. It was set up by a rather remarkable man called Deen Mahomet.

This godfather of the British curry house was a Muslim from Bihar in northern India. Deen joined the Anglo-Indian army after finding himself an orphan at the age of 11. He travelled widely with his regiment and, when he left the army, ended up in Cork in Ireland with an Irish wife. Having lived a rich and varied life already, you'd think Deen would have been content to slow down a bit, but no, aged 50 he decided to try his hand at the restaurant trade, and moved to London. His idea was to serve an Anglicised version of authentic Indian food. What Deen offered was not cheap and it was quite different from the chop houses and taverns which were his competition. Since all the gentry had their own chefs – who could, if their masters so desired, rustle up a curry and replicate exotic favourites – the great and the good didn't come in numbers, and nor did anyone else. It looked like Deen didn't quite get his market right.

Unfortunately, he went bust within three years. But in addition to a very interesting life, which included a travel memoir published in 1794, Deen's venture into the restaurant business has not quite disappeared from London's culinary map. On the site of the Hindostanee Coffee House stands a building called Carlton House, which bears a plaque to his memory. From that false start springs the mighty chicken tikka masala, part of our authentic London cuisine (and officially Britain's favourite dish) along, of course, with sweet and sour king prawn balls.

While we are on food of the exotic East, you might be familiar with Gerrard Street in Soho as the hub of Chinatown in London, festooned with lanterns to celebrate the arrival of the Chinese New Year when I last walked past. This is the place to get your pak choi and five-spice, ginger spice, sporty spice, scary spice and, if you are flush, posh spice. But Gerrard Street is not the original hub of the Chinese community in London, or the home of its first Chinese restaurants and grocers. Again, you have to go further east, to the docks in Limehouse. Chinese sailors were employed by outfits like the Blue Funnel shipping company, and many of them stayed in London for one reason or another – maybe they fell in love with jellied eels and pies, mash and liquor? Unsurprisingly, shops and cook-houses grew up around the docks to cater for them, at places like Mandarin Street near the Westferry Docklands Light Railway station and Ming and Canton Streets. The presence of this small Chinese community, which was not much more than 100 people, is now memorialised in these street names. The slum clearances in the 1930s and the Blitz pretty much wiped everything of substance away, but it is fair to say that Limehouse is the original homeland of London's Chinese takeaway. But while we might be able to trace the origins, a bigger mystery remains. Who first asked that controversial question: 'Are we all sharing or each ordering our own?'

Having a takeaway these days might seem to us as something of an extravagance because it is assumed that most homes have an oven, even if they aren't used. A hundred or so years back, many fewer households, particularly those in the slums of the city, had an oven of any sort, and then there were the people who lived most of their lives on the streets. Buying hot food from street vendors or cook shops was not unusual. For some it was a way of keeping body and soul together.

Staying with the Victorian takeaway keeps us in the east of the city, among the urban poor and the immigrant communities settling in the East End. And now I want to move on to a dish which is closer to the hardened arteries of my own heart and a meal synonymous with everything that is great about Britain: fish and chips.

Just mentioning those two humble items together whets the appetite. Before I go in search of what claims to be the site of the first fish and chip shop in Britain, I want to dig about a bit and trace the origins of these two culinary companions. Let's start with the fried fish. It is generally accepted that fried fish was brought over to London by Sephardic Jews, possibly from Portugal and possibly as early as the seventeenth century. The Jewish community, like many immigrants entering the capital, did not stray too far from the port and settled in east London. The Bevis Marks synagogue in Nelson Street, EC3 was founded in 1701 by the Sephardic community and is one of the oldest and most beautiful synagogues in Britain. It's a testimony to the long and rich cultural heritage of the Jewish East End. There is a brilliant organisation called the Jewish East End Celebration Society which has a website crammed with amazing information about this part of London's cultural life, including suggested walks which take you through landmarks of that community. So when did fried fish stop being a Jewish delicacy and move out of its originating culture to become a street food of the poor?

In 1839 fried fish makes an appearance in Dickens' novel *Oliver Twist*, which I, like many others, first came to know through the rose-tinted version of the musical *Oliver!* All rather jolly and uplifting. For those who have not seen or heard the musical (where have you been?), one of the songs provides the very title for this meander on food. But if you have seen the musical, you'll know that there is no sequence of the Artful Dodger putting in an order for ten cod, six hake and nine haddock plus chips and scraps and a saveloy for Nancy. Actually, there is no great fish and chips sequence in the book either, but it does hold an important 'plaice' in the fish and chips story. You may remember that Dickens set the site of Fagin's den in the roughest slums of London. We know it must have been a dire spot because it was very near to the site of one of the fresh-water drinking fountains that were installed to try to keep the poor out of the pubs, on Holborn Viaduct, just on the corner of Giltspur Street.

The viaduct would not have been there in Fagin's day because it's a mid-nineteenth-century embellishment following slum clearance of the kind of squalid tenements that Fagin and his gang inhabited. So you'll have to forget the viaduct is there and ignore the Tesco Metro on the south side and the shiny glass and red-stone offices of one of London's premier law firms, Lovells, which sit on the north side of the street, west of the viaduct, and rise up from Farringdon Road below. Clearly they wouldn't have been there either.

It's hard to get a sense of the place as it was in Dickens' day, but if you turn down Snow Hill, walking west down the slope towards Farringdon Road, imagine a narrow alley running off it into one of the lost streets of London, a real street called Field Lane, 'a narrow and dismal alley leading to Saffron Hill', says Dickens. Here is Fagin's den, fighting for space, light and air with the 'coffee shop, beer shop and fried-fish warehouse'. Now I come to think of it, having consulted some maps of the area, in particular the Reynolds 1857 map of Sir John Snow's London, which shows this part of London before the viaduct was in situ, I'm blowed if those lawyer's offices aren't on the spot of Fagin and Dodger's fictional old home. What a glorious heritage for a law firm! 'You've Got to Pick a Pocket or Two' springs to mind as I amble past, humming.

But I am not interested in the law; what I am in search of is evidence of the origins of fish and chips in London. And I think I've pinpointed Dickens's 'fried fish warehouse' from this mooch around the streets of the city courtesy of Reynolds' map. From Dickens and another Victorian writer, G. W. M. Reynolds, author of *The Mysteries of London*, we know that the fried-fish business was pretty well established in London in the 1830s.

'What about the chips?' I hear you roar. Surely the fried potato is a British thing, created by Boudicca's head chef from spuds the ancient Britons grew in the fertile fields of Hertfordshire? Well, no, not quite. Walter Raleigh or some Tudor importer brought the spud back to London from the New World, and – batten down the hatches and prepare to be shocked – the chip is a French invention. *Non, impossible, sacré bleu!* One theory is that the chip came over to London with another wave of immigrants, again a group escaping religious persecution, this time the protestant French Huguenots. What we do know is that they are definitely a French thing. They are, after all, known the world over as 'French fries', though that is not a phrase that I use or encourage, especially not in London, though I'd give dispensations to travellers to America, to avoid the embarrassment of being given a plate of crisps.

Back to Dickens. He is a key figure in the history of fish and chips. In *A Tale of Two Cities*, chapter five, Dickens tells us that for 'a farthing' – so it's even cheaper than jellied eels – the poor and starving of Paris ate 'husky chips of potato, fried with some reluctant drops of oil'. So, even allowing Dickens a bit of artistic licence as an observer of life in the French capital, that, as far as I am concerned, puts the chip firmly in the bosom of the French Republic. Also, for the lovers of language among you, and arguably as important as his entire literary legacy, Dickens, writing in 1859, gives us a very early use of that beautiful word 'chips' to describe the cut fried potato. But do not fear, I am not going to reveal that the French also invented the fish and chip supper, because it is the genius of the British inventive spirit that teamed these two elements to create one of the world's great dishes.

So, now I think we are ready to head for the site of London's first fish and chip shop. I know you are salivating and your tongue is pricking at the thought of salt and vinegar, but the bad news is that the original fish and chip shop is no more. We can at least go and pay our respects, however. So it's back to Bethnal Green tube station. Here are some directions. Walk south away from the tube down Cambridge Heath Road towards Mile End Road. Because the original shop has gone, we need to collect some fish and chips en route to do this properly, so walk on past Cephas Street and you'll find a lovely old-fashioned-looking fish and chip shop, with a 1960s sign adorned with orange swimming fish welcoming you to The Fish Plaice at 86 Cambridge Heath Road. Once you've got your food, you need to retrace your steps to Cephas Street and then do a right into Cleveland Way. On Victorian maps of London, like the Reynolds Shilling Map of 1895, this is marked as Cleveland Street. But I am assuming you have a dog-eared A–Z like me. The street name has changed and clearly a lot of the Victorian buildings have been bombed and rebuilt, though part of it looks old enough. Walking down Cleveland Way, mouth-watering purchase in hand, you are now paying tribute to the first fish and chip shop in the world. It was opened by a Jewish cook and entrepreneur called Joseph Malin in 1860. I am guessing that his grub must have been good because fish and chip shops began to multiply.

Now, there are competing claims that a certain Mr Lees in Mossley, near Oldham, opened the first establishment. He would have been selling your northern chip, which is, of course, merely a peeled potato cut in half and chucked in the fryer, not the superior London chip. But until the social history of fish and chips in Britain produces new evidence, I am sticking to my guns on this. I say it's a wonderful London multicultural triumph – a Huguenot, Cockney, Jewish thing.

While fish and chips is lovely, with the best will in the world, I couldn't eat it every day. I couldn't necessarily say the same thing about French pastries, however. Despite its Italian heritage, Soho was a focal point for the Free French in the Second World War, and the French House on Dean Street was a tiny patch of Paris in London. But there are other French landmarks with just as illustrious a history as the French House, including the Pâtisserie Valerie on Old Compton Street and a particularly fine French patisserie called Maison Bertaux, the oldest in London. It's unmistakably French, from the mini bottles of Perrier water holding flowers that sit on the tables outside, to the piles of croissants in the window, next to the glazed apple tarts and cream cakes sitting in paper cases that always seem too small to hold them. And when you venture in, the mirrors behind the counter proclaim 'Liberté, Egalité, Fraternité' in unmistakable French script. I've purchased many a fine tart from here and been beguiled by Michelle Wade, its marvellous current proprietor. Michelle has been a fixture here for years, having started out as a Saturday girl. She took over the patisserie from the previous owners, Monsieur and Madame Vignon, in 1988. They had run the place since 1923. A patisserie has been here since 1871, so it is quite a legacy. I've yet to ask Michelle about the origins of French fries, but she has told me about her past participations in Bastille Day celebrations, which included bare bosoms and judiciously placed cream horns. Is it any surprise that the spud question went completely out of my head?

But just as I couldn't live on fish and chips alone, I can't really live on cakes either, not even those made by Michelle. I love Italian food and I love Italy. One way or another, having spent a lot of time growing up in and around Soho, I've always been conscious of the smells of Italian delicacies from the shops like Camisa's, the grocer's, and the cafes like Bar Italia, and restaurants like Gennaro's, now the site of the Groucho Club, or Little Italy. I must have absorbed those smells and held them in my memory bank as markers of flavoursome food. I've also come across many people involved one way or another in catering and restaurants, and learnt a bit about the business from them. In Italy being a waiter or barista is a very honourable tradition. Perhaps that's why one of Soho's legendary maître d's is Italian. Her name is Elena Salvoni and she must be in her 90s now, but still going strong at her restaurant in Charlotte Street, L'Etoile, a French name disguising the warmth of Italian hospitality on offer there.

About 40 years ago, Elena was running an Italian restaurant called Bianchi's on Frith Street in Soho. The restaurant occupied a spot just next to Bar Italia and she was a fixture of Soho life during that period. Unsurprisingly, she knows my mum too, but we astonished her recently when we had lunch together at L'Etoile, as until that day she had never connected the two of us.

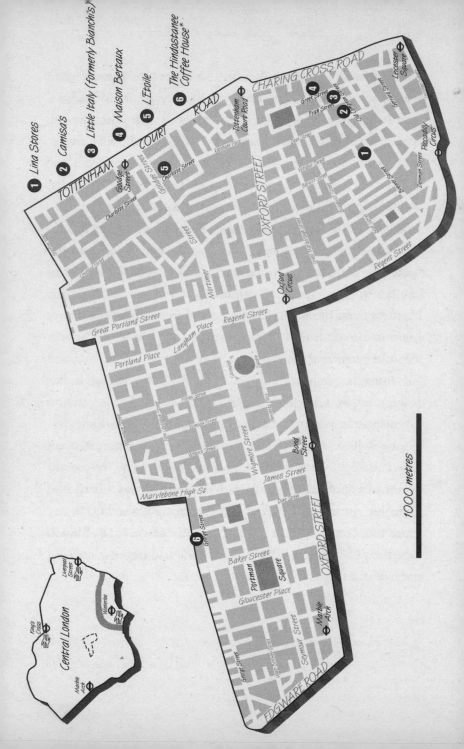

1 Lina Stores
2 Camisa's
3 Little Italy (formerly Bianchi's)
4 Maison Bertaux
5 L'Etoile
6 The Hindostanee Coffee House*

Central London

King's Cross
Liverpool Street
Marble Arch
Waterloo

TOTTENHAM COURT ROAD

CHARING CROSS ROAD

OXFORD STREET

Goodge Street
Charlotte Street
Goodge Street
Charlotte Street

Tottenham Court Road

Greek Street
Frith Street
Old Compton Street

Gerrard Street
Leicester Square

Piccadilly Circus

Brewer Street
Denman Street

Regent Street

Oxford Circus

Mortimer Street

Great Portland Street
Regent Street
Langham Place
Portland Place

Harley Street
Wimpole Street

Cavendish Square

Wigmore Street
James Street
Bond Street

Marylebone High St

George Street

Duke Street

Baker Street
Portman Square
Gloucester Place

OXFORD STREET

Seymour Street
George Street

Marble Arch

EDGWARE ROAD

1000 metres

Elena's reign at Bianchi's in the 1960s and 1970s is thought to be such an important cultural phenomenon that its menus and bookings diaries are now exhibits at the Museum of London in the Barbican. Once upon a time, the place could have hosted Christina Onassis, Maria Callas, and Beryl Reid on the one hand, and Ringo Starr, Francis Bacon and Tariq Ali on the other. The names that appear on the bookings' diary is a comprehensive list of pretty much every person that played a significant role in the social and cultural life of the nation. Leafing through her autobiography, *A Life in Soho*, published in 1990, every page is full of A-list stars, and not the ragbag that you see in *Heat* showing off their knickers after falling out of nightclubs in Mayfair. This was an age of innocence, before people were just famous for being on the telly.

Elena recounts how one evening she sang 'A-Tisket, A-Tasket' with Ella Fitzgerald as they both descended the stairs of the restaurant, and on another night joined Labour Party officials and the leader of the TUC, Bill Sirs, in a rendition of 'The Red Flag'. That world may have disappeared, but Elena, a hard worker, keeps going. If you visit L'Etoile, you'll no doubt be impressed by the white linen, comfortable, deep, velvet seats and sparkling glasses, but it's the walls lined with signed photos that catch the eye. If you want to step back in time and dwell among the stars of a gentler time, treat yourself – the photos alone are worth the price of a plate of asparagus risotto.

Mr Bianchi has passed away and there is no longer a Bianchi's on Frith Street. It's rather sad that the name just survives as a memory and as artefacts in the Museum of London. At least the site is still home to an Italian restaurant. You remember that I said that Bianchi's was next to my old favourite, Bar Italia? Well, the restaurant on that site now is run by my friend Anthony Polledri and is called Little Italy. Anthony is following in his grandfather's footsteps and has worked for the family since a teenager. As I am in the habit of taking my coffee at Bar Italia and using it as a surrogate office, I have got to know Anthony pretty well. Actually, Anthony has a sixth sense when it comes to my demeanour, proffering a kick-start, or a toe-tapper as he calls it, often served in a tea cup with a stick of celery, just at the right moment, when he can see me flagging during a meeting. Little Italy, in contrast to Bar Italia, is a contemporary venture, a mix of plush dining rooms and swanky bar, but rather than relax in its charming surroundings, I ask Anthony if he can help my culinary education by letting me into his kitchen. Having seen the starched linen and gauzy drapes in the upstairs dining room, I don't let on that my only professional chefing experience is working a pastry machine in a pie and mash shop. Though there's no denying I was a dab hand at shovelling parsley into a steaming pot of liquor, I don't think that information would strike quite the right tone.

I hope Anthony might start me off on *insalata tricolore* – avocado, tomato and mozzarella salad in the colours of the Italian flag – as critically it involves no culinary skill and no heat, and therefore a limited chance of a spark igniting Frith Street. But, reckless of the consequences, Anthony chucks me an apron and in a flash there is a naked flame and I am cooking.

In contrast to the front of house, the kitchen is all very utilitarian – polished steel and hard metal with chefs in whites and hats. It's a narrow galley kitchen and is run with military precision. I set to work on risotto. Thank goodness I can make risotto. Anthony gets the butter going in the pan, a few handfuls of Arborio rice follow, and then I start getting instructions. 'Give it a stir,' says Anthony – it's not merry banter any more. It's one thing cooking in your own kitchen, but it's all very different when you are among a load of Italian chefs. I've been learning Italian for years but in that environment, all of a sudden every word I knew went straight out the window.

Risotto is simple, but like so many great Italian dishes, it requires a lot of attention. You have to keep at it, adding stock and giving it a stir. You need to concentrate. There I am, ladling on the stock as the rice soaks up the liquid, conscious of half a dozen pairs of eyes on my every move. Then Anthony offers me butter to loosen the gloopy mixture that is building in the pan. I am in the zone now, and the risotto is nearly there; a touch more butter and it goes all glossy, then a spoonful of Parmesan to add that creamy richness. Anthony tells me to take it off the heat, and obediently the pan scuttles across the stove. 'Add a bit more Parmesan,' says Anthony, and given it's his kitchen, I won't argue. It has a lovely sheen now. I've gone all Nigella Lawson. I stir – no, I wrap – the melting Parmesan in among the nuggets of glossy golden rice. It's a pan oozing with promise. I am so excited I start talking enthusiastic but ungrammatical Italian, extolling the virtues of food, glorious food. After all that effort, the general view in the kitchen is that my risotto is not too bad at all. Talk about being damned with faint praise.

Using all that Parmesan turned my mind to Samuel Pepys, who I have already tried to credit with the invention of the doner kebab. Much of the London he knew went up in smoke in 1666. Like me, he did like a good meal, and what I like about him in particular is the fact that when preparing to leave his house as the fire drew nearer to his home on Seething Lane, near the river not far from the Tower of London, one of his last acts was to bury his Parmesan cheese in his garden. There was no more room on the cart and he obviously couldn't bring himself to give it away or leave it to the flames. So what else can you do with such treasure but bury it? You've got to admire a man who risks his life for his cheese. Pepys escaped the bubonic plague of 1665 and he and his house escaped the Great Fire of 1666, though it did burn down in another fire in 1673, so there's nothing to visit now. You can, however, pop your head inside a beautiful old church, St Olave's, just at the top of Seething Lane on Hart Street, where the old fellow found his final resting place, though I am sorry to say that he never did find his cheese.

It's a lot easier to get the exotic ingredients needed for your risotto now. We probably take it for granted that we can buy Parmesan cheese in the high-street supermarket. But this is quite a recent phenomenon. It was really not that long ago that you had to make a special journey to a special shop in Soho.

Imagine explaining that to your wife or girlfriend! Elizabeth David, one of the great cookery writers in the years BD (before Delia), gave readers of her book *Italian Food* specific directions as to where ingredients could be sourced. She was pretty worried about the availability of good Parmesan in 1954. 'It is exceedingly rare to find good Parmesan in this country,' she said, and the only places to go were 'the Italian shops of Soho'. Goodness only knows what you were meant to do if you were reading Elizabeth David's book and lived in Redruth or Runcorn. Anyone wishing to cook Elizabeth David-style food in 50s Britain who couldn't get to Soho would've struggled to find even the very basic ingredients we take for granted today, such as olive oil, which was only available from Boots, where it was sold to alleviate earache! To be fair, it's still pretty handy for earache, but we've also got some culinary uses for it now.

One of those stores saving Elizabeth David's prosciutto in 1954 was the Italian grocer's Camisa's on Old Compton Street that I remember from my youth. This shop is a survivor, despite the changing face and feel of Soho over the last 40 years. It is packed with all the food smells of Italy, and is extraordinary in a very straightforward, ordinary sort of way. In the window are great sparkling chunks of Parmesan, like rocks quarried from the Parmesan mines of Reggiano. Inside is a counter brimming with dishes of olives and homemade ravioli, and on the shelves opposite is enough dried pasta to weather a year-long siege of Soho. Lina Stores on Brewer Street is another treasure trove of Italian delicacies whose layout hasn't changed since the 1940s. We owe a debt of gratitude to these two Soho stalwarts for their ground-breaking contribution to helping Britons discover that spaghetti doesn't really grow on trees, and for continuing the good work despite an onslaught from the supermarkets. Fortunately for Camisa's and Lina Stores, ordinary, authentic Italian grocers are pretty rare in London, and so both have loyal and regular customers. They come from far and wide to purchase their fresh pasta here.

There is a similar loyal fanbase for another grocer's up in Muswell Hill, Martyn's, which has been there since 1897. It's not Italian, but it has its own peculiar heritage and, like both Lina Stores and Camisa's, it has kept on keeping on. It sits among a parade of shops on Muswell Hill Broadway. There is a pleasing late-Victorian uniformity to the street, even down to the repeated fan-and-shell mouldings above doorways and windows. That's because the buildings along the Broadway are all part of a planned scheme.

Here, among the usual chain stores, failing banks and mobile-phone stores, which I swear seem to breed along the high streets of Britain, is this independent food shop which seems to be bucking the trend. If you don't care to buy your food by walking up and down aisles, and you want to have a good look at your prunes before making your regular purchase, Martyn's is the grocer's for you. I, for one, welcome the thought of asking for half a pound of brazils and a man behind the counter handing me a packet with the comment, 'Your nuts, sir.'

Martyn's was one of the very first tenants on Muswell Hill Broadway and has been in the same family from the date of that late-Victorian building boom. Just as well, as the mosaic tiles in the doorway spell out the family name in little brown-and-cream squares.

Once you do step over the threshold, you'll find comforting jars of lemon curd along with cardamom seeds, preserves and pastes, grains, nuts and dried fruit. The old mahogany counter runs the length of the shop and behind it the shelves reach up to the ceiling. There's even a set of old brass scales. There is nothing lurid or brash or branded here, except Martyn's own brands of packeted tea, herbs and spices and the old tins of 'Golden Brandy Snaps' and Peek Frean's 'Princess' biscuits which are now used to store coffee beans.

The colours are all muted creams, browns and greens, like a Farrow & Ball paint chart. But this is not a heritage shop: the goods are real enough and the customers are loyal. I met one of them on my last visit, a young lady called Hettie Bowers, who at the age of 100 still comes in for her coffee.

I suspect Hettie would agree with me that over the last 100 years, food on offer in the capital has certainly become more diverse and, in the absence of chalk and lead, much improved. Individual restaurants and cafes come and go with changing tastes and styles, and each new generation often wants something a bit different. The fact that some dodgy diners that overcooked your carrots have perished to make way for the array of new arrivals is probably not to be mourned. But the disappearance of places like the New Piccadilly cafe is why I now cherish places like Cooke's, the Lorelei and Bar Italia, and shops like Martyn's, Camisa's and Lina Stores all the more.

These once ordinary, everyday places, which are not part of a chain or big brand and are sometimes just a bit off the beaten track, are becoming extraordinary and exceptional because fewer and fewer of them exist. Perhaps if we know more about the history of these places and how they've come to be where they are, we will make more effort to patronise them and, who knows, make a difference to their chances of survival. In an attempt to do my bit, I hope the various stories in this chapter will encourage us all to cherish some of the long-standing gems that are out there. But somehow I feel frustrated and even forlorn about the whole thing. Perhaps it is low blood sugar that has made me a bit maudlin, and I need some food inside me. It's too early for a kebab. I feel I ought to have something traditional, so perhaps I'll see if I can find a place selling that Huguenot/Jewish fusion food that seems to have become all the rage.

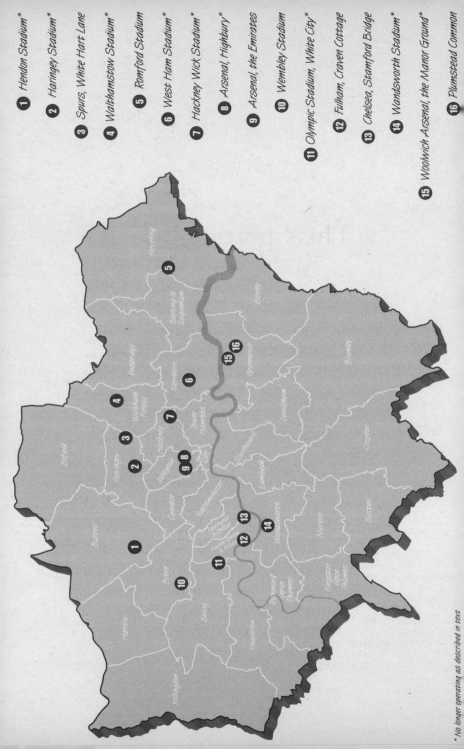

1. Hendon Stadium*
2. Haringey Stadium*
3. Spurs, White Hart Lane
4. Walthamstow Stadium*
5. Romford Stadium
6. West Ham Stadium*
7. Hackney Wick Stadium*
8. Arsenal, Highbury*
9. Arsenal, the Emirates
10. Wembley Stadium
11. Olympic Stadium, White City*
12. Fulham, Craven Cottage
13. Chelsea, Stamford Bridge
14. Wandsworth Stadium*
15. Woolwich Arsenal, the Manor Ground*
16. Plumstead Common

* No longer operating as described in text

CHAPTER EIGHT

This Sporting Life

Ilike watching all sports. I would happily sit down with Beau Brummell and chums and watch competitive raindrop racing. It has also been observed in my house that if the TV screen is mainly green and there is a ball rolling around, I am instantly transfixed. Although for my own sanity, my family draw the line at crown green bowls. While I am very happy to cheer on the lads of many colours from the comfort of my sofa, you can never beat the live experience, and I learnt from an early age that it sometimes takes a bit of grit and determination just to get to a game, let alone the perseverance needed to stick it out through thick and thin. And I'm not just talking about extricating myself from the pub.

There are two spectator sports that play an important part in my personal sporting landscape, and they've experienced contrasting fortunes over the last 50 years. They are both sports that we went to watch in our droves every week from the 1930s through to the 1960s: football and greyhound racing. Before the Second World War, greyhound racing came close second to football in that often-run race, the popularity stakes – not quite a photo finish, but it gave football a good run for its money.

Sometimes the two sports shared some of London's most glamorous grounds, like Wembley and my home turf Stamford Bridge. There were 220 tracks across the country, with weekly attendances topping five million. Despite the BBC's refusal to broadcast commentaries on the big meetings, like the Greyhound Derby, it had a huge following. The BBC didn't consider greyhound racing to be a desirable or useful sport, and its working-class roots didn't appeal to the bigwigs who saw the Oxford and Cambridge Boat Race and Wimbledon as jewels in the crown of the broadcasting calendar and the epitome of British sporting endeavour. The BBC only started covering greyhound racing because its popularity made it impossible not to. In 1953 the BBC showed three races, but dared not broadcast the results of any other races for fear it would encourage gambling among the masses. Isn't it nice to be treated like adults?

But while football is now London's dominant sport, greyhound racing is in terminal decline, very much on the last of its four skinny legs. Given the close association of these two sports, which often shared both stadiums and supporters, and their contrasting fates, I thought I would take a closer look at their history in the capital, which means boldly going where I have not ventured before and revisiting a few old haunts too. I'll start with greyhound racing, as I think football will be able to survive without my immediate attention, while the whole greyhound racing business looks extremely fragile, Walthamstow dog track having turned off the power to the electric hare in the summer of 2008 after 76 years in business.

Racing and hunting with hounds have ancient roots. Tombs of the pharaohs are adorned with images of hounds, and historians think that Cleopatra indulged in a bit of dog racing, presumably when she wasn't chasing Mark Antony. Maybe she combined the two. I can imagine it now, with Sid James as Mark Antony dressed as the rabbit in *Carry On up the Dog Track*. Yes, I like it.

Elizabeth I loved her hounds and she is credited with establishing the rules for competitive game hunting with hounds, where two dogs were pitched against each other to hunt down their prey. At the start of the 1600s, competition using hounds to hunt hares – known as hare coursing – was all the rage. After a morning's hare coursing you'd head off to the Globe Theatre for an afternoon play. Perhaps you'd fail to find a laugh in *A Midsummer Night's Dream* while indulging in the new fad of smoking tobacco. Presumably, it would then be a few pints of sack and on to a thrash-lute club to dance a few quadrilles, before heading off for an eel pie and then home to bed. The perfect end to the perfect day.

The modern version of this sport, despite its noble British

ancestry, was actually developed in America and then imported back to the mother country. The Americans had applied a bit of technology to the process, inventing the mechanical 'lure' or dummy hare, and bringing it into the cities. Greyhound racing of the kind enjoyed until recently at Walthamstow is a twentieth-century phenomenon. The first meeting round a track with a mechanical hare actually took place at the Belle Vue Stadium in Manchester in July 1926, which even I can't claim is in north-west London. The first meeting in London was at the old 1908 Olympic Stadium at White City in June 1927.

Reminiscing about the old days with Carolyn Baker, whose dad owned Romford dog track, I discover that in the 1920s, before the mechanisation of the sport had come to Romford, they had an ingenious method of pulling the lure (which was nothing more than a flea-bitten bundle of rags with ears) along at speed. This involved putting a car up on bricks and attaching the wire of the lure to the rim of one of the tyreless wheels, and then it was a case of clutch in, select gear and foot hard down to the floor. The wheels of the car spun round while the car went nowhere but the lure got wound in like a yo-yo. So next time you see a car on bricks, don't rush to conclusions about the theft of a set of alloys – perhaps you've just missed some urban hare coursing.

The revolution in greyhound racing came to Britain when Charles Munn, an American entrepreneur, bought the licence to exploit the mechanical hare outside the USA. Instead of a bundle of rags pulled around a field on a wire, a sprightly little rabbit could now be set off, like a furry train on a monorail, to run round and round a track, race after race. In the 1920s Munn's innovation proved to be a great success. Cities took to the sport and in London dog tracks were incorporated into some football stadiums, including Chelsea, which already had a big running track around the perimeter of the pitch. Stamford Bridge hosted dog racing from 1937 through to 1968. Unfortunately, I never saw any greyhound racing at the Bridge, but I certainly saw a few people being chased around that old track in my time!

There are differing opinions on how many dog tracks London boasted, but about 15 were in operation at any one time. As well as Wembley and Stamford Bridge, White City was the big greyhound venue, attracting crowds of up to 100,000 to its meets. White City has been demolished now, but the same site currently hosts the BBC, those greyhound racing lovers. I am informed you can still see the chasing of tails and packs running around in circles, and all without a bunny or greyhound in sight. Haringey, Hendon and Hackney Wick have also gone, and there's no longer dog racing at West Ham, Walthamstow or Wandsworth. I don't know what's wrong with London's Hs and Ws.

In the heyday of the sport, Romford had to compete with these and other London greyhound stadiums for business, and Carolyn recalls her father experimenting with special events to keep the punters coming to his track. One of his more radical and imaginative innovations was novelty racing with cheetahs. No, I didn't believe that either, until photographic evidence was produced to prove the point. The novelty lasted for two weekends in the 1930s. They quickly learnt that they had to use real bait to get the big cats to run, and they also had problems controlling the beasts when they weren't running. I'm not sure I'd have been too keen to be in the crowd. The experiment didn't last long.

I don't think it's the risk of being savaged by wild animals that keeps the good folk of London at home rather than at the dog track these days. But there are now so many other activities competing for our leisure time, like pilates, which hadn't been invented in 1927, and the TV, computer games and the internet – and you haven't even left home yet. The virtual world is your oyster. Now that the sport is slowly losing its visibility in popular culture, it's hard to imagine just how important greyhound racing was in the sporting calendar.

One of the best-loved dogs of the pre-Second World War era, and probably the star that really got Britain excited about the sport, was a hound called Mick the Miller, whose career spanned 1929 to 1931. Originally owned and trained in Ireland by Father Martin Brophy, legend has it that he was so impressive on his first run out at White City that he was auctioned then and there on the steps of the stadium for 800 guineas, the price of desirable house in a leafy London suburb or two. During his brief British racing career, he won 46 out of 61 races and was the first dog to be a double Greyhound Derby winner, the top prize of the greyhound racing calendar.

He was the sporting pin-up of his day. His mush appeared everywhere. On his retirement, he even starred in a film loosely based around greyhound racing called *Wild Boy*, playing the title role. Released in 1934, having gone way over budget, the thin plot revolved around an unscrupulous greyhound owner trying to stop his rival, and the owner of our eponymous hero, from winning the Greyhound Derby. I think, actually, it would make a rather marvellous plot for a Duran Duran comeback promo. Simon Le Bon in flat cap, nervously smoking a roll-up while trying to nobble John Taylor's dog. No? Not enough yachts? Oh well. Scrolling down the list of credits, I spotted that among Mick's co-stars were Flanagan and Allen. That's Bud Flanagan, who once shared the bill with my mother-in-law and whose own mother ran a fried fish shop on Hanbury Street in Spitalfields. Which takes us back to that Huguenot/Jewish fusion food again.

When Mick the Miller died, he was so highly treasured that he was stuffed and exhibited in the Natural History Museum, which, rest assured, was an accolade. Mick was there on display until 2005, when he was moved to an offshoot of the Natural History Museum in Tring. It's a bit out of my catchment area, but apparently you'll find him on his plinth in Gallery Six.

My passion for dog racing was probably at its most fervent when, along with my fellow band members, I actually enjoyed a stint as owner of a greyhound, Nutty Boy, who briefly raced out of Walthamstow. We were very excited about his potential, and we had some great nights out, taking on the likes of Vinnie Jones – on the track, I hasten to add. But Nutty Boy didn't reach the heights we'd hoped for, because of illness rather than lack of class.

After Mick the Miller, the sport found other heroes and remained popular through to the 1960s and 70s. Imagine this: even in 1966, when we all had World Cup fever and were innocently singing 'World Cup Willie' without even thinking of sniggering, a greyhound meet at Wembley took precedence over a World Cup match between France and Uruguay. All the group one games except this fixture were played at Wembley, but the France v Uruguay match had to be played instead at another great greyhound venue, White City Stadium, while the dogs had their day at Wembley.

Greyhound racing had something of an ironic revival in the 1980s, when city workers discovered the sport, and it was plonked back on to the cultural map when Blur featured greyhounds on the cover of *Parklife*. But there has been no real resurgence in interest. Now it's a sport that is struggling to keep its place in the affections of the public. Greyhound racing has always been closely allied with gambling, so the 'lure' of other betting opportunities, especially online gambling, has also had a role in the decline of the sport.

As you'll have gathered, I am all for being 'there', wherever the 'there' is, rather than experiencing something vicariously on a computer screen. To get a taste of this fast-disappearing spectator experience, you could do worse than head out east to Romford for a night out. But if you do go, I recommend that you follow this golden rule: put your betting money in one pocket and your real money in another and don't confuse the two, because if you do, you may have trouble getting home.

So there you are at Romford, standing on the terrace on a

crisp late-winter evening, and – putting the newish hospitality area to one side, with its restaurants and bars – the terraces are reminiscent of a lower-league football club in the 1970s: functional and intimate rather than glamorous. But you are quickly transported away from reality, even with no cheetahs on the race card. It has to be said that dog racing is improved when it's experienced as a nocturnal event. The sky is a deep black, an unnatural colour only ever achieved under floodlights. There is a sense of adventure in the air – or is it just the aroma of Woodbines and spilt lager? The arena at night, under lights, suddenly seems to acquire a touch of glamour. The crumbling stadium, the slightly tattered advertising hoardings, the litter, all recede into the half light. The rest of the world and all its aggravations and demands can be forgotten. The bookies' stalls entice you, the lights of the bars of the stadium twinkle and beckon you in. All wrapped up against the cold, you get a race card and give it your utmost attention. In my case, it's all done scientifically. I eliminate the name of any dog that in any way might suggest disappointment or failure. Using this patented system to identify the winning hound, I stride to the bookie certain that I'm going to get it right this time, just like the England World Cup squad of 1982.

When I am about to hand over hard-earned cash, book-makers are so welcoming and full of promise. At the dogs, they always seem to congratulate me on my choice – 'Certainly got a chance' – which is merely a grudging statement of the fact that my dog had actually made it on to the track, had not savaged its owner or refused to enter its trap. But hope springs eternal and I immediately have a sense of camaraderie with fellow gamblers, whose dreams I share for just a minute or so.

There goes the electrified bunny round the inside ring, up go the trap doors, all of a clatter, off go the greyhounds in their little orange, blue, black and white racing waistcoats. And there goes my money, down the drain. Like England in 1982, the campaign begins with optimism but ends in broken dreams. At the end of the night, the steps of the terracing at Romford are covered with discarded dreams and betting slips, mine included. One of the great mysteries of dog racing is why you are always standing next to some delirious winner when you are losing.

Romford has not been my lucky track. But the track at the now-defunct Walthamstow dogs, well, that has been a scene of triumph. Aside from each race night with Nutty Boy, one of my best nights out at Walthamstow dogs was enjoyed in the company of my cousin, Hector, on the occasion of his stag do. Twelve Welshmen were let loose in London, and I was their guide and chaperone. We had a superb time in Soho and then we determined to enjoy a spot of dog racing. I can't quite recall how we got our party up to Walthamstow, but we were having a jolly time at a table in the terrace restaurant, despite losing money on every race on the card. Then out of the corner of my eye I saw the elegant figure of Jimmy White, snooker supremo, with a few mates in tow, who seemed to appear out of the night shadows like a vision.

There were only about three races left and it was apparent Jimmy and his mates weren't betting. They were just sitting, fags in mouths, counting out wodges of cash on their table. Big wodges.

Jimmy is one of the few people who deserves his billing as a London hero, and is an eminently likeable chap to boot. Having seen him around over the years, I went up to say hello and, with a vague sense of responsibility for my group, who could barely rustle a cab fare at this point, find out what was occurring. Among the pleasantries, it was intimated to me that a certain dog in the last race might be worth the punt of a penny or two, and there were a fair amount of pennies in Jimmy's hands as he strode to the teller.

Now as any betting man will tell you, a true tip is an elusive creature and even a tip based on inside knowledge can never guarantee a winner. So it was with this in mind that I approached the bookie with some trepidation. In my hand was the contingency fund, which I was holding in reserve in order for there to be some evening left back in town, should things turn out badly for us. To be frank, they already had. But by making a bet at this late stage, I was breaking my golden rule.

Jimmy and his mates had only come for the last race. Did they know something? They must. They better had. All eyes were on me as I returned to our table, the little table lamp dimmed, the distorted trumpet fanfare sounded and they were off! And so were we. The dog came out of the traps first and won by a mile. What a feeling, second only to standing in front of the teller as she counted out the readies, lots of them, an experience I have had so rarely I can count them on the fingers of one mitten. Thanks, Jimmy.

At 5.30 that morning I was standing on Frith Street in Soho and still had £800 of my winnings in my pocket. A cabbie I knew was chatting to my friend Anthony Polledri outside Bar Italia. He had had poor business all night and was about to give it up. My family had decamped to Kent for the weekend and I was flagging and wanting to go home. My last Champagne Charlie act of the night was to say to the cabman, 'Take me to Whitstable and don't spare the horses.' There can be few finer things than munching on a cheese and ham croissant, cantering up hill and down dale, through the misty Kentish countryside, in a black cab, first thing.

The closure of Walthamstow, the scene of this rather wonderful night of adventure and some other convivial evenings, is a loss to me and to London. It even holds a place in David Beckham's heart because it's where, as a teenager, he earned a few bob collecting empty glasses. Presumably, David could only do this when Manchester United had away games in London. Life is full of tough choices, and I guess David will just have to learn to live with regret in his mansions in Milan and LA.

David chose football, as so many of us now do. So let's have a look at how the competing sport of football staked its claim on the hearts and minds of Londoners at the end of the nineteenth century. As the story unfolds, what becomes clear is that numbers and availability of spectators had a huge impact on the location, architecture and destiny of some of London's football clubs 100 odd years ago. The players were very much an afterthought.

In the early days of football in London, the success of a team was as much about the spectators and where the ground was as the standard of football itself. In the interests of research into Fulham's footballing history, I chanced upon an old Fulham FC coaching film from the 1930s. I have to say that even now I could probably back-heel a ball with greater skill and confidence than the two chaps in their long shorts.

To be quite frank, if we spectators hadn't come to games in the 1890s in search of a bit of light relief, entertainment and camaraderie, there wouldn't be any professional football teams in London. No stadiums, no legacy and no football songs like 'Blue Day', the one I recorded with Chelsea's 1997 FA Cup squad. I'm prepared to argue the toss over the contribution to culture that I made with that particular musical outing, but I feel I'm on firmer ground when I draw attention to the importance of spectators in the emergence and development of football in the capital.

As one of the inheritors of this noble band and as one of the hundreds of thousands of football fans who collectively form part of the fabric and history of the game, not just in London but across the UK, let me just share with you one of my first efforts to see a game on my own at the Bridge (Stamford Bridge, of course). I spent my early years near to the ground, so there was no real doubt about where my loyalties would lie, particularly as at the time Chelsea were the team of the moment – the King's Road boys, full of flair and ambition.

I was football crazy, football mad. As a kid, like every boy I knew, I played every lunchtime at school, then after school in the street or the park. Like every player in our daily kick-abouts, at some stage during the game my imagination would take wing and transport me to Wembley – the old Wembley with the twin towers, mind you. Why they never incorporated them into their new Wembley, I shall never know. I still dream of them now. The next goal I'd score would not be any old goal – in my head, it would be the winning goal in an FA Cup final. Then I'd throw my arms in the air – victorious – and run around like everyone did, screaming, 'Yeeeessssss!' It often left me a bit hoarse, and having no voice left after football is something that has haunted the rest of my career. I still struggle to restrain that full-throated cry, even in my home.

My love of football was not confined to just playing the game. My bedroom wall was covered with team photos. I lived and breathed that team: Osgood, Hudson, Harris, Hutchinson, Hollins, Webb, Bonetti, etc. Indelibly etched in my mind, even to this day. At night I dreamt football, and each night the dream was the same. There I was at Stamford Bridge, clad in my blue shirt, blue shorts with the white stripe, white socks, Chelsea lion on my chest, Osgood on my left, Hudson on my right, jogging out on to the pitch as the Shed roared its adoration. Oh, to be eight again.

I had fallen in love with Chelsea Football Club. While I was practising my turns and overhead kicks, I was also memorising names. I was learning about the club's history. Then, aged eight, I took my first tentative steps in European football. I'd like to say it was as the second striker 'in the hole', but sadly it was in the stands. But don't think for one minute that because

I was not playing I had only a passive role in the match. This could not be wider of the mark. That day, I gave my all.

Chelsea were in the Cup Winners' Cup. We had won the FA Cup that summer, in two titanic battles against the supposedly impregnable hard men of Leeds. It was 1970, and on a dark, wintry Wednesday night in November we were due to entertain CSKA Sofia. That makes it sound as though me and my mum were laying on a spread of cold meats and pickled eggs for the Bulgarian hordes and, of course, I would have happily obliged. The welcome they would have got round our house would have proved warmer than the reception they got at Stamford Bridge, because at least we had electricity at home. Not for the first time, the Chelsea stadium was less than fit for purpose. The floodlights had failed and the game had to be postponed. As a nine-year-old, I knew I was never going to be allowed to go to that night game, but this technical hitch was the first of a number of pieces of good fortune that befell me and my chums in the ensuing 24 hours.

Now, these were the days before cheap flights and before big money had been lavished on football; they were also the days of the Cold War and restrictions on travel. The Bulgarians took the view that rather than go to the aggravation and expense of rearranging the fixture, they might as well stay over and play the game the next afternoon in the light. Presumably they had been assured that even in the degenerate capitalist West, with their crap stadiums and unreliable power supply, the sun would still rise the next day.

Rise it did and bathed west London in its golden rays, or so it seemed to me. Sofia and Chelsea agreed to play the game on Thursday lunchtime during school hours. My school, Park Walk, was within earshot of the ground and, what's more, easy walking distance for an eight-year-old boy. The news of the rearranged fixture spread around the neighbourhood quicker than a winter vomiting bug. As I gambolled merrily to school, innocent as a lamb, I was plotting how I would bunk off undetected. What would be the path of least resistance? How best could we avoid detection? By the time I caught up with my mates, I had already planned an escape route to the ground at lunchtime. The brainpower I was applying to this project was considerable. I was rigorous, I was obsessive, I was precise. I now realise that if I had applied a modicum of this brainpower to my schoolwork I could have been running the country by the age of 18.

Unfortunately, my headmaster had also learnt of the fixture rearrangement. I say 'unfortunately' because, quite contrary to all logic and reason, he took an entirely different view of the matter from us boys. He announced at assembly, to those of us who had not had the wit to have feigned illness and so absent themselves from his unjust realm, that no one was to leave the school premises during the lunch hour. Why the old stinker hadn't given us the afternoon off was incomprehensible.

Lunchtime duly came and a phalanx of boys charged at the school gates only to find them firmly bolted. Much clambering and scrambling followed, and some unlucky souls got pulled down off the gates and never even left the school premises. We had taken our first casualties, but about 30 of us had got out. Off we ran up Park Walk, heading for the Fulham Road. As we passed side streets we were joined by groups of other boys, of all ages and sizes, escapees like ourselves, on the run and with one destination in mind – not the neutrality of Switzerland, but the partisan terraces of Stamford Bridge. We were careering up the middle of the road now, drunk with our success and feeling safety in numbers, turning and whirling in the air like salmon, but then we turned into the Fulham Road and pretty much stopped in our tracks. There they were: a squadron of school inspectors, strung across the street in their battle dress of belted blue rain macs. They all looked the same, like identikit Blakeys from *On the Buses*.

We advanced at walking pace and, almost as if in response, the inspectors stretched their arms out, creating a blue wall across the road. We could have been back in the playground playing a rather one-sided version of British Bulldog. Just as we were about to have a face-off in the Fulham Road, we heard a great clamour from behind us and we turned to see our Head and assorted teachers, well worked up, running towards us. We faced assault on all sides. It seemed like we were well and truly stuffed. There was no chance of getting away with anything now, but we might as well go down with honour, so into the valley of detention rode the 40-odd of us and onwards we charged.

We took further casualties in the ensuing melee. I remember some kids being brought down with rugby tackles that would have graced Twickenham. But me, I was one of the smallest, and dived under the outstretched arms of a school inspector and just ran and ran. I got to the corner of Edith Grove, lungs bursting, stopped to take a breath, looked up and there she blew: Stamford Bridge. I looked around me; about ten of us had made it, all the little ones. The high five had not been invented then and I can't recall quite what we did to congratulate each other, but our joy was unbounded. At that moment I thought I could hear angels playing their trumpets, a beam of white light shone down from the heavens and I swear that God, with a great blue-and-white beard, parted the clouds and sang, 'Zigga, zagga, zigga, zagga, oi, oi, oi' in approval. After all that effort I had faith. I knew God couldn't let us down. My first experience of European football at Chelsea ended in victory, and, believe me, this was not something I was going to get used to in the following 20-odd seasons.

When I began my enquiries into London's fast-vanishing football history, I must admit to being less than thrilled to learn that Chelsea's formation and location was strangely linked with two London rivals. As with all family trees, when you start poking about you always turn up something a bit unexpected, like the fact that Auntie May served time for racketeering in boot polish during the Boer War. Well, when I started testing my own knowledge of football in the capital, I was more than a little alarmed to learn about the links between Chelsea and Fulham, and via Fulham, Arsenal. Yes, ARSENAL!

Arsenal are now a north London team, but they were

originally a 'works team' from the royal armaments factory and took their first name, Dial Square, from the specific workshop within the Royal Arsenal at Woolwich where they all worked. Chelsea's near neighbours, Fulham FC, were originally a church team called St Andrews Church Sunday School FC of West Kensington, to be exact. Both were teams rooted in the life of their local community. I almost want to convince you that Chelsea are the original team of the famous Chelsea bun bakery, The Old Chelsea Bun House (well, Millwall originated at a jam factory on the Isle of Dogs, so why not?). Or perhaps that we were a team made up of orderlies and recovering patients from the Chelsea and Westminster Hospital. Unfortunately, neither would be true. So, what are the origins of Chelsea FC? I hear you ask.

There's a long and a short answer; it's a bit like a question on the origins of the First World War. You might say that the 1914–18 war kicked off after the shooting of Archduke Franz Ferdinand. While that short answer is true in part, this assassination was really only a further expression of the crisis in the Balkans. Similarly, you could say that Chelsea were a team invented by property speculators with a spare stadium, but again, it's more complicated than that. A more complete answer is that Chelsea were really a product of the turmoil and change taking place in football at the turn of the century, as teams struggled to get established and secure a fanbase.

So the answer is a bit of a saga, but in telling it I'll also take you on my own personal safari through London's football past. Looking more closely at Chelsea, Fulham and Arsenal, because they are connected, it becomes apparent that the origins and early history of these three clubs collectively shed a bit of light on the history of football in the capital.

My search for landmarks of a bygone era doesn't quite begin with Chelsea, given their somewhat mysterious appearance out of the west London mists. But, in pursuit of football's early days in London as seen through the blue-tinted lenses of a Chelsea supporter, I can take you to one of London's less fashionable quarters.

You need to travel south-east out of London, beyond the Thames flood barrier in Woolwich, heading out to the North Sea. On the south bank of the estuary is Plumstead. It is not a very accessible suburb of the capital, which is probably why Her Majesty's Government have built Belmarsh prison there.

In addition to a prison, this part of London also contains a few obscure venues and landmarks of football's history in the capital. Forget the now dearly departed twin towers of Wembley, there are lost treasures of ye olden days of football to be found 'south of the river, and I don't mean Bobby Charlton's comb.

Plumstead – yes, Plumstead, not the rather grander-sounding Woolwich – was the former home of a club that claims to be one of the London big boys and one of the greats of the British game – it's the true home of Arsenal, who were born here in 1886. Spurs fans good-heartedly josh their north London neighbours with a chorus or two of their take on 'Abide With Me': 'F**k off back to south London'. So I wondered just what Arsenal's original home turf was like and what traces of Arsenal's early days are still around. Now, as you've gathered if you don't live in Plumstead, you've got to really want to come here because it is not somewhere you are likely to chance upon. There is only one train line and no tube. Alighting at the station, I confess the world is not exactly your oyster – if anything it is more your burger or your KFC. I am looking for traces of Royal Arsenal or, as they soon became, Woolwich Arsenal.

I shouldn't be starting here at all. As football aficionados know, football really kicked off in an organised way in the North and Midlands, not down here in London. Though the FA had their cup competition going by 1871, it was being con- tested by the public schools' old boys' teams and regimental sides. It was Aston Villa, Accrington, Derby, Notts County, Stoke, West Brom, Wolves, Bolton, Blackburn, Burnley and Everton that were the first teams among the founding group of 12 to contest a league title, and the runaway winners of the first football league championship were the twelfth club to complete the hallowed dozen: Preston. It wasn't till 1894 that the southern league got going.

Take Woolwich Arsenal for example. Many of their first players were exiles from up north – in fact, north of up north. Among their founders was a Scot, David Danskin, formerly of Kirkcaldy Wanderers, along with ex-Notts Forest player Fred Beardsley, a goalie rather than a striker like Peter. Arsenal's first kit was a kind of homage to Nottingham Forest Football Club, Beardsley having prevailed upon them to send a full set of their old shirts for his new, soft, southern team. All very practical and utilitarian and so very different from the disposable kits of today, with the Premier League teams churning out half a dozen variants on their kit a year.

Arsenal flitted about a bit down here. Their first ground and their real home was Manor Field, which sounds rather grander than Plumstead Common, where they also had a kick-about in the earliest days and which remains a fine piece of open land. Arsenal fans can still run around on Plumstead Common pretending to be Jack Humble or David Danskin. Yes, there really was an Arsenal player called Humble – it's hard to imagine a more unsuitable name for a Premiership footballer now. Looking back at the names of players from that era tells a story too – they are all called Fred or Bill or Jack, not a single Wayne or Steve, and you can forget your Didiers or Cristianos.

Manor Field, near the railway station, had been part of an old pig farm, and when Arsenal started playing there was not much more than an enclosed field, though it was renamed the Manor Ground by its footballing tenants. Now what sort of cold-hearted cad would want to picture Arsenal's origins as a team of Forest has-beens playing on a pig farm in south London? The Manor Ground was a bit of a dead loss because, despite being enclosed, the best view in the early days was from outside the ground standing on a sewer. Mmm, I'll say no more.

Step in local entrepreneur George Weaver, who had made a fortune selling mineral water. Now there's a chap ahead of his time. Seeing the growing popularity of the game, he built a stadium called the Invicta Ground with stands and terracing which could take crowds of up to 20,000. Arsenal went to play there in 1890, but as soon as they'd had a couple of successful seasons, the owner of the Invicta Ground got greedy and hiked up the rent. Not an unfamiliar story over the past 100 years of football. Arsenal, who had just turned into a professional club, could not afford the increase and so, after three years, they decided to go back to the Manor Ground.

The Invicta Ground was demolished by the mineral-water tycoon, who made more money by building houses on the land. Arsenal fans can still mark the spot with a mooch up Mineral Street, named after the source of his fortune, which runs behind Plumstead High Street and along Hector Street where, according to official Arsenal historian Phil Soar, some of the gardens still retain the concrete terracing from the 1890s.

To complete this part of the story, Arsenal – now known as Woolwich Arsenal, and the first London club paying its players and playing in the football league proper – ended up buying the Manor Ground and building a terrace in front of the sewer, presumably in an attempt to force more punters to pay to watch. The Manor Ground did not prove to be a happy home for the club and the pitch is now buried under the Woolwich industrial estate. There's no obvious sign of their former presence; it's a rather utilitarian and bleak urban landscape.

If you have sloped around the streets of Plumstead, you have earned a drink. You can find one of those on Plumstead High Street by visiting number 67, formerly the Green Man and a quite fine-looking Victorian pub. Now it's one of those chain Irish theme pubs, O'Dowds. The reason for going in here in particular is because this is one of the pubs where, just over 100 years ago, the Arsenal team used to change. They had a choice of either here or the Railway Tavern at 131 Plumstead Road, which is now the site of the Greenwich Islamic Centre, so still worth a visit but not perhaps for a Guinness.

The world of football has changed dramatically since those days. When I see the wonderful Chelsea Pensioners watching a match at the Bridge it leads me to think about what the game was like when they first went to see a ball being kicked. Players have gone from changing in a pub and knocking a ball against a brick wall as part of their warm-up to earning £125,000 a week and driving their Ferraris into them! It is an extraordinary transformation.

At this point, let's hop on the train away from the marshes of south-east London back to terra firma in Fulham to pick up the Chelsea/Fulham story. At the end of the 1890s football was booming in the north-west and Londoners were getting the football bug. Two brothers called Gus and Joseph Mears owned a building firm in west London, and in about 1896 were asked to do some work for Fulham Football Club laying out the ground at a new site, overgrown and neglected, running along the banks of the river. The land has a romantic past: it was part of hunting grounds once owned by Anne Boleyn, Henry 'who ate all the pies' the Eighth's second wife. It's known as Craven Cottage because a later owner, Baron Craven, built a cottage in this beautiful riverside setting. But forget the rural idyll – as far as Fulham were concerned, it was land suitable for football. The club were keen to have a home of their own. They'd had their fill of moving around and, like Arsenal, changing in pubs, in their case the Eight Bells on Fulham High Street. They were ground-sharing with Wasps Rugby Football Club in 1894, when the club purchased the scrubby bit of wasteland, Craven Cottage, on which they would build their permanent home. It looks like the Mears brothers liked the sport and saw the potential to make some ready money from it, just like George Weaver. After all, there were all these people turning up to stand in the cold and shout themselves hoarse while paying for the pleasure, and you didn't even have to provide any real facilities.

In the same year that they completed the work at Fulham, 1896, the Mears boys spotted a great location in west London that could be developed into a football venue. There was a major omnibus terminus at Farm Lane, a couple of streets away from the prospective ground, a growing local population and a tube station called Walham Green, which we now know as Fulham Broadway, a short walk away. They were convinced, *Field of Dreams* style, that if they built a football stadium, the spectators would come – and come in numbers – although there was the small matter of not actually having a football team.

The spot they had in mind was Stamford Bridge Athletic Ground, but they could not get hold of it until eight years later. By the time they got the land in 1904, they had various options. One was to make a quick turnaround on the purchase and sell the land to Great Western Railway as a fuel depot; the second option was to develop it a bit and get Fulham Football Club to move in as tenants. The third and least attractive option was to build a football stadium and start their own team.

The Mears brothers approached Fulham to try to entice them up the road to a lovely, spacious new ground. Fulham faced a bit of a dilemma. If you know this part of London, Fulham's ground is an absolute gem to behold and something of an oddity because of its location. It is right bang on the banks of the Thames and known widely to the non-footballing public as one of the markers for the Oxford and Cambridge Boat Race.

So, picture this: on the south side the ground is bordered by the River Thames, and on all the other sides it's surrounded by rather nice Victorian houses, and at the Putney end the leafy green of Bishop's Park. The site is worth a packet nowadays. Expansion of the ground and facilities was always going to be a problem for the club, but the Fulham directors of 1904 baulked at the offer from the Mears brothers for a move to Stamford Bridge Athletic Ground. Instead, Fulham decided to improve their own site a bit more.

This time, and perhaps not surprisingly, the Mears' firm did not get the contract. The Fulham board did not mess about, and they called in an engineer who had a growing reputation for his work on football stadiums. His name was Archibald Leitch, a Scotsman who during this period effectively invented how football grounds should look and whose simple formula was implemented by clubs up and down the country for the next 70 years. His trademark ground was a covered grandstand along one length of the pitch distinguished by a gable in the middle, often adorned with a clock or club symbol, with open terraces on the other three sides. A design he perfected with one of his first commissions south of the border at Craven Cottage.

Now, I have a particular interest in Craven Cottage and Fulham for three reasons. The first is the decision by Fulham in 1904 to stay put rather than move to the Bridge. It was momentous, and if they had their time again I wonder if the directors would have made the same choice. The impact of their snub to the Mears boys had a dramatic impact on football in the capital. If Fulham had moved to Stamford Bridge there would have been no Chelsea, because there would have been no need to create a new team to play at Stamford Bridge. So I guess I'd have been a Stamford Bridge regular supporting Fulham as my team. Perish the thought. The new Stamford Bridge-based Fulham would have had room to develop and expand, and with bigger crowds and income . . . who knows?

My fondness for Craven Cottage is also rooted in the fact that it's the first ground I ever went to, at the tender age of five. The magic of that introduction to the game, on the banks of the Thames, has stayed with me ever since. And the final reason for my interest in Fulham is the stadium itself. While Stamford Bridge has been through some horrendous periods of demolition and rebuilding over the years, Fulham has survived bloody but unbowed and retains the only stand from the Edwardian era in London pretty much as it was originally constructed. It's even retained its wooden seats, which contrary to expectations are actually very comfy and warm to the bum.

Craven Cottage is place of real footballing nostalgia and even a hard-hearted old Chelsea supporter like myself couldn't fail to have a soft spot for it, particularly as Leitch, its original designer, also designed the first stand at Chelsea, which is pretty much identical to the stand at Fulham.

One of the pleasures of Fulham's ground is the very fact that it is constructed by Leitch to fit so unobtrusively into its neighbourhood. Walking down Stevenage Road, you'd never know you were patrolling the back of a football stand unless you cross over and look up and see the floodlights. The man who was keen on this sympathetic design was Henry Norris, Mayor of Fulham, a property developer and house builder who also just happened to be on the board at Fulham. At the time of this construction project, Norris was the man at Fulham's helm. He wanted the exterior of the main stand to blend in with the masonry and brick-work of the surrounding streets, which were full of rather splendid family houses, many of which were built by Norris's own firm.

The facade of the stand is all a bit of a con really because standing on Stevenage Road from the outside of the ground, what you see is regular red brick and what look like stable doorways with half-moon windows above. Look above ground level and there is a fake first-storey row of grander windows with carved masonry, followed by another layer of subterfuge and more windows. An innocent to the area might be wondering just what that building is. Could it be a warehouse, perhaps, with floors of offices above?

But the glory is on the inside. If you get a chance to go behind the brick facade, do it on a day when you aren't going to be distracted by the trifling matter of a game. (I went with the world authority on the football grounds of Great Britain, Simon Inglis.) Behind the fake stable doors, you'll find yourself standing on the concrete concourse and above your head are great iron girders, joists and bolts, all made on the banks of the Clyde and shipped down to London ready to be assembled, like a huge Meccano set, in the closed season. A triumph of functional design.

Once you are out from underneath all that iron and sitting in the stand, you can glance across to Leitch's version of the Baron's cottage. It looks like a poor man's version of the pavilion at Lord's Cricket Ground, with wrought-iron pillars and balcony. But it also has that cottagey touch, with the two chimney pots front and back. You could imagine the players coming in at half time on a cold February afternoon and warming their socks on the stovepipe while toasting their crumpets on the hot coals.

So what about those entrepreneurial builders Gus and Joe Mears? When Fulham spurned their offer to move to Stamford Bridge Athletic Stadium, the Mearses had a ground with no team. Legend has it that they were wondering what to do when their mate Fred Parker set out a plan of how they could make money from football. Parker was so determined to win them over that he continued his argument despite being bitten on the leg by Gus Mears' terrier. Convinced by Parker's persistence, the small matter of having no team did not seem to worry anyone too much. First things first, what on earth were they going to call this new team they had just created out of thin air? The three of them bandied some names about over a few drinks in the Rising Sun, just over the road from the main entrance to the ground.

Abramovich's predecessors rejected the names London FC and Kensington FC, and settled on Chelsea FC. They got Leitch – who else? – in to sort out the stadium, and Chelsea FC were off and running. It was 1905. A brand-new team with no players had been born, the marvellous brainchild of a group of west London property speculators.

If you care to venture into the same pub for a drink now, it's been renamed and is now the Butcher's Hook. On the occasion of the club's centenary, I was there for an event, the first time I'd been in for a while. The club dedicated every year of its 100-year history to someone who they felt had made a contribution to Chelsea's illustrious heritage, and they very kindly gifted me the year 1997, for my cup-winning song 'Blue Day'. (Not that I felt I'd won it single-handedly of course.) I was thrilled with the honour, which was not a state of mind shared by the clientele of a certain QPR-leaning pub on Portobello Road after my mate Alf slipped that particular song into their jukebox one match day and selected it 14 times in a row. Now I come to think of it, perhaps I should have had a few other years too. Perhaps, for example, the year I stood with a measly crowd to watch the mighty Blues struggling to a titanic 0–0 with Coventry. Actually, the whole lot of us should have got some reward and commendation just for being there.

I'm proud to have my name put to 1997, and am almost as proud that the good people at the marvellous Chelsea independent magazine *CFCUK* started a campaign to get a small flight of steps leading out of an alley from the ground, that I have taken an occasional stumble up, named the Suggs Steps. My life is almost complete!

Let's roll back to the arrival of Chelsea on the scene in 1905. It affected Fulham big time. The two teams were now competing for spectators, but Chelsea had a bigger ground and, like Arsenal, had enrolled in the football league. Only six years after the redevelopment of Fulham's ground by Leitch, Henry Norris, their chairman and the local property magnate, seemed to think that Fulham needed to 'push on to the next level', which meant more space and more spectators. Perhaps his thoughts were prompted by the successes of Chelsea, the new kids on the block. Chelsea, with their massive goalie captain, 6 foot 3 inch and 20-stone Willie Foulke, who probably intimidated all onrushing strikers with his sheer bulk, won promotion from the football league's second division in only their second year. It looked like Norris thought Fulham's ambitions were too limited. Perhaps they had missed a trick by not moving to Stamford Bridge?

Norris scouted around for better options for his ambition and money. He saw that Woolwich Arsenal, a steady enough outfit out in the sticks in south-east London, were now in debt, having taken on the burden of borrowing money to buy their own ground, thus becoming one of the first clubs to learn that getting into debt and embarking on expensive building projects can be a recipe for disaster. Somewhat controversially, Henry Norris defected to Arsenal, perhaps seeing an opportunity to develop a team in his own image, like the Mears brothers' creation of Chelsea. And they say there's no loyalty in football now! Norris took Arsenal to a new ground to make a new start, and so begins the story of Arsenal at Highbury.

If you were going to make money from football in London, you needed to be able to get bums on seats or feet on stands. That meant two things: you needed to be based somewhere that was easy for potential supporters to get to, and you needed a site that could be developed to accommodate them. Norris secured a lease on playing fields in Highbury in north London which belonged to St John's College of Divinity. The lease was countersigned by the Archbishop of Canterbury, no less. Though a blessing from on high was probably welcome, what was crucial for Norris was that the land he had secured was bang next to a newly opened tube station called Gillespie Road.

Again, Leitch was called in to design the first stadium, which opened for business in 1913, but the iconic ground associated with the club took shape in 1931, when Highbury was completely redeveloped and local residents were invited to come and empty their rubbish at the north and south ends of the ground to build up the banking for the terraces. Apparently, a helpful coal merchant reversed his horse and cart too near to the footings for the north bank stand, and in he went with the whole shebang. The poor nag could not be rescued from the hole and was buried where she fell.

While this escapade shows that even during the 1930s the horse was a familiar sight on the local streets of London, the new Highbury Stadium was meant to be all about modernity and looking to the future, and was beautifully designed in the style of the moment, art deco.

If you should chance to travel up on the Piccadilly line, it is still worth stopping off at Arsenal tube station – the cheeky fellows even got London Transport to rename Gillespie Road after them, the only club in London with their own tube station. Even though Arsenal have moved around the corner to their new stadium – the Emirates, at Drayton Park – remnants of their old stadium at Highbury survive. Like Fulham's Leitch stand and cottage, the art deco facade of the east stand on Avenell Road is considered a unique relic of football in London, and it has been listed. It is a thing of beauty, with its stylish mouldings and sweeping windows. A touch of the magic of the place has gone though because behind the marble and the glass aren't club officials complaining to the FA about a disputed incident that they didn't see or the reek of liniment, just floor upon floor of luxurious flats.

Arsenal and Chelsea supporters seem to have a lot to thank Fulham for, one way or another. Chelsea's very existence and Arsenal's success seem to be strangely entwined with Fulham, and the history of both teams seems largely based on the ambitions of builders to make a bit of cash.

I have heaped praise on Fulham's ground and traced the early fortunes of Arsenal to their arrival at Highbury, but what of good old Stamford Bridge? 'The only place to be/ Every other Saturday/Is strolling down the Fulham Road.' Now that sounds like a good song. I don't go to every match, but every time I do go, I get the same feeling of anticipation, and regardless of what has happened to the game – or the product or brand or whatever it is now called – it will always be my first love. 'Meet your mates, have a drink, have a moan and start to think, will there ever be a blue tomorrow?' Faces you haven't seen for ages having heated discussion in the pubs, kids skipping down the road with brand new scarves, happy as I was the first time I went.

I've got my memories. In particular those days in the Shed, a kind of oversized car port with a corrugated roof at the south end of the stadium. It barely covered a third of the crowd on the south terracing. Then there was the occasional river of piddle coming down the terracing from the lavs at the back. There you were, squashed in the crowd, literally feeling the noise, in the words of that great philosopher Noddy Holder. The place was becoming a bit of a footballing shanty town: different-shaped stands higgledy-piggledy around the ground, and facilities that were next to nought. Much as I loved it, it was falling apart as I stood there.

For each new generation, the memories will be different. The stadium that drew me in like a magnet and then enfolded me in her loving embrace has gone. Now all that remains of the stadium I first visited as a child is a bit of the old Shed end wall that has a little blue plaque on it to mark its survival through years of turmoil and bankruptcy.

That old ground did have to go, but building new stands for largely absent spectators nearly brought about the club's demise. Having won the European Cup Winners' Cup in 1971 against the might of Real Madrid, I guess we thought glory would always be ours. We pulled down the old Leitch stand and commissioned some fabulous architects, Darbourne & Darke, to redesign Stamford Bridge at a cost of £6 million – a mere bagatelle to us kings of the King's Road. We were going to start with a 'stand of the future' with a built-in heating system wafting warm air, presumably perfumed with rose petals picked at dawn, around the posteriors of the spectators. Just this one stand was going to cost £1.6 million and, remember, these are 1972 prices – a loaf of bread cost about 8 new pence, we had just gone decimal, and a pint of beer was about 13 new pence. We were committing ourselves to selling a lot of burger buns and pints of lager for years to come.

One side of the ground was laid to waste while we waited and waited for two seasons for the new East Stand to emerge from the rubble, 'massive imposing, ruinous' as Simon Inglis notes in his book *Football Grounds of Britain*. The monster stand that was created still looks modern 30 or so years after it was completed. It's on three levels, with a steeply raking upper tier which seems to defy gravity and a roof that hangs like a claw over the blue seats below. Again, I can't do better than Simon's observation that when it was first unveiled it made the rest of the ground look like 'Neolithic ruins'. This was going to be the beginning of the new grand plan – the whole ground was to be redeveloped in this style.

The problem was that it was built just as the world was going into recession in the early 1970s. The stand was built for the boom times, not an economic slump and, what was worse, it was matched by a slump in our performance on the grass. Soon after our lovely new stand was ready for the bottoms of Chelsea fans, Chelsea were sitting at the bottom of the league. Then we were relegated, and if you were old enough, you wept into your 13p pint.

Spectators weren't exactly clamouring to come to Stamford Bridge anyway. Football was not in the least bit fashionable, not completely unjustifiably, and the papers were full of stories about hooliganism. I remember clearly there was genuine embarrassment in certain circles to have a football supporter in their midst.

Being a Chelsea supporter, it helped that I developed the emotional range to deal with Kipling's 'triumph and disaster' over the course of an afternoon without feeling the need to call a football phone-in show for support or counselling. Not that there were any. And while I have not missed a wedding or a funeral in favour of football, I admit that I have been sacked. In fact, I was sacked from Madness because I went to a game rather than to work. I'd been struggling to cover my tracks when missing our regular Saturday afternoon rehearsals, only to discover, when flicking through the now-defunct *Melody Maker*, an advert for 'a semi professional singer' along with our keyboard player's phone number. Fortunately, the replacement only lasted a few weeks, and I was back. I've managed to have a relatively successful career with the band ever since and still follow my beloved Blues, with no sign of another replacement being sought in the small ads. Although I'm sure there have been one or two moments when they wish they could!

I went on to have two lovely girls who've been coming to the Bridge since they were six, and still do on occasion, even though they're now both in their 20s. As for me, I still go as often as I can, although Madness duties do mean that I'm not always around. And despite the over-commercialisation that tests my love on an almost weekly basis, the thrill of the live spectacle excites me as much as it ever did. But it's a real shame that standing terracing has gone. I would have loved to see a new Shed. It would be cheaper for the fans and more cost effective for the clubs because you can get more than twice the number of people standing as seated, and the atmosphere created is far more vibrant. Some German clubs have managed to overcome the health and safety concerns and have adapted stands very successfully to allow for safe standing, so where there is a will, there is a way.

I know the clubs care about the fans and the standard of facilities nowadays is wonderful, but I can't help but feel that if football was more affordable then more families would go to the games. And that should be seen as being important. Multiple generations attending together and sharing the experience – as happened to me and as I've done with my children in turn – is surely essential to protect the long-term health of the game. It is the supporters who keep the whole thing alive. We are the people who care about the result, the race or the raindrop, if only for the duration of the event until normality resumes and we remember we still have to do the washing-up or walk the dog. Without spectators, greyhound racing will wither and die; and without fans and atmosphere, what is a football ground?

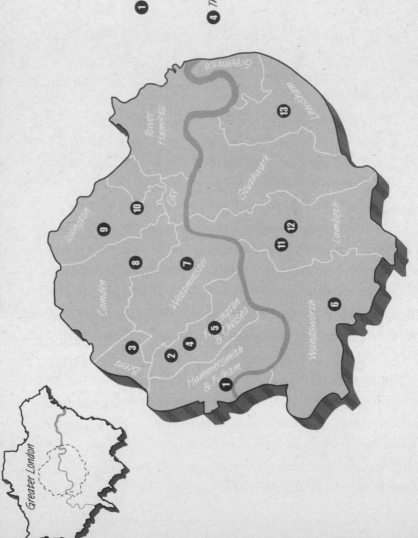

1. The Odeon, Hammersmith* (now called the Hammersmith Apollo)
2. The Electric, Portobello
3. The Gaumont State, Kilburn*
4. The Gate Picturehouse, Notting Hill
5. The Coronet, Notting Hill
6. The Granada, Tooting*
7. The Eros Cinema, Piccadilly*
8. The Odeon, Camden
9. The Odeon, Holloway
10. Screen on the Green, Islington
11. The Brixton Astoria* (now called the Brixton Academy)
12. The Ritzy, Brixton
13. The Rivoli, Brockley*

* No longer operating as described in text

CHAPTER NINE

Cinema City

I'm not proud to admit it, but as a young kid I was in a gang whose membership spread right across the country. Each Saturday morning I'd meet up with fellow members of my local branch in a dark, cavernous building on the Fulham Road. All of us wore luminous badges emblazoned with our gang's logo, but none of us stood up for the National Anthem when ordered to do so by a rival gang known as the Management. Yes, this band of brothers (and sisters) was mad, bad and dangerous to know. We went by the name of the ABC Minors.

For me, and countless others of a certain age, the Saturday morning pictures were a ritual and a riot. Parents would happily wave their kids off to the local ABC cinema, under the impression that they'd spend three trouble-free hours watching a selection of Children's Film Foundation movies, cartoons, westerns, The Three Stooges, Zoro and Flash Gordon etc., unaware of the ice cream- and sweet-chucking mayhem that would ensue the second our rallying song was sung and the lights went down. I can still recall 'The ABC Minors Song' to this day, which was all about shouting with glee, having a sing-song and being great pals, all jolly and happy and innocent.

It was so twee, it made the Ovaltinies theme tune sound like some of the more ribald choruses I would be singing a few years later in the Shed. However, it used to strike abject terror into the hearts of usherettes, projectionists, cleaners and cinema managers all over the country every Saturday morning, as they sought to contend with the major nuisance wrought by the ABC Minors. Happy days.

As I entered my teens, my local haunts were the Holloway and Camden Odeon cinemas. Both are still standing, but not as the massive one-screen movie houses I remember: they were converted into multiplexes over 30 years ago. And what a shame my daughters' generation can't share the extraordinary experience of sitting in the front row of the circle, looking down, through a haze of cigarette smoke, on what looked like a million people, all completely absorbed in the overhead, flickering projection of the film. In those days, of course, smoking was still permitted, but only on the left-hand side of the auditorium. How the smoke was supposed to recognise the boundary, I was never quite sure.

Having acquired half-price tickets as minors, we would

then proceed to sit in the smoking section, on the backs of folded-up seats so as to look as tall as possible, but it didn't always work. The eagle-eyed usherettes were wise to this ruse and before the film started they would scan the area left of the aisle for any shrimp-like creatures smoking cigarettes almost as big as their heads. If you felt the torch beam linger on your face for more than a second, the game was up and you would be ejected by the ear with an accompanying observation that you had to be 14 for junior admission and 16 to smoke and that you couldn't have it both ways. Later, of course, the problem was reversed, as I tried to look 18 in order to get into X-rated movies.

Besides my north London favourites, we sometimes ventured further afield in search of celluloid fun. There were some really quirky cinemas around London in the 70s, and plenty of real dives, or flea-pits as they were infectiously known. Some had a bit of a reputation and, believe me, if a cinema did have a reputation it was best to be in the know.

The Eros Cinema, on the corner of Piccadilly Circus and Shaftesbury Avenue, seemed like a perfectly harmless place to while away an afternoon. After all, this bijou art deco picture house only screened classic cartoons. As with a lot of cinemas at the time, it had a rolling bill of features, which meant that when one cartoon ended, another began. So once you'd paid your entrance fee you could watch as many films as you liked. While I was enticed by the prospect of an endless bill, that wasn't the main attraction for some of its clientele and I wonder whether I should've been paying more attention to the name of the place: it was, after all, a venue named after the god of lurve.

I ventured in and purchased my ticket. This was not printed up with information about the seat and time of the show plus your inside leg measurement and star sign, as we have come to expect, but like an old bus ticket printed on coarse, thick paper, just proving you had paid. In fact, I could have done with just a bit more info. The place was pretty busy, even at 3 p.m. on a Monday afternoon. But my mind was on the screen and a pomegranate my mum had bought me. An unusual item to take to the pictures, I'll grant you, but I'd never seen one before and had been treasuring it for this moment, keen to find out what was inside the tough, waxy skin.

As it turned out, the pomegranate was not the only unusual occupant in the stalls. The Eros was one of the pick-up joints for the rent boys of Piccadilly Circus and their clients. I was in the dark about its notoriety, but after the auditorium lights dimmed and we were plunged into darkness, conversely I began to see the light. I think it would be fair to say that at the Eros most of the action took place at the back of the stalls rather than on the screen.

Removing the pomegranate from my trouser pocket, I groped around trying to tease my way into this mysterious fruit bursting with exotic promise. Unfortunately it refused to yield to my clumsy advances and shot out of my grasp and under the seat in front. Calamity! I had to retrieve it. But I moved too slowly, and as I left my seat and started to grope around under the seat in front of me, my pomegranate began its inexorable roll towards the screen and I followed it.

Why I decided to take a pomegranate to the cinema and not a bag of wine gums, I'll never know. Perhaps it was going cheap and my mum was feeling the pinch. I certainly did. Whatever the reason for the fruit – and, by the way, how ahead of the times was my mum providing her son with such a healthy treat? – I'll never forget that first pomegranate. It is forever associated in my memory with the unexpected sights, and sounds, of the stalls on my one and only visit to the Eros. I suppose it's a kind of Pavlovian moment, only I don't have to taste a pomegranate, I just have to see one and my mind immediately conjures up a recollection of . . . cartoons.

Today the building which housed the cinema is a Gap clothing store, but if you want to catch a glimpse of the Eros my pomegranate and I knew, here's a bit of trivia: the cinema's exterior was used in the final sequence of *An American Werewolf in London*. Ah-hoooo! That's got to be showing somewhere on an endless bill.

These days, of course, a trip to the cinema can be a pretty luxurious affair: plush seats, air conditioning, tasty refreshments, including, no doubt, pomegranate juice (which would've saved me a whole lot of trouble). Sometimes they even throw in a decent film as well, just to complete the package. But on the whole, today's cinemas are comfortable rather than flamboyant, with none of the character of their distinguished forebears. It was all very different at the beginning of the last century, when moving pictures first seized the imagination of London's entertainment-seekers.

Back in the first decade of the twentieth century, films were shown in old music halls, disused shops, fairgrounds and even railway arches, as there weren't any purpose-built cinemas. A trip to the flicks was a pretty risky business in those days because nitrate film stock was highly flammable and could burn even underwater. Following a string of fires in the early 1900s, the government decided enough was enough and introduced an Act of Parliament to protect filmgoers from the risk of going up in flames. Fire-resistant projection booths were required from then on, and this put an end to makeshift cinemas and sparked a picture-house building boom.

Within months, London was awash with purpose-built cinemas, many of which had the word 'Electric' in their names, which reveals much about the novelty of electricity back then. Indeed, the oldest surviving purpose-built cinema is the Electric on Portobello Road in west London. The projectors started turning there in 1910 and today it's still one of London's smartest picture houses. Among the other handful which are still in business are the Electric Pavilion in Brixton, now known as the Ritzy, and the Empress Electric in Islington. This one's dropped the 'electric' moniker as well and is today called the Screen on the Green, the scene of many an all-night Clint Eastwood fest. All of them have had to weather many storms to make it through to the twenty-first century.

Most of the purpose-built early cinemas, like the three above, were all very similar in style, with barrel-vaulted ceilings and richly decorated auditoriums all on one level. Others, which were converted from other buildings, vary in style. If you take a trip to Notting Hill Gate you'll find two examples not more than a few yards from one another: the Gate cinema and the Coronet. The former, located at 87 Notting Hill Gate, at first glance looks far less impressive than its grand rival, but beyond its drab facade lurks a glorious auditorium with ornate panelled walls and a coffered ceiling with decorative Edwardian plasterwork. The Gate underwent a programme of refurbishment in 2004, including the installation of plush velvet seating and some additional double 'love' seats. I don't know if this is a nod to the Gate's decadent, racy past, but in 1879 the building operated as the Golden Bells Hotel, an upmarket brothel. A surviving register from 1911, the year the 'hotel' swapped red lights for house lights and was converted to a cinema, reveals that trade that year was still brisk, with over 100 gentlemen booking in to its 15 rooms in one day. However, after the bell tolled for the hotel, the Gate began life as the – surprise, surprise – Electric Cinema before switching to the Embassy in 1931. The cinema's anonymous facade is the result of Second World War bombing which destroyed the original exterior, including its ornate domed roof.

However, if it's a domed roof you want then you only need to head left out of the Gate's front doors and wander past half a dozen shops to the corner of Notting Hill Gate and Hillgate Street. Here you'll find the splendid Coronet Cinema. The facade of the Coronet is quite striking, with painted stone, giant classical pilasters and a short round tower crowned by said dome. Originally built as a theatre in 1898, the Coronet became a cinema in 1923 and was designed by W. G. R. Sprague, the architect responsible for the earlier mentioned Camden Palace, who was a prolific theatre designer and spent four years articled to the great Frank Matcham. Two of Sprague's most notable creations are the Aldwych and Wyndham's in the West End, but this one's a little cracker too and pretty much in original nick, despite a few scares over the years, such as demolition threats and plans to convert it to a McDonald's. A second cinema was built on the stage of the theatre in 1993, thus keeping the main auditorium intact.

The Coronet has had a cameo role in several adverts and films over the years, including a scene in Richard Curtis's *Notting Hill* featuring Hugh Grant and Julia Roberts who were doubtless blown away, as was I, by the auditorium's 'plaster ornaments in Louis XVI manner; two elliptically-curved balconies; and square enriched architrave to the proscenium'. There, now you know, but you don't have to be au fait with the technical details to have your head turned by the Coronet's charms: it's as pretty as a picture house can be, even if it didn't begin life as such.

Capacity in the early cinemas rarely exceeded 600 and if you fancied sitting in the posh, padded tip-up seats it would cost you a shilling, payable at the entry box, which was open to the street. If, however, you only had threepence to spare, it would buy you a lowly place on a bench situated at the front of the auditorium. Just to add insult to ignominy, you'd also be made to enter the cinema through a separate side entrance. Oh, the shame! But if you think three old pennies was the cheapest admission, you'd be mistaken. Some cinemas allowed admittance in exchange for empty jam jars. I don't know if these cinemas were run by the WI as a sideline or whether they were an offshoot of Tiptree Jam, but clearly glass had a price. I wonder if an empty jar of Duchy Originals Organic might get me a plush seat today? Actually, forget the big conglomerates like the WI. Ownership of the first purpose-built cinemas was largely in private hands, but small chains did emerge in those fledgling days. A gentleman glorying in the name of Montagu Pyke was one of the early pioneers of chain cinemas and had several picture houses around London. He even has a Weatherspoon pub named after him on Charing Cross Road, which stands on the site of the last cinema he built. Make mine a double bill!

Of course, the films back then were silent and accompaniment was provided by a pianist or a small orchestra. Despite the relatively primitive nature of the early films, according to modern tastes at least, cinema caught on in a big way and when the talkies arrived in the late 1920s it became even bigger. This meant that most of the early cinemas degenerated into flea-pits, as they were unable to compete with the huge, temple-like movie theatres that began to go up. Most have gone, of course, while others found new uses, like the Rivoli on Brockley Road opposite Crofton Park Station in south London, which was converted into a ballroom when the craze really took hold in the 50s.

The Rivoli began life as the Crofton Park Picture Palace in 1913 and was built in the style of the Electric cinemas I mentioned earlier. It remained independently owned throughout its time as a cinema, having become the Rivoli in 1931. The last waltz for the Rivoli as a picture house came in 1957, and it ended with a double bill featuring *The Nat King Cole Story* and *Reach for the Sky*, the Douglas Bader biopic starring Kenneth More. Today the Rivoli's a glorious mix of art nouveau elegance and fabulous 50s kitsch and is, remarkably, one of London's last, if not *the* last, remaining public ballroom.

I've always had my own rather particular style of dancing, and although I've heard it called many other things, it didn't stop me from shuffling into a few ballrooms during my youth. In the late 1970s I used to be a regular at the Gresham in Archway, north London, which was one of a series of dance halls catering for émigré Irish men and women. I would always arrive late on Saturday nights. However, I didn't necessarily go for the dancing: no, I acquired my dance-hall habit on account of the draconian licensing laws that prevented pubs from selling alcohol after 11 p.m. These ballrooms were oases in a desert of dryness for thirsty teenagers because, for some strange reason, they were permitted to sell alcohol way past last orders, which was why they attracted Daniel Farson and were also a draw for young, adventurous men like me.

These venues were traditional Irish dance halls and felt like they had been transported lock, stock and Guinness barrel from rural Ireland. Men would stand on one side of the hall, jackets off, in white shirts and ties, eyeing up the women opposite, and when enough drink had relaxed the atmosphere they would approach the girls and ask for a dance. Even for an urban yobbo like me, it was a charming reminder of days gone by. I don't think many youngsters bother with preliminaries like that any more. In those days girls were probably warned by their mothers to be careful about having a dance with a stranger because it might lead to, well, you know . . . court-ship!

Some of the large art deco cinemas that took London by storm in the 1930s were, as I mentioned earlier, still function-ing when I was in my early teens, but they were pretty run down and either on the way out completely or about to get a multiplex makeover. What I didn't realise then, of course, was that these vast, usually empty, single-screen cinemas were among the last of a breed that began dying out from the late 50s onwards, when television began to rule the entertainment roost. When I later played the Hammersmith Odeon with Madness, which became a music venue in the early 60s, it was hard to take in that this place was once a cinema because it was so massive. I simply couldn't imagine 3,500 people sitting in this auditorium all watching the same film. It really hit home just how big an attraction the cinema was when these places were built. Apparently, 23 million people went to the cinema each week in the UK in the 1930s which, in old money, was half the population. It was such a regular weekly event that people rarely checked what was on before they set off. So let's rewind to those times.

When the talkies arrived in 1928 so too did the big three national chains – Gaumont, Odeon and Associated British

Cinemas – and the next decade saw the great age of cinema-building. These weren't just any old cinemas, they were escapist fantasies with marble staircases, glittering chandeliers and uniformed staff. Some were built in the style of Egyptian temples while the art deco Odeon cinemas became the embodiment of 1930s architecture.

Hollywood films were big business back then, and the chain cinemas made a point of ensuring that the fantasy world their patrons saw on the screen was matched by the interiors of their picture houses. Many of London's big, luxury cinemas have long gone with the wind, but it's not a total disaster movie on the giant 1930s cinema front: salvation for some arrived through religion, bingo or rock'n'roll, so thankfully the Big Smoke still has some blockbusting examples to feast your eyes on.

The Brixton Astoria is regarded as the first 'atmospheric' super cinema and had room for 3,000 patrons when it first opened its doors in 1929. Built in the Italian Renaissance style, the cinema was taken over by the Odeon group in the 30s, but it had to reinvent itself several times in order to stay standing. Today it can accommodate 5,000 screaming patrons, having had the seats in the stalls removed, and is, of course, now known as the Brixton Academy. It became a concert venue in 1982, having spent many years as a demolition-threatened warehouse. Fortunately, unlike most ageing film stars, the Academy never lost its looks: it's managed to retain most of its original features and underwent extensive renovation work a couple of years ago. It's now a Grade II listed building, so it should be around in all its 1929 glory for decades to come.

The Academy was pretty massive, but it wasn't the biggest cinema back then. That accolade goes to the Gaumont State Cinema in Kilburn, which had room for over 4,000 punters. The State is currently empty, having served time as a ballroom and bingo hall, but salvation of a sort is just around the corner. When you are looking to save an old gem like the Gaumont State, you've got to think big and you can't think much bigger than God. Turning its back on lascivious dancing, the devil's music and gambling, the Gaumont State is set to become a church. It's a remarkable art deco building and Kilburn's most identifiable landmark, with its 120-foot skyscraper tower – modelled on the Empire State Building – which once used to house a fully equipped radio studio. The interior isn't too shabby either, with its huge, gilded foyer complete with a vast chandelier that's a replica of one that illuminates the banqueting hall at Buckingham Palace.

I've mentioned that London scored a few notable firsts when it came to cinemas and moving pictures, and this trend has continued into the twenty-first century. The Granada Cinema in Tooting has recently been awarded a Grade I listing by English Heritage and is the first cinema in Britain to receive this accolade, which puts it in the same bracket as the Tower of London, Westminster Abbey and the Houses of Parliament.

Built in 1931, it will come as no surprise that, with room for over 3,000 punters, this picture palace ceased to function as a cinema long ago. In its heyday more than three million people came to watch films at the Granada, but the number of patrons attending each year had dropped to just 600 a week by 1971. By anyone's calculation, that's one heck of a reduction. The Granada had occasionally moonlighted as a concert venue over the years and played host to an array of stars ranging from the Andrews Sisters to Jerry Lee Lewis. Even the great Frank Sinatra played consecutive nights here when he was on the comeback trail in 1953.

But there was to be no comeback for the Granada as a cinema after 1973 when the final curtain fell following a week's screening of *The Good, the Bad and the Ugly*. Things might have turned ugly for the Granada if plans to build an office block on the site had gone ahead. But, perhaps taking the lead from their famous fictional son Citizen 'Wolfie' Smith, star of the Robert Lindsay sitcom that brought a satire on left-wing politics into our front rooms in the 70s, the good folks of Tooting were up in arms about the plans and threatened to revolt. Fortunately, the local council saw sense and slapped a preservation order on the cinema. As Wolfie used to cry, 'Power to the people!'

The Granada eventually became a bingo hall in 1976. Why was it that bingo came to the rescue of so many cinemas? Luck really. The decline in cinema attendances coincided with the liberalisation of the gaming laws in 1960, which allowed commercial bingo halls to set up. Bingo became hugely popular and big venues were required by companies such as Mecca. Empty cinemas fitted the bill perfectly and, fortunately, the transition generally didn't do too much damage to the fabric of the buildings. At the Granada, for example, only the seats in the stalls needed to be removed in order to make the house a home for the bingo brigade, which is more than a relief because the place is a treasure.

The Italianate facade of the Granada, including four tall pillars topped by Corinthian capitals, gives the cinema a stately appearance which belies the flamboyant splendour that awaits beyond its front doors. Once inside, the dazzling brilliance of the place left me gobsmacked and I dare say it had the same effect on the full house that turned up on its opening night in 1931, when over 2,000 punters were turned away at the door.

The interior was designed by Russian theatre-set designer Theodore Komisarjevsky, who apparently ransacked a textbook of gothic details in order to make the punters feel they were entering a palace when they walked into the Granada. He certainly succeeded. I'm not sure how authentic the styling detail is, but if you want one word to describe the Granada, I'd plump for 'opulent'. If you want two, then I'd go for 'beyond opulent'. Komisarjevsky clearly wasn't a man who thought less was more.

When you step off the Mitcham Road and into the Granada you are confronted at once with a splendiferous sight. The interior features a marble foyer and staircase, where vast moulded columns support arcading topped by painted heraldic lions. Dazzling chandeliers and candle-effect wall-lighting illuminate this double-height foyer and its fancily carved ceiling. Once up the stairs on the way to the circle, you're greeted by a spectacular hall of mirrors. This looking-glass arcaded cloister is topped off by a gently arched, flower-encrusted ceiling from which hang Moorish-style decorative candelabras. For a moment it's easy to forget you're in south London and it's possible to feel as though you've stumbled down some mysterious sci-fi corridor into a medieval palace in Moorish Spain. If you get past the hall of mirrors without getting a bit of a blast from the heady mixture of gothic, Romanesque and Moorish design you've already encountered, then the auditorium is sure to blow you away. Here there are mural paintings of troubadours and wimple-wearing damsels, huge gothic and Romanesque arches, vast stained-glass windows and a ceiling that is so elaborately carved that it would have given Michelangelo a run for his money in the effort and exertion stakes.

The 1930s are remembered for the Great Depression, but a visit to the Granada must have lifted people's spirits in that period of strife. I can only imagine what it must have been like to watch a movie in such opulent surroundings, but a game of bingo here put a spring in my step and if I'd won, it would have been hard to resist the temptation to shout, 'Our house!' As long as you don't mind too much about being beaten by ladies of a certain age at a game of chance, I recommend you go and give it the once-over. I'm sure it'll put a smile on your face too.

The surviving cinemas are living monuments to an age when entertainment in London was experienced socially. It was the golden age of the 'good night out' because entertainment at home was, at best, limited to the gramophone or a sing-along around the piano, or, from the 1920s onwards, the wireless. I've always liked the idea of people getting dressed up for a night on the town and I love thinking about all the millions of multi-denominational Londoners who still do – although I'd advise you to leave the pomegranate in the fruit bowl and stick to popcorn.

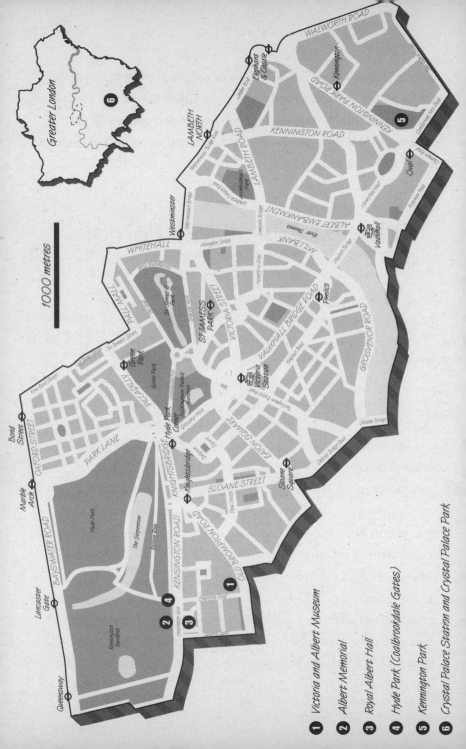

Greater London

1000 metres

WALWORTH ROAD

Elephant & Castle

Kennington

KENNINGTON PARK ROAD

LAMBETH NORTH

KENNINGTON ROAD

Westminster

LAMBETH ROAD

ALBERT EMBANKMENT

Oval

WHITEHALL

River Thames

Vauxhall

MILLBANK

Abingdon Street

St James's Park

PALL MALL

ST JAMES'S PARK

Pimlico

Green Park

VICTORIA STREET

VAUXHALL BRIDGE ROAD

GROSVENOR ROAD

Bond Street

OXFORD STREET

Hyde Park Corner

Victoria Station

Marble Arch

PARK LANE

Green Park

Buckingham Palace Gardens

KNIGHTSBRIDGE

Knightsbridge

EATON SQUARE

BAYSWATER ROAD

Hyde Park

KENSINGTON ROAD

SLOANE STREET

Sloane Square

Chelsea Bridge

Lancaster Gate

The Serpentine

OLD BROMPTON ROAD

Queensway

Kensington Gardens

1 Victoria and Albert Museum
2 Albert Memorial
3 Royal Albert Hall
4 Hyde Park (Coalbrookdale Gates)
5 Kennington Park
6 Crystal Palace Station and Crystal Palace Park

CHAPTER TEN

The Park that Time Forgot

I accept I am no palaeontologist but I do have one dinosaur-related a fact which I have personally verified and which I am now happy to share with you. For more than 140 years, a small colony of these ancient creatures has been living peacefully in a leafy corner of south London. Good, eh.

The story of how these unexpected residents took possession of their slice of the capital involves a motley assortment of characters, including Queen Victoria's husband Albert, a brilliant but ruthless scientist who fought with Darwin and founded one of London's great museums, and a humble farmer's son who made his name by propagating Britain's very first dwarf banana. Its plot features the greatest show in the history of London (and I'm not talking about

Starlight Express), an event which left its footprints in every corner of the modern city and paved the way for some of London's best-known buildings. It's a story of high finance and big ambitions, international intrigue and personal vanity. And it all begins with a greenhouse.

Not just any old greenhouse, mind you. This isn't Uncle Ted pottering around on the allotment, instead think of the greatest greenhouse the world has ever seen. A greenhouse so whopping that you could grow enough tomatoes in it to feed Britain for a year and still have plenty left over to go squidgy in the fridge. A greenhouse so glorious that it attracted visitors from around the globe and came to be known as the eighth wonder of the world. A greenhouse built to house the greatest show on earth. A greenhouse they called the Crystal Palace.

It was created, of course, not for tomatoes, but for the Great Exhibition – the celebrated Victorian extravaganza which, for a few glorious months in the summer and autumn of 1851, took over a huge plot of land in London's Hyde Park to show off all that was biggest and best about the British Empire. You may remember that I came across some of the original display cabinets from the Exhibition at Floris perfumiers in Jermyn Street while following the trail of Beau Brummell through the fashionable West End. They'd been bought by the shopkeepers after the Exhibition had closed to the public and the buildings which housed it moved from the site in Hyde Park. It was this chance discovery which set my imagination running: what other remains from this legendary event had survived in the modern city, and where might I find them? This led me via

Hyde Park to south London's very own Jurassic Park and an encounter with the aforementioned dinosaurs.

The legendary exhibition was dreamed up by Henry Cole, one of those great Victorian movers and shakers who dipped his fingers into a whole smorgasbord of different pies over the years. His impressive CV includes central roles in the creation of the Penny Black – the world's first postage stamp – and the building of the Royal Albert Hall, although his forthright approach to fundraising also made him, according to Prime Minister Lord Derby, 'the most generally unpopular man I know'. High praise indeed, although it didn't prevent Cole from being appointed in 1850 as the boss of the Society for the Encouragement of Arts, Manufacturers and Commerce, an impressive-sounding outfit of the great and good dedicated to ensuring that the British Empire continued to lead the world in just about anything you can think of. Always on the lookout for new ideas, Cole had gone to Paris to visit their national exhibition and returned home to England with his imagination on fire. Duly inspired, he hotfooted it back to the Society and argued the case for a bigger, better version of the Paris show to be staged in London – Hyde Park, to be precise. He pitched his plan for a great international exhibition to none other than Prince Albert, Queen Victoria's husband, who was president of the Society and, like every good Prussian, a champion of all things British.

With Albert throwing his full weight behind proceedings, you might have thought it would be a mere bagatelle to get the show up and running. But it seems that there were plenty of people who didn't like the idea one bit. Some worried about the sheer number of people likely to descend on London from the farthest-flung corners of the kingdom, bringing a tidal wave of death, disease and destruction in their wake, which were genuine fears back then, it seems.

In 1848 Karl Marx and Friedrich Engels had published *The Communist Manifesto*, much of it written, by the way, in the British Library in London. The same year had seen a string of revolutions in other European countries, and in London the Chartist movement had organised a mass demonstration in Kennington Park, south London, as part of their campaign for greater democracy – a show of strength which prompted the government to deploy 8,000 soldiers and 150,000 special constables in case things got feisty.

As it turned out, the day passed off peacefully, but the fear of large crowds with the potential to turn nasty lingered on, which is why some people thought the idea of an exhibition in the park was a bad one. According to *The Times*, 'The whole of Hyde Park and, we will venture to predict, the whole of Kensington Gardens, will be turned into a bivouac of all the vagabonds of London so long as the Exhibition shall continue.' Others were especially concerned about the threat posed by foreign tourists. An MP called Charles Sibthorpe predicted the return of the bubonic plague to the capital, while the nationalist *John Bull* magazine, in an astonishing display of spluttering xenophobia, quaked at the prospect of 'the influx of large masses of visitors, whose moral standard in their own homes is considerably below our own'.

As if all the opposition wasn't enough to put them off, there was another challenge for the organisers to deal with: a suitable home had to be built to house the extravaganza. They launched a competition, inviting any interested parties to submit ideas for the building. These days, of course, the whole process would be much simpler – simply launch a TV show, complete with public voting and a panel of judges, all expertly marshalled by Bruce Forsyth, who may, now I come to think of it, perhaps have visited the 1851 show as a young man. Members of the Great British public would be encouraged to throw their hats into the ring and make an exhibition of themselves in the hope of being selected to help make an exhibition for the rest of us. But the Victorians opted for something more modest.

The competition was launched in March 1850 and would-be builders were given a month – that's four whole weeks – to cook up a suitable plan. They were only being asked to create a building fit to accommodate the greatest show on earth – how much more time did they need? Two hundred and forty-five designs were submitted, but almost all of them were, to use a technical architectural term, complete pants.

Unfazed, the organisers decided to take matters into their own hands and challenged the members of their own building committee to come up with an alternative scheme. Since the committee included Sir Charles Barry, the man who designed the Houses of Parliament, plus a whole toolbox full of legendary engineers, they weren't exactly going out on a limb here. If I tell you that, in the end, most of the design they came up with was the work of a certain Isambard Kingdom Brunel, the man who gave us the Clifton Suspension Bridge and the SS *Great Britain*, you may expect to have your socks blown off by his solution to the plan. But please don't remove your shoes in anticipation.

When Brunel, puffing no doubt on an improbably large cigar, closed his eyes and dreamed the impossible dream, he saw not the glittering glass palace which would eventually house the Exhibition, but bricks instead. Millions of bricks. Fifteen million, to be precise, all cunningly arranged to create what a later critic suggested would have become 'a vast, squat, brick warehouse four times the length and twice the width of St Paul's'. Big, I grant you, but not very beautiful. Perhaps unsurprisingly, Brunel's plan did not send the pulses of the committee racing, although it would probably have been enough to earn him 'Man of the Year' at the annual knees-up of the British Brick-makers Association. It's worth remarking that Brunel's failure also meant a narrow escape for south London football fans: had things turned out differently they might have found themselves cheering on not Crystal Palace, but Brick Warehouse Wanderers instead.

Having bumped into Brunel's brick wall, the Exhibition committee needed a plan C. With the fate of the Exhibition swinging in the wind, an unlikely hero stepped centre stage to save the day. He was a farmer's son from Bedfordshire by the name of Joseph Paxton. Paxton had started his working life as a humble gardener (think Alan Titchmarsh with whiskers) but worked his way up to become head man on the estate of the

Duke of Devonshire (think Alan Titchmarsh with whiskers and a top hat). Along the way, he'd notched up a series of impressive firsts, including the propagation of that miniature banana I mentioned earlier, and, at the other end of the scale, a giant Amazonian waterlily with five-foot leaves. But how did these horticultural achievements, impressive as they were, equip Paxton with the skills necessary to succeed where a man like Brunel had failed? What use are green fingers, when it comes to designing a major public building? We didn't turn to Titchmarsh when we were planning the Millennium Dome, and Monty Don has not, as far as I am aware, been consulted on the new Olympic Stadium taking shape in east London.

This is where the greenhouse enters our story. Paxton's boss, the Duke of Devonshire, owned vast tracts of land in Derbyshire. His main residence was Chatsworth House, where Paxton had built a massive greenhouse to accommodate the Duke's collection of rare and exotic plants (277 feet long and 67 feet high since you're asking – the greenhouse not the collection). When Paxton got wind of the problems that the Exhibition organisers were having in coming up with a suitable design, his mind turned to glass and iron. According to legend, the actual moment of inspiration struck on 11 June 1850. By now Paxton was an eminent man and, as is the way with eminent men, he was invited to sit on the board of various organisations, including the Midland Railway. During a tedious committee meeting – is there any other sort? – he grabbed a piece of blotting paper and began to doodle designs for a huge glass-house based on the Chatsworth model. You can still see what must surely rank as the most famous piece of blotting paper in the world, a fiercely contested honour, at the Victoria and Albert Museum in Kensington.

Paxton pocketed his blotting-paper design and headed back to Chatsworth, where he set his team to work on a more detailed plan. Within days he was travelling south to present his scheme to the Exhibition committee in London. He made the journey by train, and at the station at Derby he bumped into none other than the eminent inventor Robert Stephenson, the man who designed the Rocket (steam train not ice-lolly). He gave Paxton's plans the once-over followed by the thumbs-up, a verdict which was later seconded by the committee. They green-lit the greenhouse and the Crystal Palace was born, although its famous name was dreamed up by a writer for the satirical magazine *Punch*, which had closely followed the contest to design the building.

Whatever way you look at it, Paxton's Palace was a mighty impressive affair – a monumental glass and iron structure which enclosed a space six times bigger than St Paul's Cathedral and boasted more than a million square feet of glass. Thankfully, the show was planned for the summer months, so at least there was no need for double-glazing. Even so, it took a team of more than 2,000 workers 22 weeks to put the thing together.

Eagle-eyed visitors to Hyde Park today will notice that the gargantuan greenhouse which accommodated the Exhibition is no longer to be found there. But even though the building has long since departed the stage, you'd think there might be other clues to help one get a sense of the scale of the place and the magnificence of the event it housed, an event which has passed into London legend, alongside similarly iconic moments, such as the great ice fairs on the frozen Thames in the seventeenth century and the first Madness gig in the Dublin Castle.

When I pitch up, I'm armed with another old map to help me get my bearings. Not just any old map, mind you, but a copy of the one produced by the publisher Joseph Cross of Holborn Hill, which was specially printed (on silk and coloured by hand, no less) in 1851 to cash in on the expected influx of visitors to the capital. Thanks to Mr Cross and his cartographers, I knew that the Palace – represented by a pleasing brick-pink rectangle on his silken sheets – was built on the grassy strip which divides South Carriage Drive on the southern edge of Hyde Park and Rotten Row – or horse highway number one, as I prefer to call it – to the north.

Having parked my scooter on a nearby meter, I point my compass north and stroll up Exhibition Road, dodging the traffic on Kensington Gore and entering the park through the Coalbrookdale Gates, a magnificent pair of cast-iron gates specially made for the Exhibition by the people who built the famous iron bridge across the Severn gorge in Shropshire. In 1851 the gates were on display within the Crystal Palace itself, before being moved to their current location once the show had closed. This is my first encounter with the surviving fabric of the Exhibition in Hyde Park and a promising omen of good things to come. Glancing to my left, I can see the Albert

Memorial – the grand statue erected by Queen Victoria in memory of her beloved husband after his untimely death in 1861, aged 42. Albert was one of the prime movers behind the Exhibition and, on closer inspection, I'm pleased to see that he's clutching a rolled-up copy of the show's catalogue in his bronzed fist. Another promising sign.

Turning to the east for a minute's walk brings you to the strip of greenery where once the mighty Palace stood. Pace out its length, all 1,800 feet of it, then stop to survey the scene. You'll see plenty of green but no sign of a greenhouse. No surprises there, but I had hoped to spot the remains of a few foundations or something to suggest that this patch of lawn had once been the site of one of the capital's great structures. All you can do is close your eyes and try to imagine what it must have been like to stand on this very spot on 1 May 1851, when the Crystal Palace finally opened to the public.

According to the historian Lord Macaulay, Paxton's wondrous creation was 'a most gorgeous sight; vast; graceful; beyond the dreams of the Arabian romances. I cannot think that the Caesars ever exhibited a more splendid spectacle'. To get in on day one you had to splash out on a season ticket: three guineas for blokes, two for the ladies, around £225 and £150 respectively in today's money. Entry on days two and three was a little more affordable at £1 per person, but still a small fortune for most Londoners. It wasn't until 26 May, a full 25 days after the grand opening, that the hoi polloi were allowed in for a shilling, and there was plenty of speculation in the press about how they'd behave once they got there, as

Henry Mayhew remarked: 'For many days before the "shilling people" were admitted to the building, the great topic of conversation was the probable behaviour of the people. Would they come sober? Will they destroy the things? Will they want to cut their names on the panes of the glass lighthouses?' As it turned out, most people behaved themselves pretty well. A month after it opened, on 6 June, Charlotte Brontë paid a visit. I'm guessing the esteemed author of *Jane Eyre* didn't trash the place, and nor did any of the other visitors she encountered, as she later told her father in a letter: 'The multitude filling the great aisles seemed ruled and subdued by some invisible influence. Amongst the thirty thousand souls that peopled it the day I was there not one loud noise was to be heard, not one irregular movement seen; the living tide rolls on quietly, with a deep hum like the sea heard from a distance.'

I won't trouble you with all the facts and figures surrounding this legendary event but here are a few of the highlights. The show included 112,000 separate exhibits, divided into 30 different classes of item. A glance at the original Exhibition catalogue reveals that one minute you might be admiring the world's biggest diamond – 'the Great Diamond of Runjeet Singh, called "Koh-I-Noor" or Mountain of Light' – the next you could be scrutinising samples of guano or seagull poo. There were paintings and sculptures, machinery and weapons, costumes and curios from all corners of the earth: something, in fact, for everyone. During the six months it was open to the public it received more than six million visitors, about the same number as turned up for the Millennium Dome, which was open for a whole year. The figure is even more impressive when you remember that the total population of Britain at the time of the Great Exhibition was only around 21 million.

Refreshments were provided by Messrs Schweppe, who supplied more than a million bottles of soft drinks and nearly two million buns during the months the Exhibition ran in Hyde Park. The Exhibition also marked a notable first which would probably have come as a relief to those who polished off all that pop. A chap called George Jennings, manufacturer of water closets, set up London's first public conveniences – the so-called Retiring Rooms – which were enjoyed by more than 827,000 visitors over the course of the Exhibition. Just imagine the queues. A penny was enough to pay not only for a comfortable sit-down, but also a towel and comb and even a polish of your boots. The euphemism 'spending a penny' originated from Jennings' loos.

The show was a triumph. It generated receipts of £522,000 and a profit of £186,437, which was used to buy the plot of land in South Kensington where London's great museums were later built. Many of the exhibits themselves later went on display in the new Victoria and Albert Museum, where you can still see them today, alongside Paxton's famous scrap of blotting paper, without which the whole show might never have happened.

Once the last visitor had been ushered out of the building, there was just one more small question to attend to. How do you dispose of the world's biggest greenhouse? Some people, including Paxton, wanted to leave it in Hyde Park, a reasonable enough plan, you might think, in view of how successful the show had been. Others wanted to see the back of the building. Our old friend Colonel Sibthorpe, who'd opposed the Exhibition from the start, stepped into the fray once more, arguing that the Palace was 'a transparent humbug and a bauble' and should be demolished immediately. Parliament was persuaded and the contractors who had put the whole thing up, a company called Fox and Henderson, were just preparing to knock it all down and sell it for scrap when Paxton and a consortium of businessmen cooked up a new scheme to save the Palace from the clutches of the demolition squad. They persuaded Parliament to sell them the building on a buyer-to-collect basis. Their plan involved relocating the building to a new site, where it would be rebuilt and fitted out in even grander style than the original to become the world's first theme park.

Paxton and his pals, imaginatively styling themselves the Crystal Palace Company, raised half a million quid from investors, upwards of £35 million in today's money, to pay for the scheme, which would see the Palace travel, lock stock and barrel-vaulted ceilings, south to Sydenham Hill, a leafy countryside retreat 20 miles away from Hyde Park itself. That's an awful long way to transport thousands of tons of glass and iron, especially in the days before motorised transport. The job was done by a fleet of horse-drawn carts, rattling their way along the roughly cobbled streets and bumpy country lanes which linked the heart of the city to the country estate at Sydenham.

Having failed to track down any substantial traces of the Palace in Hyde Park, I decided to make a rare foray over the Thames and into south London in my quest for crystal. I opted against a horse-drawn cart and took the train instead, winding my way from Waterloo and through the suburbs of south London. Half an hour later, I arrived at Crystal Palace Station, a stop-off purpose-built to cater for visitors to the new and improved attraction, which said hello to the public for a second time on 10 June 1854. The original plan had been to open in May, but that was scuppered when someone pointed out that the new statues of naked men which adorned the interior of the Palace might be considered too anatomically accurate for the delicate sensibilities of the Victorian public. Only after their privates had been removed or covered with fig leaves – the statues', not the visitors' – was it considered safe to start selling tickets.

By coincidence, my first port of call as I left the station at Crystal Palace and headed out into the park was another statue: a giant bust of Paxton himself, still standing sentinel over his former domain. Like just about everything else in this story, it's built on a larger-than-life scale: even his sideburns are almost as tall as me, and when you add on the height of the pedestal he's perched on, the whole edifice must be more than 20 feet high. Thank goodness he isn't wearing a top hat as well, or the whole thing would pose a serious hazard to low-flying aircraft. Today Paxton's gaze is directed down the slope of the park towards the south-east, which means his reward for putting this place on the map is a glorious view of Penge for the rest of eternity. Meanwhile, his back is turned to the spot at the top of the hill where his mighty Palace once stood until it was destroyed in a fire which lit up the sky for miles around on the night of Monday, 30 November 1936. Today a mound covered by trees and shrubs marks the last burial place of the charred remnants of Paxton's marvellous building.

I head up the hill towards the mound and amble along the remains of the Italian Terraces, ornate walkways which once heaved with visitors, but today are all but deserted. Ahead of me, a lone walker pauses to take in the view while his jaunty Jack Russell cocks a leg on a plinth which supports a statuesque sphinx, the last exotic survivor of the decorations which adorned this section of the walk when the park was in its pomp. It's difficult in such circumstances to conjure up a sense of the glitz and glamour which once made it so special, but my eye is soon drawn by another survivor from the original structure, which brings to mind waterworks of a more impressive style and scale.

A year after the park itself opened, Paxton unveiled a new attraction: two mighty water towers designed by Paxton's pal Brunel powered water down the hill to feed a series of fountains scattered through the landscaped gardens which surrounded the building itself. These twin edifices – each 85 metres tall – supported tanks containing 1,200 tons of water each, which could be released to surge through a network of pipes at a rate of 120,000 gallons a minute. Once the deluge had reached its destination, it spouted to the surface from one of more than 11,000 jets. Old black-and-white photos of the fountains in action reveal that they were a very impressive sight, like a whole series of watery palm trees, reaching hundreds of feet into the south London sky.

Between the wars, John Logie Baird, the man who invented TV as we know it, set up a workshop in the south tower here and made some of the very first TV transmissions anywhere in the world. But when the Second World War broke out, the authorities decided Brunel's towers would provide a convenient landmark for German bombers as they navigated their way towards targets in the capital, so they were demolished. I have to admit this seems a little random to me, given that they didn't try to add to the confusion by camouflaging the Thames or painting a colourful rural mural on the side of the Houses of Parliament. The north tower was blown up in a single Fred Dibnah-style explosion, the south tower was picked apart brick by brick for fear of damaging surrounding structures. That's why the base of the south tower can still be seen in the park today.

Next door to the tower is a small museum full of things that help you to get a sense of what the place looked like in its early years – paintings, photographs and, better still, the curator, a highly knowledgeable man called Ken Kiss, who offers to show me one of the park's best-kept secrets, an underground treasure which is off bounds today to all but a fortunate few.

As we head back up the hill towards it, Ken tells me how, within a few years of opening, the Crystal Palace was pulling in more than two million visitors a year to this previously remote and rural area beyond the city's boundaries. In the early years of the park, two new railway lines were built to cater for all the visitors who flooded here. Along the routes of those new lines there was a boom in house-building, which created many of the south London suburbs I'd passed through on my own journey to the park. The first line ends up at Crystal Palace Station; the second line, built by the London, Chatham and Dover Railway, came to a halt at the north-west tip of the park, on what is still known today as Crystal Palace Parade. This second station disappeared many moons ago, but the underground subway that funnelled visitors from platform to Palace lives on beneath the rumbling streets of the modern city. These days it's out of bounds to the public for safety reasons, unless you know the man with the key to this hidden chamber of secrets. And I do.

It doesn't look much from the outside – a slightly bedraggled courtyard sprouting with weeds leads on towards an archway of bricks, which frames a gloomy cavern beyond. Once we reach the entrance, I peer into the darkness for a moment, before stepping inside. It's a few moments before my eyes adjust to the low light and I begin to see why Ken was so keen to show me this place. When the park was in its pomp, more than 8,000 visitors per hour would have passed through this walkway en route to their big day out. It may have been built for a functional purpose, but that didn't stop the Victorian railway engineers who built it from pulling out all the stops when they designed this link between the workaday world of trains and platforms and the wonderland that lay beyond.

I begin to spot pillars, spreading out in all directions from where I stand. They leave the paved stone floor as slender columns but grow wider as they reach towards the roof to create a vaulted ceiling 25 or 30 feet above my head, maybe more. The pillars and ceiling were built of the same patterned red-and-cream brick which was used in the old St Pancras Hotel in King's Cross, but it's not that familiar landmark they remind me of. I'm standing in a south London subway, but it feels more like a miniature Moorish palace. For the first time today, I'm able to make the imaginative leap back in time to the days when this place echoed with the footsteps of all those excited Victorian day-trippers, surging from the trains and on towards the marvellous sights that lay beyond the turnstiles, just a shilling away. No one needed to make this place look as good as it did, but it was all part of the show. They did things with style back then, and this was a suitably grand entrance to the grand old park.

Buoyed up by this glimpse of the magnificent entrance, I banish all thoughts of my earlier arrival at the modern-day Crystal Palace Station and of the canine barbarian doing his worst to the statue of the sphinx. Instead I stride off to explore the rest of the park with a new spring in my step. It's shortly after this that I stumble across the dinosaurs.

Ah yes, those dinosaurs. Here they come at last, trundling over the horizon and into my story. You'll find them down at the bottom of the hill, grazing peacefully on a series of small islands in the centre of a placid lake. They haven't moved from here since they settled in the park in the 1850s, which will probably confirm what you might already have begun to suspect: these unlikely survivors are not flesh, blood and bone, but man-made creatures. Today, while almost everything else from those early days has disappeared completely or decayed into shabby old age, they still look in surprisingly good nick – helped, no doubt, by a recent £4 million makeover.

This Victorian Jurassic Park was conceived by Professor Richard Owen, one of the most colourful and controversial characters in Victorian science. He had been recruited by Paxton and his colleagues to devise a headline-grabbing attraction to help launch Crystal Palace mark two in its new location south of the city. There were no dinosaurs on display in the Hyde Park show: these lumbering beauties were specially commissioned to cause a stir in Sydenham.

Owen, born in 1804, was a brilliant anatomist who had risen to become one of the leading scientists of the day. He was also a great believer in public education, and would later be the driving force behind the establishment of one of London's greatest cathedrals of learning: the Natural History Museum in South Kensington. In the late 1820s he was appointed by the Royal College of Surgeons to be the assistant curator of their Hunterian Collection, an assemblage of 13,000 medical curiosities – human and animal – which had been left to the College by one of its distinguished members, John Hunter. You can still see his collection today if you visit the Royal College of Surgeons at Lincoln's Inn Fields in London. Owen's work on the collection gained him a reputation as one of the most eminent anatomists of the day, and all sorts of weird and wonderful animal remains found their way to his dissecting table over the years. One of his jobs was to study the remains of unusual creatures which had died at London Zoo, and legend has it that one day his unfortunate wife returned home to discover a dead rhino blocking the entrance hall.

Owen's work also brought him to the attention of the British Association, who asked him to provide a report on the many mysterious fossils which had recently been discovered across the country. He soon realised they were unlike any other animal remains he had ever seen and coined a new term – 'dinosaur' or 'terrible lizard' – to describe the huge creatures from which they must have come. It was a name that stuck, even though there has subsequently been much debate as to whether dinosaurs were even cold-blooded, let alone actually lizards. Over the coming years, as more and more dinosaur bones were discovered, Owen made it his business to be seen as the world's leading authority on the subject, ruthlessly sidelining anyone else who tried to stray on to his palaeontological patch. So it was no surprise that, in 1852, the Crystal Palace Company came knocking on his door after they'd decided to create a dinosaur display for the new park in Sydenham.

Owen jumped at the chance to create this new attraction. To help him realise his vision, he enlisted the help of an artist and sculptor called Benjamin Waterhouse Hawkins. Owen provided Hawkins with his estimates of the likely shape and size of the creatures, based on his careful scrutiny of the excavated bones. Hawkins then worked to create life-sized models of the mighty beasts – no mean feat when you remember the stature of the creatures he was dealing with. Here, in Hawkins' own words in a lecture he gave in 1854, is what went into the construction of the iguanodon, just one of the models on show at Crystal Palace: 'four iron columns nine feet long by seven inches diameter, 600 bricks, 650 five-inch half-round drain tiles, 900 plain, 38 casks of cement, 90 casks of broken stone, making a total of 640 bushels of artificial stone. These, with 100 feet of iron hooping and 20 feet of cube inch bar, constitute the bones, sinews and muscles of this large model, the largest of which there is any record of a casting being made.'

It sounds like more than enough to build a decent-sized house, and, sure enough, the dinosaurs themselves are built on a monumental scale. Alongside mighty beasts like the iguanodon and megalosaurus, you can find three partially submerged ichthyosaurus models, a labyrinthodon, a family of elk-like megaloceros and some pterodactyls. As far as I have been able to ascertain, the plans did not include a life-sized model of a Raquel Welch-style huntress, in all her *One Million Years BC* stone-age finery. I have a feeling that such an addition would have made the display even more popular with the great Victorian public, or the male half of it at least.

Although the size of the creations is the first thing that strikes you as you approach these islands that time forgot, a closer look reveals that Hawkins was obviously a highly skilled artist. As I step up to the mighty iguanodon – surely the star of the show – to take a closer look, I forget Hawkins' long list of ingredients from the builders' merchants and marvel at the finished thing. To my untutored eye this beast looks pretty convincing. The horn on the end of his nose is particularly impressive.

Which just goes to prove once and for all how little I do know about dinosaurs because, as it turns out, the models here are riddled with inaccuracies. They certainly bear very little resemblance to later visualisations of the creatures, which is hardly surprising when you consider that in many cases Owen and Hawkins were basing their models on the evidence contained in just a few small fragments of bone. They were also pioneers in an entirely new field – the models here were built several years before Darwin shocked the Victorians with his theory of evolution – so they can surely be excused the many errors in their designs, including the impressive nasal appendage sported by the iguanodon: later palaeontologists discovered that this horn-like bone was in fact one of the iguanodon's claws.

The dinosaur display – for all its glorious inaccuracy – was a sensation and the star attraction of the park in its early years. To mark the completion of its construction, Owen organised a celebratory dinner for 21 Victorian worthies. He obviously had difficulties getting a table at the Ivy, since the meal was actually dished up at a table placed inside the belly of the iguanodon itself. I've eaten in some strange places in my time, but never one quite as idiosyncratic as that. I only hope there were no vegetarians present.

The display you can see today is impressive enough, but

Owen and Hawkins had originally planned something even more dramatic. Besides building more dinosaurs, they intended that the artificial lake in which their islands were situated should rise and fall as though the tide was coming in and out, revealing or submerging different parts of the display according to the time of day. In the event, the cash ran out before the design could be implemented and today the water levels are fixed. Only the ducks who paddle on the pond know what murky prehistoric survivors are lurking beneath the surface here.

There's an interesting postscript to the story of the Crystal Palace dinosaurs. Hawkins was blamed for pushing the project over budget and decided to try his luck in pastures new. A few years later he surfaced in New York, where he was commissioned to build a new set of dinosaurs to go on display in Central Park. By now, many more fossilised remains had been discovered, which meant that the New York examples Hawkins created were far more accurate than the London prototypes. Instead of the chunky, bulky elephants on steroids I saw grazing in Crystal Palace Park, the drawings of his New York creations show a far more anatomically accurate set of creatures, with elegant long necks and slender limbs. There are no misplaced digits gracing the noses of this impressive collection. But if you happen to find yourself in New York these days, don't bother to go dinosaur hunting in its great park. It seems that Hawkins had a falling out with some of the city's corrupt politicians, including the notorious William Magear 'Boss' Tweed. Anyone with a passing interest in

American politics – or, indeed, with the classic 1970s series *The Dukes of Hazard* – will know that it is always a bad idea to pick a quarrel with a man whose nickname is 'Boss'. Sadly, Hawkins did exactly that and paid the ultimate price. Tweed despatched a gang of his finest thugs to break into Hawkins' workshop and trash his dinosaurs. I don't think he woke up with a megalosaurus head in his bed, but he certainly got the message not to mess with Mr Tweed and left the city soon afterwards. It's said that today their remains are still buried somewhere in Central Park, lying in wait to confuse the archaeologists of the future.

The Crystal Palace dinosaurs may have topped the bill when the park first opened, but, over the years, they found themselves upstaged by a string of other new attractions. In 1864, for example, a pneumatic railway was built, which enabled visitors to enjoy a 600-yard trip down a brick tunnel in a railway carriage which was sucked through the tunnel at a speed of 25mph by a vacuum-creating steam engine. I'm not sure I understand the physics, but I can't think of many better ways to spend a sixpence.

The park continued to offer Londoners a big day out right through to the early years of the twentieth century, even staging 20 cup finals between 1895 and 1914 – none of them contested by Chelsea, sadly. But its best days were behind it. During the First World War it was used as a naval supply depot and although it reopened as an amusement attraction in 1920, the end was in sight. The fountains no longer flowered, and the massive fire which finally destroyed the place in 1936 almost came as a relief, putting the tired exhibition out of its misery once and for all.

But still – marvellously, miraculously – the dinosaurs survive. They've stood firm through everything the last century or so could throw at them, including the bombs of the Luftwaffe. And they may even live to see a new Crystal Palace rise on the site of the original. If some recent reports I've read about in the papers are to be believed, there are plans afoot to try to build a new version of the original.

That's what I love about London most of all – the sheer resilience of the place and its dauntless capacity for reinvention. So where better to end my journey through the endlessly surprising city I'm proud to call my home than here, a place where even the mighty dinosaurs themselves are still not quite extinct? There they stand, still grazing solemnly in the park that time forgot: the megalosaurus, the ichthyosaurus and the mighty iguanodon himself – still wondering why a so-called expert stuck his thumb on to his forehead, and still waiting patiently for the tide to turn.

Further Reading

This Bright Field William Taylor (Methuen, 2000)

Soho in the Fifties Daniel Farson (Michael Joseph, 1987)

Absolute Beginners Colin MacInnes (MacGibbon & Kee, 1959)

You're Barred, You Bastards Norman Balon (Sidgwick & Jackson, 1991)

Beau Brummell: The Ultimate Dandy Ian Kelly (Hodder & Stoughton, 2005)

Beau Brummell: His Life and Letters Lewis Melville (Hutchinson, 1924)

London: A Literary Companion Peter Vansittart (John Murray, 1992)

The Horse-World of London W. J. Gordon (Kessinger, [1893] 2008)

London Labour and the London Poor Henry Mayhew (Routledge, [1851] 1967)

The Mysteries of London G. W. M. Reynolds (Keele University Press, [1869] 1996)

Italian Food Elizabeth David (Macdonald, 1954)

Football Grounds of Britain Simon Inglis (Collins Willow, 1987)

Soho Judith Summers (Bloomsbury, 1989)

The London Compendium Ed Glinert (Penguin, 2003)

The London Nobody Knows Geoffrey Scowcroft Fletcher (Penguin, 1962)

Making the Metropolis Stephen Halliday (Breedon Books, 2003)

England in Particular Sue Clifford and Angela King (Hodder & Stoughton, 2006)

Index